# THE

# LEBANESE

# COOKBOOK

Ghillie Başan

# THE
# LEBANESE
# COOKBOOK

Exploring the food
of Lebanon, Syria
and Jordan

LORENZ BOOKS

# Contents

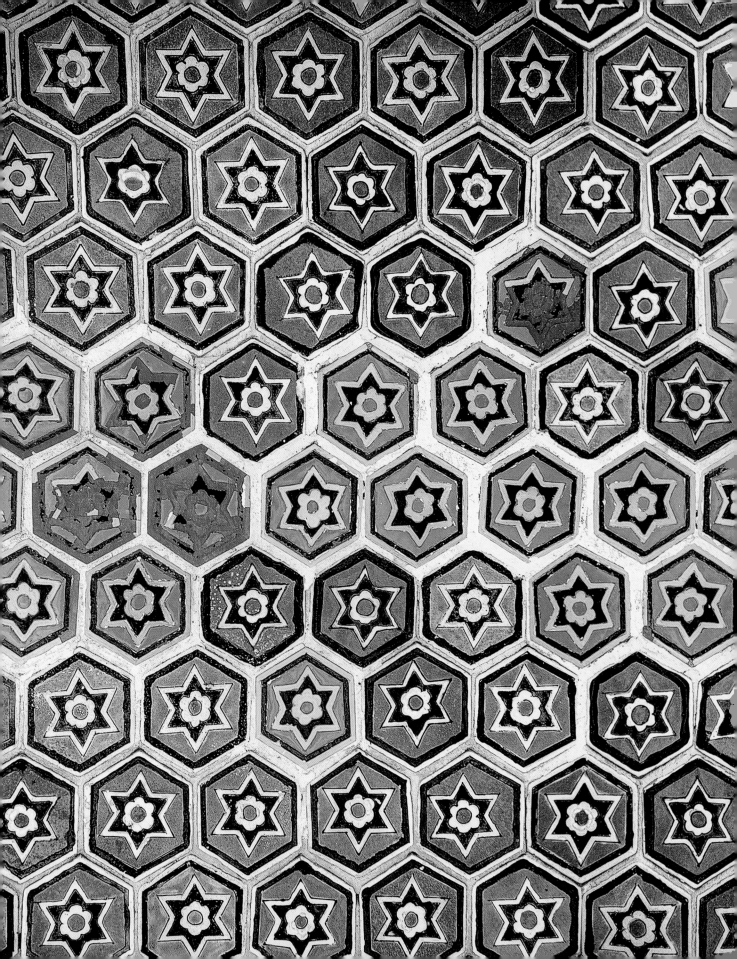

# A cuisine steeped in history

This book is my celebration of the food of the Fertile Crescent, with recipes for all the most mouthwatering dishes of the region, alongside background detail and stories. I hope to inspire a deeper knowledge of this most beautiful part of the world, where a love of food and a sense of satisfaction in sharing it with others has always been such an intrinsic part of daily life. In a time of conflict these culinary traditions matter more than ever, with the coming together of friends and family to eat, drink and talk.

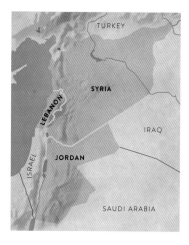

Above **The regions of Lebanon, Syria and Jordan contain distinctive geographical areas: coast, mountains, and fertile valleys.**

Opposite top **Tripoli is Lebanon's second-largest city. The Kadisha River finally meets the Mediterranean sea.**

Opposite bottom **Beautiful beaches abound along the coast.**

# Culinary passion and community spirit

The food of Lebanon, Syria and Jordan takes me on a journey – a simultaneous dip into history and a scoot through modern life – where every dish has a connection to stories, passions, old traditions and new. Visiting this region is never dull as life unfolds before your eyes with chaos in the noisy streets, colour in the busy markets, and a feast of flavour wherever you go.

If there is one thing that can unite communities it is food: the garlicky hummus and tangy smoked aubergine dip; spicy falafel and juicy fattoush; hot buttery pastries that melt in the mouth; comforting rice dishes and bean stews; classic kibbeh in all shapes and sizes; and moreish milk puddings and fritters in scented syrup. There are Muslim feasts and Christian celebrations, Jewish and Armenian traditions, Palestinian communities and Arab heritage – there's a little bit of everything under this vast culinary roof.

Lebanon, Syria and Jordan are three neighbouring countries once referred to as the Fertile Crescent. It is a region of rich produce and distinguished culinary tradition but with long periods of turbulent history. Ancient battles and modern politics, conflicting religions and recent war and terrorism have all affected the landscape and lives of people, forcing many survivors to migrate, but the culinary roots are strong and binding, full of memories of home. For some, survival has become a way of life as communities gather what little they have, light a fire or charcoal stove, and cook a meal together.

Having visited war-torn Beirut when it looked beyond repair and Syria when it was thriving in its architectural glory, it is devastating to see this destruction and loss but comforting to know that things can change and see small signs of healing and hope. Lebanon has always tempted us with seasonal treats and a flourishing international food scene, Jordan attracts visitors to its unique desert landscape and Bedouin traditions, and Syria will surely return to better days. Where there is food and community there is hope, and the culinary culture of the eastern Mediterranean is one of the oldest and strongest there is. So this book celebrates the food that holds these communities together, and the regional culinary heritage that every family shares.

Collectively, the cuisines of Lebanon, Syria and Jordan could be regarded as traditional Arab food at its best. The Lebanese are proud of their appetising mezze and *kibbeh*, the Jordanians are renowned for their meat dishes and for Palestinian recipes, such as *makloub*, that came to the country with the large population of refugees, and the Syrians lay

claim to many of the more piquant specialities of the region, including *muhammara* and *lahm bi ajeen*. Dairy produce, fruit, vegetables and pulses are of prime importance in the region, resulting in hundreds of healthy, sustaining dishes. Everyone talks about food, the dish they are preparing that day or what the new season will bring to the table. There is excitement in the air whenever there is cause for celebration – a reason to feast. From the cradle to the grave, food is so subtly embedded in the mind and so neatly intertwined with life that there is a feast to mark every personal milestone and every act of faith. If ever there was a reflection of the human spirit, it is surely the culinary heritage of this region, as even among the rubble of a bombed neighbourhood, or in the dry heat of a simple Bedouin camp, there is always food being cooked, offered and shared in ancestral style. The preparation of it is not a duty but a joy.

## The Fertile Crescent

We now know Lebanon, Syria and Jordan as three separate countries but, if we look back at the history, they were once part of the Ottoman Empire, Greater Syria and the Fertile Crescent of Mesopotamia, bound by a common language and an ancient heritage in a vast region that also covered modern-day Israel, Iraq and a portion of Turkey. A shared culinary culture was rooted in the peasant cooking of the fertile plains and mountain pastures, combined with Persian and Ottoman influences.

The name 'Fertile Crescent' was attributed to a vast crescent-shaped region with rich soil and a good climate conducive to large-scale production of grain and vegetables. Even in medieval times, the variety and abundance of the crops astounded visitors. Recording their impressions of the Bekaa and Jordan Valleys, these early travellers described olive trees bursting with fruit; figs, mulberries, sugar cane and aubergines in terraced fields; corn, beans, a variety of squashes; and plump purple grapes dangling from their vines. Specific regions were known for their vegetable specialities: Damascus produced the best asparagus; Ashqelon was known for its onions; Tripoli was famous for its taro; and the best cucumbers were cultivated in the Bekaa Valley.

The agricultural production and village life in the grain-growing regions of the Fertile Crescent have barely changed over the course of time. The land is still tilled by oxen, and groups of women work side by side in the fields, returning to their village as night falls. There are often orchards of peaches, apricots and pomegranates and small vineyards around these rural villages. Old wooden carts laden with plump melons and tomatoes sit in courtyards, and the pretty yellow heads of sunflowers are laid along the edges of the dirt country lanes to dry in the sun so the seeds can be extracted. Young boys often tend the goats or

Top **Vineyards in the spectacular Bekaa valley, the most fertile area of Lebanon.**

Bottom **The *Cedrus libani*, a species of evergreen conifer. Native to the mountains of the eastern Mediterranean, the tree is the national emblem of Lebanon.**

sheep while the women thresh the wheat or grind the corn. There is as much culinary activity on the rooftops as there is indoors: the flat roofs provide an ideal surface for apricots, figs, plums, raisins, wheat and corn to dry in the sun alongside trays of pulped tomatoes and peppers. It's delightful to wander around these villages and chat to the children who often seem so well nourished and happy in their soil-rich home.

After the First World War, the Fertile Crescent acquired the name of the Levant States, which referred to the French mandate over Syria and Lebanon. Later Lebanon and Syria became independent states, Jordan became a kingdom, and Palestine and Israel were partitioned. The terms 'The Fertile Crescent' and 'The Levant' now refer to modern Lebanon, Syria, Jordan, Palestine, Israel, and Iraq. Egypt, Iran, parts of Turkey and Cyprus also come under the banner of the Fertile Crescent. To keep things simple in the recipe section of this book I refer to the collective region of Lebanon, Syria and Jordan as the eastern Mediterranean.

# Mountains, rivers, desert

The landscape of Lebanon, Syria and Jordan is amazingly diverse, from arid desert to green valleys, and flat flood plains to high mountain peaks. Although Lebanon is by far the smallest of these three countries, it is also one of the most productive, with a long coastline and relatively few barren areas. The coastal strip of Lebanon and Syria is hot and dry, but heavy dew often forms during the night to keep the fruit and vegetables well watered. Much of Jordan, on the other hand, is desert. All three countries have substantial river valleys and flood plains with long hours of sunshine for crops and grazing but, geographically, this part of the eastern Mediterranean is a land of contrasts.

Lebanon | This small country has a rich and varied landscape, which divides quite naturally into three main regions, all running from north to south. The first is the coastal region, a mere 2 or 3 km (1–2 miles) of flat terrain giving just enough space for the major towns to gain a foothold before the mountains begin. These sea ports became important trading centres in the early medieval period, dealing in all kinds of foodstuffs. There is also room on the coastal strip for growing vegetables and fruit, particularly citrus fruits, with orchards and fields packed into this small fertile space.

The second region is the Lebanon Mountains, where the terraced lower slopes sprout almond and olive trees. These mountain peaks rise to over 3,300 metres (10,800 feet) in the north of the range and most are topped with snow throughout the year. Crossing the mountains was a risky enterprise hundreds of years ago, but now the routes are well established.

Top **Bsharri village is famous for being the birthplace of the poet Khalil Gibran, and the location of the remaining original cedars of Lebanon. It perches at high altitude above the imposing Kadisha Valley.**

Bottom **The medieval Jaabar Castle (or Qalaat Jaabar) is sited on an island in Lake Assad, in Syria, connected by a causeway.**

Top **The surreal desert landscape of Wadi Rum.**

Bottom **The beautiful buildings, monuments and carvings in the red sandstone at Petra in Jordan are world-famous. The ancient structures were carved into the hill by the Nabataeans in the second century** CE.

The third main geographical area in Lebanon is the fantastically productive Bekaa Valley, nestled between the Lebanon Mountains to the west and the Anti-Lebanon Mountains to the east. This is a valley rich in agriculture of all kinds, from settled farming to nomadic herding. It has changed little over the centuries. The eastern Anti-Lebanon Mountains protect the Bekaa Valley from the heat of the desert in Syria, and the highest peaks of these mountains, like those of the Lebanon Mountains, are snow-covered for much of the year. This area is more thinly populated than the western side of the country, and the border with Syria snakes along the top of the range.

## Syria
Flowing through the northeast of Syria is one of the great rivers of the Middle East, the Euphrates. This mighty waterway cuts through a dry, rocky, desert landscape, giving the river banks and flood plains sufficient moisture to grow wheat, cotton and sunflowers, as well as a variety of vegetables. In the south, mountains give way to a cultivated plain, the Al-Ghab, through which the Orontes River flows. Irrigation from these two major rivers plays a vital role in the country's agriculture.

In the south a high mountain range, the Jebel Libnan ash-Shariqiyya, separates the arid land of Syria from the fertile Bekaa Valley in Lebanon. Damascus, Homs, Hama and Aleppo are surrounded by areas of intensive farming, including wheat and other cereal crops, but inland to the east, away from the sea and the mountains, lies an enormous expanse of seemingly endless, stony desert, broken only by the oasis of Palmyra which, in ancient and medieval times, was an important centre for camel caravans plying the trade routes.

## Jordan
Many people visit Jordan to go to the Dead Sea, Petra and Wadi Rum in the desert, which is visually spectacular although the only plants that grow there are cacti and scrub grazing for the hardy sheep and goats that thrive in these regions. Jordan's most dominant feature is the fertile valley of the 251-km (156-mile) Jordan River, which is fed by water from the Sea of Galilee, the Yarmouk River, and countless little streams from the high plateaux. The river valley forms part of the Great Rift Valley, and runs the entire length of the country, from the Syrian border in the north, past the Dead Sea, to the Gulf of Aqaba and the Red Sea in the south. The pine forests of the northern part of Jordan give way to cultivated slopes bearing eucalyptus, olive and banana trees, and most of the Jordan Valley is lush and fertile, providing citrus fruits and vegetables, and good grazing for livestock, although the Dead Sea area is too salty for cultivation.The east bank plateau, divided by deep gorges, is home to the main cities of Jordan, including Amman and Karak. Crops such as cereals, pulses, olives, and fruit are grown although the wadis (valleys) are often dry in the summer, so small plots and gardens require constant watering. The remaining 80 per cent of Jordan is arid desert.

# An ancient heritage

The vast area called Greater Syria was located at the crossroads of major trade routes so it witnessed many settlements and empires, from the early Egyptians, Canaanites, Hittites, Assyrians, Greeks, Romans, Arabs, Crusaders and Ottoman Turks right up to the French and British occupation in the 20th century. These have all left an influential stamp on the geographical, cultural and culinary landscape.

The research of archaeologists has confirmed that around 8000BCE agriculture was already being practised by the early settlements in the Fertile Crescent of Mesopotamia, which was also referred to as the 'cradle of civilisation'. Wheat and barley were the principal grains, resulting in a variety of leavened and unleavened breads baked in clay ovens or on flat stones; meat was roasted whole over an open flame, or preserved in its own fat; milk was transformed into yogurt, cheese and butter; and olives were pressed for oil.

With a history of trading with far-flung countries and centuries of productive cultivation in the fertile fields, it is no wonder that the cuisine of the region grew and prospered with distinction.

## Phoenicians and Persians

As far back as the 12th century BCE, the seafaring Phoenicians dominated the coastal colonies of the eastern Mediterranean, trading in shrubs and herbs, spices and perfumed oils, fruit, nuts and dried fish. The rise of the Persian Empire from 558 to 330BCE, spanning a vast territory from Russia in the north to Egypt in the south, and from Greece in the west to India in the east, made an even bigger impact on the regional cuisine. Persia's merchants also spread their empire's culinary skills, introducing some wonderfully exotic ingredients such as pomegranates, saffron, aubergines and lemons, as well as the inherent belief in the art of pleasing the eye as well as the palate.

## The Roman and Byzantine Empires

The Romans were the next great power to annex the countries of the Fertile Crescent, and in doing so they linked India to Rome by sea, extending the trade routes even further. This was a period of industrious culinary productivity, with the discovery of many spices and scents and their uses in both food and medicine. When the Roman Empire split in two in CE 395, the eastern half became the Byzantine Empire, which governed Greater Syria until the early 7th century. The reign of Emperor Justinian I and Empress Theodora in the 6th century saw the further spread of culinary traditions as their great feasts embraced Indian, Persian, Armenian, Greek and Syrian dishes.

Top **Part of the ancient Roman site of Palmyra, near Damascus in Syria; the ruined Arab castle Fakhr-al-Din al-Maani can be seen on the hill behind.**

Bottom **Delegates from the subject lands of the Persian Empire, which included most of what is now Lebanon, Syria and Jordan, bear gifts for a ceremony in this bas-relief, c.515BCE.**

Above **Pressing olives for oil probably dates back 4500 years in the regions of Jordan and Israel.**

## The Golden Age of Islam

The spread of Islam in the 7th century had a huge impact on the culture and cuisine of the region, as it travelled from Asia to North Africa and Spain. Along the way, the invading Arabs converted most of the diverse inhabitants to Islam and imposed religious restrictions on culinary practices, although some Christian communities hid in the mountains of Lebanon and in cave dwellings in Syria and Anatolia, holding on to their religious traditions. The Golden Age of Islam flourished during the Abassid dynasty from the 8th to the 12th century. The culinary culture included an emphasis on etiquette and tableware, as well as visual creativity of the dishes. A number of culinary manuals were written during this period, with an emphasis on manners, diet and health, such as the 10th-century *Kitab al-Tabikh* by Ibn Sayyar al-Warraq.

## The Ottoman Empire

In the year 1258, a son named Osman was born to the chief of a Turkish tribe in Anatolia. This boy later established the Ottoman (Osmanlı) Empire, which ruled a vast territory encompassing the Balkans, the eastern Mediterranean, Arabia and North Africa for the next 500 years. The impact of the Ottoman Empire on the culinary culture of the region was particularly significant in the 16th century, when the Ottomans and the Spaniards came to an agreement that the goods brought back from the New World would be transported via the North African coast to Egypt and Constantinople. This arrangement meant that New World ingredients such as chilli peppers, tomatoes and corn were distributed throughout the Ottoman territories, finding their way into the cuisine with ease. It was during this time, too, that coffee was discovered, probably in Ethiopia, spreading by the middle of the 15th century to Yemen, Arabia, and the rest of the Empire.

The rulers of the Ottoman Empire had a reputation for extravagance. A list of the foods served at a feast held by Suleyman the Magnificent, Sultan of the Ottoman Empire from 1520 to 1566, is as follows: barberry and almond soups; noodles; pigeon, peacock, and mutton kebabs; savoury pastries; meatballs; savoury rice dishes; saffron rice pudding; carrot and quince jellies; sponge cakes soaked in syrup; sweet pastries; almond and pistachio sweetmeats; sweet preserves made from cherries, pumpkin, peaches, aubergines and melon; and many varieties of bread. After ruling for half a millenium, the Ottoman Empire collapsed with the defeat of Turkey in the First World War, but its culinary legacy is evident in the cooking of the region today.

## Recent history

After the Second World War, Lebanon and Syria became independent states, Jordan became a kingdom, and Palestine and Israel were partitioned. Since then the crescent-shaped region of Lebanon, Syria and Jordan has been involved in terrible conflict. Yet through the worst of times, the shared culinary history and enthusiasm for food and cooking has not wavered.

# Feasts and festivals

Lebanon, Syria and Jordan are home to a range of ethnic and religious groups. Arabic is the principal language and the majority of the region's population is Muslim, with a minority that includes Christians, Jews, and breakaway Islamic groups. All of these contribute to a melting pot of languages and dialects, as well cultural and culinary customs. The regional culinary calendar flows from one Islamic religious feast to another, interspersed with Christian celebrations.

Christmas | At this time of the year, the Christian communities generally celebrate with an exchange of gifts and a roasted bird, or a leg of lamb, just like Christians in other parts of the world. One exception is the Armenian community, which celebrates Christmas on 6 January, the Epiphany, with mounds of sticky *awamat*, deep-fried fritters bathed in honey or syrup. Both days are public holidays.

Easter | This is the most important date of the Christian calendar. On Good Friday, when devout Christians abstain from meat, a variety of vegetable and pulse dishes are prepared, such as *mujaddara*, rice cooked with lentils, and a sour bulgur soup called *shoraba zingool*. The sourness of this soup is intended to remind Christians of the vinegar given to Christ on the cross. On Easter Sunday, platters of *ma'amoul*, semolina cakes stuffed with walnuts or dates, celebrate the end of Lent.

Ramadan | As the vast majority of the population is Muslim, the month of Ramadan plays a very important part in the year. During Ramadan, the ninth month of the Muslim calendar, all adult Muslims fast between sunrise and sunset to mark the revelation of the Quran to the Prophet Muhammad. A simple meal, *suhur*, is prepared before dawn and is designed to fill the stomach for the daylight hours ahead. It normally comprises a hearty soup and bread. *Itfar*, the meal that is consumed once the sun has gone down, is much more extensive, perhaps involving savoury pastries, meatballs or kibbeh, stuffed vegetables, and numerous sweet dishes such as baklava, milk puddings, fruit compotes, and *ma'amoul*, the little semolina cakes. Drinks such as sherberts made from carob and tamarind are served to accompany dishes of roasted lamb and chicken with rice, and dates are always placed on the table at religious feasts as a reminder that they were the only food for the Prophet when he was fasting in the desert. The purpose of Ramadan is to teach self-discipline, a necessary virtue when submitting to the will of God, and to instil understanding and compassion for the poor, who experience hunger all year round.

Top **Ananias Christian church in the Old City of Damascus in Syria.**

Bottom **Sayyida Zeinab mosque, in Damascus.**

**Eid al-Fitr** | Once the month of Ramadan comes to an end, it is time to celebrate with a great deal of merriment and feasting over a three-day period. Friends and neighbours exchange gifts, buy new clothes, and visit their relatives to share good food of all kinds. Two public holidays are set aside for the event, to make up for the previous month of restraint.

**Eid al-Salib** | One of the most celebrated feast days among the Christian communities is Eid al-Salib, or St Helena's Day, on 8 September. Legend says that Queen Helena, the mother of the Roman Emperor Constantine, found the True Cross of the crucifixion on a hillside above Jerusalem and demanded that fires be lit in watchtowers all the way to Constantinople. To commemorate this legend, bonfires and fireworks light up the sky, as Christians, and Muslims too, gather together to dance and feast in the streets, and vendors sell kibbeh and other delights late into the night.

**Eid al-Barbara** | Another Christian celebration that Muslims enjoy is St Barbara's Day, with festivities similar to Halloween. The children dress up in masks and devour bowls of *kamhiyeh*, wheat or barley sweetened with sugar and decorated with pomegranate seeds.

**Eid al-Adha** | Also called Eid el-Qurban, this is a feast day that is respected throughout the Muslim world, and marks the near-sacrifice of Isma'il, or Isaac. Each family that can afford to buy a ram will take it home and share it among the family members and sometimes with the poor in their area. The meat is cooked in soups, stews and kibbeh, the intestines are stuffed and grilled, and the tail is boiled and served as a delicacy with pitta bread and yogurt. Nothing is wasted.

## Family feasts and traditions

Special foods are also associated with the main events of life, such as birth, marriage and death. When a baby is born, a traditional cinnamon-flavoured rice pudding, *meghlie*, is served to family members and visitors. When the baby's first tooth comes through, the family typically prepares sachets of sugar-coated almonds and chickpeas to distribute to friends and family.

Wedding feasts are lavish affairs, often involving an entire village. Stuffed vine leaves, pastries, pilaffs, kibbeh and puddings are all prepared for the celebration, and some dishes specifically symbolise fertility or prosperity for the new couple. Funeral traditions do vary from region to region, as some families mark the occasion with a feast, while others simply prepare a traditional halva to offer to those who have come to pay their respects.

Top **Dried fruits, sweetmeats, cakes and pastries are made in huge quantities for many feasts, and the meal eaten at the end of the day during Ramadan will finish with a delicious array of sweet pastries.**

Bottom **Family gatherings may have a more contemporary feel now, but the tradition of preparing and eating food together is still very important.**

# Culinary customs

The Arab traditions of hospitality and sharing are deeply ingrained in the psyche of most of the region's population, especially the nomadic Bedouin, the people who perhaps have the least to share. Over the last few centuries, writers and travellers have commented on the dignity and courtesy of the Bedouin, often describing their gracious hospitality when they have stopped at a tent in the middle of the desert.

When it comes to culinary culture, most of the traditional customs are still observed. Even the youngest members of the family are deeply courteous and hospitable. Hospices, guest-houses and private homes have provided free food and shelter for travellers throughout the region's history and they still do so to this day. When a host welcomes a guest it is normal to hear the words 'bayti, baytak' (my house is your house), and usually it is sincerely meant.

It is polite to offer food and drink to strangers. It is also usual to offer them the best cuts of meat, which may include the coveted eyeballs, brains or testicles, and it is impolite to refuse! Sometimes great mounds of food are consumed, which can be difficult for the guest, but it is acceptable to leave food on your plate, proving to the hostess that she has provided you with more than enough to eat.

In most households, meals are eaten sitting on floor cushions, often with everyone gathered around trays of food raised off the ground. In some traditional families the grandparents may be served in one room with the male head of the house, while the women eat with the children; in other households, the women and men may eat separately. This is not necessarily for religious reasons. In some areas, eating separately is simply a time-honoured tradition for the family. In more modern families, however, mealtime is a sociable, family event and all the members and their guests eat together.

# Islamic food rules

In the Quran, there are four categories of food that are forbidden (or not *halal*): any animal that did not have its throat cut; products made from the blood of an animal; pork; and the meat of an animal sacrificed in the name of any other God. The consumption of reptiles and beasts of prey is not officially banned, but Islamic scholars consider them harmful so they are not usually on the Muslim menu. Also, although it is lawful 'to fish in the sea and consume the catch', not all Arabs eat shellfish. The Quran forbids alcohol, although the relevant text refers to 'wine', leaving room for argument amongst those who consume arak or other spirits.

Top **Falafel, spicy deep-fried balls prepared from ground chickpeas or beans, cooked by a street vendor.**

Bottom **A simple café breakfast of flatbread and puréed brown beans, with fresh mint, raw onion, salt and chilli accompaniments.**

# Shopping in the souks

The food markets are the heart and lungs of every community, and typify all that is best about the food culture of the eastern Mediterranean. In the Islamic and Ottoman Empires, goods of infinite variety were brought by camel caravan from Arabia, Persia, Armenia, Byzantium, Egypt, India and China, and delivered to the markets of Beirut, Aleppo and Constantinople. Still central to people's lives today, the markets range from the sprawling clusters of historic bazaars in Damascus and Amman to the rural, makeshift stalls of the mountain villages of Lebanon. In the larger indoor souqs, the shops are grouped together according to their trade in the manner of the medieval guild system, and as you walk through them you can observe artisans making kibbeh and other delicacies. If you're feeling hungry, you can buy some kebabs or falafel tucked into pitta bread, or roasted, salted pumpkin seeds in a cone of newspaper.

# The mezze (mazzeh) tradition

Nothing quite beats eating mezze under the shade of an old fig tree, or on a balcony overlooking the cobbled streets of an old town, at a table by the sea, watching the sun sink below the horizon, or indoors seated comfortably on cushions around a low table set with a tantalising array of little dishes.

The concept of mezze or mazzeh is an old one. The word is thought to have derived from the Persian word 'maza', meaning 'taste' or 'relish', or from the Arabic verb, 'mazmiz', 'to nibble at food'. The ancient Greeks and Romans enjoyed a tradition of nibbling nuts, herbs, seeds and raw vegetables, accompanied by wine. The medieval Arabs and Ottoman Turks added to the quality and variety of appetising dishes but, under the rules of Islam, they were usually offered with non-alcoholic drinks. However, in Lebanon the drinking of wine and arak, the aniseed-flavoured spirit, was not banned and the Christian monasteries produced their own wine. In Lebanon and Syria, snacks and appetisers that are served with a non-alcoholic drink, such as a glass of tea or a sherbet, are generally referred to as *muqabbalat*.

One thing that all mezze have in common is that the dishes are served in small quantities on individual plates, and everyone helps themselves. The joy of mezze lies in admiring different colours and textures, dipping bread into creamy dips, and popping succulent nibbles into your mouth. It is a wonderful way to eat and can form an entire meal, but it is also easy to forget that this spread of dishes is very often only a prelude to the ensuing meat, rice and vegetable dishes, so a degree of restraint has to be mastered.

Top **Shopping in the souks is a sociable part of daily life. The markets have a variety and abundance of fresh vegetables and fruit that can be almost overwhelming, and the aroma of spice is ever-present.**

Bottom **The tradition of mezze, the sharing of multiple and varied little dishes, is one of the most enjoyable features of the culinary culture in the Levant.**

# Cooking equipment

For millennia, waves of seafaring traders passed by the eastern Mediterranean coastline bearing goods and spices from India, the South Seas and China, and bringing with them all their own food traditions. It would be easy to assume that the illustrious culinary history would lead to the development of modernised kitchens and cooking tools but many people in rural villages still use communal ovens and a simple hearth made by piling up a few stones to contain a fire, situated in a dark room at the back of the house or outdoors. Wealthier, more modern households may possess a fixed brick range, or an electric cooker with an oven, but even in the most up-to-date buildings, the kitchen is often fairly basic with traditional cooking utensils.

In the medieval period, it used to be the custom for a father to give his daughter a gift of useful household items on the eve of her marriage. This mainly consisted of basic copper pans, a baking tray, ladles and the long thin rolling pin required for traditional flatbreads. Neither the custom nor the utensils themselves have changed much, and each newly married couple is still grateful to receive a selection of classic utensils to furnish their own kitchen.

Regardless of how intricate and time-consuming some of the dishes can be, they do not require sophisticated equipment. Of course, wealthier and more cosmopolitan members of society may have aids such as electric mixers, but to achieve good Arab food, simple tools are all that is required. The techniques of simmering, frying and baking remain the same whether the cook is using a built-in cooker in a city apartment or a tiny fire in an open hearth next to a Bedouin tent.

### Pilaffs, stews and preserves
Many households reserve pride of place in the kitchen for a large copper pot, known as a *dist*. This substantial utensil is used for simmering mixtures gently on the stove top. It is ideal for preparing rice or a bulgur pilaff, for producing a large quantity of tomato paste from the summer crop, or a seasonal batch of fruit jam and molasses. These pots are lined with tin and supported by two handles to make them easier to carry to the table when full. The copper base means that the heat of the stove is quickly transferred to the food simmering inside. The hefty size of a dist means that is an extremely useful piece of equipment, as it can contain a large amount of soup or even a whole sheep cut into joints for a feast. The dist typifies the hospitable nature of the region, always ready to cook for a crowd. A smaller version of this pot, used for everyday dishes in smaller households, is the traditional *tanjara*, which is also fashioned from copper and tin-lined, with one or two handles and a lid.

Top **Flatbreads are made daily in the traditional way. The large, stretchy *taboon* is a Bedouin or Levantine bread, cooked here over a wood-fired stove. It is perfect for wrapping round sharwama and falafel.**

Bottom **Most restaurants and many homes have a portable or permanent grill or barbecue for roasting kebabs.**

### Roasted spices and kibbeh
A spacious frying pan, called a *miqla*, made from heavy tin-lined copper or cast iron, is another important utensil for cooking eggs and omelettes, for dry-roasting spices, and for frying meatballs and kibbeh. It is ideal for cooking pieces of meat or fish quickly on the stove top.

### Baked savoury and sweet treats
For oven-baked savoury dishes such as spicy meat pies and kibbeh, most households use a circular metal tray with raised sides, known as a *siniyya*. This is also perfect for baking sweet pastries, such as baklava.

Many households still do not have their own built-in oven for baking. Villages and towns are generally provided with communal ovens, known as the *furn*, where people can purchase bread or take their home-prepared dough and other dishes to be baked. Large cuts of meat or whole beasts are also roasted in the local furn for special occasions such as religious feasts or weddings. A furn is often made from clay and is fired by wood. Flatbreads can also be prepared outdoors on hot stones in desert areas, or in the kitchen on a heavy iron griddle, known as a *saaj*.

### Succulent barbecues
A charcoal grill, the *manqal*, made out of copper, clay or metal, is frequently used for grilling meat and fish. This is often a permanent fixture in the kitchen or in the enclosed yard of a rural house. When it is made freestanding and fashioned out of metal, it becomes portable so that it can be used on balconies, in gardens or even taken to the countryside for picnics.

### Coffee pots
Turkish-style coffee is very finely ground and brewed in a long-handled pot, a *rakwi*. Arabic-style coffee is generally prepared in two pots, known as *dallahs*: the first is used for making the brew of ground coffee and boiling water, which is then poured into the second, leaving the grains behind. Coffee is always served in tiny ornate cups.

### Other useful equipment
The cooking processes are fairly simple, requiring just a few solid pots and good-quality utensils. A selection of sharp knives of different sizes is needed for preparing and carving whole joints of meat, filleting fish and chopping vegetables and herbs. Wooden spoons are typically used, often carved with beautiful patterns. A large curved spoon is absolutely vital for ladling soup or rice from the *dist*, the large cooking pot found on every stove. Metal grilling skewers are needed for kebabs cooked on the *manqal*, or barbecue. A draining dish or tin with a perforated base, like a colander, is used for draining vegetables or rice or bulgur. Bread-making requires a long, thin rolling pin for the wide flatbreads so typical of the region. And not least, a mortar and pestle is used for many kitchen tasks, such as grinding spices and coffee beans, crushing garlic, and pounding pulses.

Top **Small cups of thick black coffee are enjoyed through the day and at the end of a large meal.**

Bottom **Circular metal trays with raised sides (*siniyya*) are used for all kinds of savoury and sweet bakes, ideal for festive kibbeh, baklava and pastries.**

# Ingredients

These are the everyday ingredients that
play an intrinsic role in the cooking of the
eastern Mediterranean. With the Phoenician
and Persian legacy of trading, it is not
surprising that the stylish and vibrant
cuisine of the Levant is rich in all the senses.
Fragrant spices, herbs and flavourings
infuse and accompany the abundant
fresh vegetables, fruits, grains, cheeses and
locally sourced meat and fish. And of course
olives, oil and breads are essential
components of the daily meal.

# Spices, herbs and flavourings

Spices and herbs, scented flavourings and syrups play an important role in every dish. The ones described here are the standard ingredients kept in a *munay*, the food cellar or larder of a kitchen in a typical Lebanese, Syrian or Jordanian house.

Ancient Chinese theories of yin and yang filtered through to the Fertile Crescent in the medieval period. This involves balancing the warming and cooling properties of foods, as well as utilising their medicinal properties. Warming spices such as cumin, cinnamon, allspice, cloves, and chilli peppers are believed to improve the appetite and aid digestion. Generous quantities of fresh herbs, particularly mint, dill and parsley, are often mixed together as a warming trio to balance the cooling properties of some vegetable dishes and salads, and garlic is believed to be beneficial to the circulation of the blood.

Chillies | These fruity and fiery little peppers reached the eastern Mediterranean in the 16th century, when the Ottomans and Spaniards brought them into the region, along with tomatoes and corn. Since then, chillies have developed a leading role for themselves, particularly in Jordan and Syria, where some dishes are very fiery compared to the subtler notes of Lebanese cooking. Unripe green chillies are used mainly in salads, kebabs and grilled dishes. Some of these are tiny and extremely hot, while others are long, twisted and fairly mild. The long red chillies, known locally as Aleppo peppers, are the most common as they are extremely fruity with just a hint of fire. They are left to dry in the sun and then chopped finely or ground to a powder and sold as the ubiquitous chilli spice, Aleppo pepper.

Garlic | Indigenous to the Fertile Crescent, garlic is used for both medicinal and culinary purposes. It appears in mezze dips, nut sauces, pickles, marinades for fish and meat kebabs, and most stews and soups. In the villages of Lebanon, Syria and Jordan, whole heads of plump, healthy, strong garlic are threaded on to kebab skewers with strips of fat from the sheep's tail and grilled over an open fire. Because of its pungency, garlic is believed to hold magical powers, and strings of garlic bulbs are often hung in people's doorways to ward off evil spirits.

Sumac | Deep red, almost purple, in colour this popular spice is prepared by crushing and grinding the dried berries of a bush (Rhus coriaria) that grows wild in the mountains of Lebanon and the arid regions of Syria and Jordan. It has a sharp, fruity taste and was traditionally used as a souring agent before lemons arrived in the region. It can be sprinkled over most dishes and is a component of zahtar.

Top left **Sweet-scented rose petals.**

Top right **Resin-tasting dried mastic crystals.**

Bottom left **Aleppo pepper – the finely chopped dried chillies of the region.**

Bottom right **Often combined with mint and parsley, fresh dill is a lovely addition to many dishes.**

**Cinnamon** | This spice was first brought to the region by Arab traders from Sri Lanka and the Spice Islands, and quickly became absorbed into the culinary culture. The Ottomans added cinnamon to savoury rice dishes, stuffed vegetables, milk puddings and sweet pastries. In Lebanon and Syria it is used in a variety of sweet biscuits, cakes, and sweetmeats, as well as savoury stews and soups.

**Coriander seeds** | Along with cumin, coriander seeds are used daily. Regarded as a 'warming' spice, the seeds appear in many vegetable dishes. They emit a delicious nutty fragrance when roasted.

**Cumin** | These seeds have a distinctive taste and, like coriander seeds, emit a delightful nutty aroma when roasted. Cumin is believed to aid digestion, and is therefore used in a number of dishes that might cause a degree of indigestion or flatulence, such as *ful medames*, a dish of brown beans.

**Saffron** | Worth its weight in gold, saffron is the only spice in the world to be measured by the carat. Genuine saffron is very special indeed. It is formed from the dried orangey-red stigmas of the purple crocus (Crocus sativus), which only flowers for two weeks every October. Although only mildly perfumed when first picked, the stigmas come to life when soaked in water and impart a magnificent yellow dye with a hint of floral notes. Most of the saffron used in the region comes from Iran.

**Baharat** | A ground spice mix used to flavour meat stews throughout the Middle East. It includes eight spices: black pepper, coriander seeds, cumin, cinnamon, cloves, nutmeg, paprika and cardamom (the cardamom is often omitted in Lebanon).

**Zahtar** | A combination of thyme, sumac and sesame seeds – this much-loved spice mixture is known as zahtar, the Arabic word for thyme, which grows wild in the hills of Lebanon. It is sprinkled over bread, cheese, yogurt and salads and is a favourite seasoning used by street vendors throughout Egypt and the Fertile Crescent. It is added liberally to beans, cooked meats, kibbeh and other hot savoury snacks. Simply mix 30ml/2 tbsp dried thyme, 30ml/2 tbsp toasted sesame seeds, 15ml/1 tbsp ground sumac and 5ml/1 tsp sea salt, and rub with your fingers to release the aroma before sealing in a sterilised jar.

**Coriander (cilantro)** | The coriander plant has been used in the eastern Mediterranean for medicinal and culinary purposes since ancient times. Coriander leaves have a citrus taste which works particularly well in marinades, meat and poultry dishes, and as a garnish.

Top **No market will be without stalls selling huge bowls of spices, both whole and ready-ground.**

Bottom **Fresh herbs are used regularly and in abundance.**

Flat leaf parsley | This is probably the most popular fresh herb in the eastern Mediterranean. Large bunches of flat leaf parsley are stacked so high in the market stalls that they completely conceal the stallholder. Although it is used liberally in dishes, parsley is also served on its own to sharpen the appetite, to cleanse the palate, or to freshen the breath. The flat leaf variety has a very distinctive aroma and taste. It is used in great quantities in *fatoush*, *ful medames*, *baba ghanoush* and above all *tabbouleh*, a parsley salad with bulgur tossed through it, rather than the other way round.

Mint | This well-known herb grows prolifically in the eastern Mediterranean, finding its way into numerous salads, dips, soups (such as chilled cucumber and yogurt soup, *shorbet khyar bi laban*) and sweet dishes. With its refreshing and digestive qualities, fresh mint is one of the most useful herbs for cold dishes. The dried herb is found more often in soups and stews. Infusions are believed to relieve nausea, stomach pain and sore throats.

Rose | The use of rose petals can be traced back to the ancient Egyptians, who bathed in an infusion of roses, and the Romans, who made wine from the flowers, but the invention of distilled rose water for culinary purposes is attributed to the Persians. This spread throughout the region, from the sumptuous medieval dishes prepared for the banquets of Baghdad to the sophisticated dishes of Constantinople (now Istanbul). Rose petals are used as a garnish, and rose syrups are used in a variety of sweet dishes and drinks. Rose water is a main ingredient of the popular sherbert drink, *sharab al ward*, often served to welcome guests.

Mastic | This is the aromatic gum from a small evergreen tree (Pistacia lentiscus) that grows wild all over the Mediterranean region. The droplets of resin form little crystals, which are pulverised with sugar in a mortar and pestle. Traditionally, the distinctive flavour of mastic is added to milk puddings, jams, ice cream, marinades and the local aniseed-flavoured spirit, arak.

Carob molasses | This is a thick, dark molasses obtained from the fruit inside the pods of the carob trees that grow in the dry soil of the desert areas in Syria, Jordan and Lebanon. Traditionally, the molasses was used instead of sugar to sweeten drinks, puddings and stews. Dates, grapes and mulberries are also used to make sweet fruit molasses.

Pomegranate molasses | Unlike the carob one, this molasses is very sharp. The juice of sour pomegranates is boiled until it thickens and darkens. The molasses is used in salad dressings and marinades, and is often drizzled over dishes to add its exquisite fruity, sour note.

Top left **Fresh, dried, roasted and grilled whole on kebab skewers, garlic finds its way into most savoury dishes.**

Top right **Dried and broken-up bay leaves.**

Bottom left **Freshly pounded spice mixes zahtar and baharat.**

Bottom right **Coiled cinnamon bark emits a sweet, warming aroma.**

# Olives and truffles

A handful of olives, a chunk of cheese, some bread and a drizzle of fruity olive oil is one of my favourite snacks. In the mountain pastures of Lebanon and the fertile plains of Syria, local herders and travellers carry just these, with perhaps a few dates, to sustain them for the day.

Olives | A Lebanese dinner table would be incomplete without a bowl of locally harvested olives, which are often marinated in olive oil, thyme and lemon juice, and are invariably served as part of a mezze spread. Evergreen olive trees thrive in the dry soil and stony hillsides of Lebanon, Jordan and Syria, where they bear fruit for a long time, sometimes hundreds of years. A huge variety of olives is available in the markets of the eastern Mediterranean, often particular to a village or locality. Certain villages are renowned for different kinds of olives and for their local olive oil.

Olive oil | Collectively, Lebanon, Syria, Jordan and Turkey are the main producers of olive oil in the eastern Mediterranean and the Middle East. Olive oil is the principal cooking oil of these countries, where it has been produced for thousands of years. The Romans used it as fuel for lamps and cooking, while the ancient Hebrews used it for religious ceremonies. The cooks of the Ottoman kitchens devised recipes where olive oil was not only the cooking fuel but also the principal flavouring ingredient, requiring the dish to be served at room temperature to appreciate it. In medieval times the olive oil of Syria was much sought after, but nowadays Turkey has superseded Syria as the main producer of quality oils in the region. Generally, olive oil is used in salads and in dishes where the flavour is intended to predominate, whereas sunflower or nut oil is used for frying.

Truffles | Although truffles are more commonly associated with the cuisines of France and Italy, they have been enjoyed in Lebanon and Syria for centuries. Some varieties of Lebanese truffle, kama, are found at the roots of particular trees on the hillsides, but the Syrian variety is found in the desert. The best truffles, which are gathered and distributed throughout the eastern Mediterranean, grow in profusion around the oasis of Palmyra, situated on the ancient caravan route from Damascus to the Euphrates River. The Bedouins collect them and eat them boiled with buttermilk, or roasted in the ashes of the fire. Medieval recipes call for truffles to be boiled and dressed with oil and crushed thyme, or to be cooked with eggs or lamb. A traditional Lebanese preparation is to cut them into cubes, which are marinated and threaded on to skewers to grill over a fire or barbecue.

Opposite top **A terraced olive grove near Moukhtara, in southern Lebanon.**

Opposite bottom **This olive tree is growing on Mount Nebo in Jordan, where Moses is said to have looked out over the Promised Land.**

Below **The black and white truffles of the driest regions are mild in aroma and taste. You might see them sold in the markets still covered in desert sand, which means they need very careful cleaning.**

# Preserves and pickles

Preserving food is a long tradition, inherited from the medieval Arabs, and there are many different techniques for making sure there is plenty of food for the lean months. This seasonal activity used to be part of daily life in the region and still is in many rural homes, although most of these products are now commercially produced in the cities and available year-round. Just about every kind of food is preserved in some way: meat is preserved in its own fat; fish is dried and salted, or pickled; fleshy stone fruit, mulberries and figs are dried in the sun, as are bell peppers, aubergines or eggplants, okra, and broad or fava beans. Tomatoes and peppers are reduced to pastes, and sour pomegranates and grapes are boiled down to syrupy molasses. Preserved lemons are world-famous.

Pickling is the most popular method of preserving vegetables, fruits and nuts, partly because the results are so delicious and attractive. Individual pickles include jars of green beans, white cabbage, green chilli peppers, okra, green tomatoes, green walnuts, green almonds and beetroot. Combined pickles can range from cabbage with apricots and green almonds, to slices of aubergine wrapped around garlic or apricots, and tied in a bundle with a thin ribbon of leek or celery. Other favourite combinations include pickled turnip with a few slices of beetroot to turn them a pretty a shade of pink, or the addition of red cabbage to cauliflower to give a purple hue.

To flavour the pickling brine, vine leaves, garlic cloves, coriander seeds, cinnamon sticks, parsley stalks, allspice berries and small, thin, hot chillies are often added. The jars are then filled to the brim with apple or white wine vinegar, sometimes diluted with water, and often seasoned with salt. The pickling juice is drunk to quench the thirst on a hot day.

# Dairy products

Milk and its by-products have a central part in the culinary world of Lebanon, Jordan and Syria. In accordance with Islamic customs, milk is rarely consumed fresh, and more commonly appears in the form of by-products such as butter, clarified butter, yogurt, cheese and clotted cream. Some Bedouin use camel's milk but the majority comes from sheep, goats and (to a lesser extent) cows. Each country has a particular region where the dairy products are regarded as superior to everywhere else, such as the Bekaa Valley in Lebanon or the Euphrates Valley in Syria. Before the days of the large dairy farms and truck distribution, women from the villages used to go from door to door, selling their own milk, cheese and yogurt from large trays balanced on their heads.

Top **The classic green pepper pickle. Pickling used to be vital to the diet, as there was a shortage of fresh produce in the winter and also in the arid desert areas, but the preserves are still made and enjoyed.**

Above **The nutritious yogurt drink, laban. It is very popular in Lebanon, Jordan and Syria. It can be served plain with ice, or with a light sprinkling of dried mint, a pinch of the spice mix zahtar, or a dusting of cinnamon.**

Opposite **Cheese is a way of preserving fresh milk. Clockwise from top right: two types of halloumi, feta, labneh (yogurt cheese), and ewe's milk cheeses.**

Yogurt | Yogurt has been enjoyed in this region since ancient times and has formed an important part of the basic diet, being easily digestible and nutritious. A bowl of yogurt is often served with a meal, particularly with rice and pulse dishes, or it can be combined with other ingredients, such as herbs, garlic and vegetables, to form a dip or salad. It is also served mixed with water and a little salt to produce a refreshing drink, called *laban*, often served with ice cubes, and with a little dried mint sprinkled on top.

The yogurt of this region is generally thick and creamy, but for certain dishes, it is strained through muslin for 6–12 hours to produce an even thicker cream-cheese consistency, called *labneh* (*labna*), which is ideal for dips and sweet dishes. When strained for 36–48 hours the yogurt can be moulded into balls and left to dry before storing in olive oil.

Cheese | Records of cheese-making can be traced back to the ancient Egyptians, Greeks and Romans as well as to the early pastoral societies of the Fertile Crescent. Cheese appears in various guises, from soft white goat's cheese to hard yellowish blocks prepared from ewe's milk. The set white kind is the most versatile as it can be used in mezze dishes, in sweet and savoury pastries, in fillings for flatbreads, or simply drizzled with olive oil for a quick snack or for breakfast. For most dishes in this book, the firm white cheese of the eastern Mediterranean can be substituted with the readily available feta or the salty, springy cheese, *halloumi* (*hallum*), which is popular in Lebanon and Jordan.

Butter | Traditionally, butter was made in a churn fashioned from the tanned skin of a whole goat. The skin was partially filled with milk, and then suspended by four ropes, which were secured to the legs of the skin. The woman of the household would then sit beside the skin and jerk it to and fro until the milk was churned – an age-old tradition that is still used in the remote rural villages and by the Bedouin in their temporary camps. Depending on where you are in the eastern Mediterranean, butter can be made from the milk of sheep, goats or buffalo. It can have quite a strong, almost rancid smell and taste, which some people prefer.

Butter was used lavishly in the medieval kitchens and still is by some cooks, but olive oil and a variety of vegetable oils have superseded butter for cooking in most areas. Aleppo in Syria is well known for its delicious creamy butter, and Hama, also in Syria, gained a reputation for its clarified butter, *samna*.

Clarified butter is used in many dishes. Butter is melted until it froths and then is strained through muslin to remove the impurities, before being poured into a container to cool and solidify. Clarified butter is enjoyed for its nutty taste and aroma, is easy to make, and can be stored in a cool place for months. Because the milk solids have been removed, it can reach higher temperatures before burning, so is perfect for frying.

Top **Most dairy products in Lebanon are made from the milk of goats or sheep.**

Bottom **Almond trees in blossom in the Bekaa Valley.**

# Nuts and seeds

Nutritious and healthy, nuts and seeds of all kinds have played a huge role in the culinary culture of the eastern Mediterranean. They even appear in motifs on ceramic tiles, crockery and textiles. These are a few.

**Almonds** | The ancient Greeks are the first people known to have cultivated almonds, and the Romans, who consumed them in vast quantities, referred to them as a Greek nut. In the early Arab cooking manuals, there are records of almonds being poached and pressed for their delicate milk, which was then used in puddings and drinks.

Immature green almonds are picked while their husks are velvety soft and the whole fruit, including the husk, is eaten as a snack with a sprinkling of salt, or preserved in vinegar. Mature almonds, on the other hand, are prised from their hardened shells and then blanched, roasted, flaked or ground and employed in numerous sweet and savoury dishes, such as the dried fruit and nut compote, *khoshaf*, a dish of medieval origins that is popular throughout the eastern Mediterranean.

**Chestnuts** | Sweet, soft chestnuts in their prickly husks grow prolifically in the eastern Mediterranean and the large, hardy trees live for a long time. When they are finally felled, the strong, flexible wood is used to make orchard ladders and garden tools. They bear ripe fruit in the months of October and November so they are associated with the colder months and the familiar sight of street vendors roasting them on open braziers. Palestinians add chestnuts to *makloub*, their traditional upside-down rice dish, and all over the region chestnuts are preserved in syrup as a popular winter treat and gift.

**Pine nuts** | The creamy seed of the pine cone has a mild resinous taste and is deliciously crunchy when roasted. In ancient times, pine nuts were included in ceremonial cornucopias of fruit placed on statues to symbolise the wealth and status of individual towns and cities. The medieval Arabs added them liberally to both savoury and sweet dishes; the Ottomans added them to fillings for stuffed vegetables and vine leaves, and roasted them to scatter over puddings and dips. All of these traditions continue in the eastern Mediterranean today.

**Pistachios** | Most of the pistachios in the region come from Turkey and Iran, and they are much sought after for taste and colour. The name pistachio comes from the Persian word 'pesteh', and the genus also includes the trees from which the edible resin, mastic, is harvested. The nut can be used in all sorts of creative ways, both sweet and savoury, such as in baklava, salads, rice dishes and stuffed meatballs.

Top left **Sweet preserved chestnuts are given as treats and gifts.**

Top right **Sesame seeds are often sprinkled over breads and pastries.**

Bottom left **Dried almonds are usually blanched before using.**

Bottom right **Walnuts, the king of nuts, in their shells.**

Sesame seeds | These tiny, teardrop-shaped seeds seem almost indispensable in the Arab culinary world. Black (unhulled) or white, they are sprinkled over a variety of savoury pastries and breads, such as the bread rings, *semit*, which are sold on every busy street, on the quayside, in bus stations and markets. Sesame seeds are added to salads, marinades and spice mixes such as zahtar, and they are crushed for their oil and ground to a versatile creamy paste called tahini. The seeds are harvested while still immature – they tend to burst out of their pods and scatter everywhere when they are ripe, hence the famous command 'Open sesame!' in Ali Baba and the Forty Thieves.

Walnuts | These large, wrinkled nuts have long been regarded as the 'king of nuts', in accordance with the Latin and Greek myths that the gods ate walnuts, while mere mortals lived on acorns. The immature green nuts are often pickled or preserved in syrup, while the ripened ones are pressed for their rich, pungent oil, or used in a variety of puddings, sweet pastries and salads. Perhaps their most famous role in the eastern Mediterranean is in the popular red pepper and walnut mezze dish, *muhammara*.

# Vegetables

In a region known as the Fertile Crescent you would expect to find vegetables. And what a choice you have. Abundant harvests and endless dishes are prepared with them – mezze, pickles, salads, stews, pilaffs, jams and puddings. Vegetables have featured in the cooking of the region since ancient times, attaining glory in the medieval period, then influenced by the cuisine of Persia. They are held in the highest esteem.

Aubergines (eggplant) | The most useful vegetable of all is the aubergine, which is known throughout the region as 'poor man's meat'. Originally from the Indian continent, aubergines first appeared in Persia, where the conquering Arabs fell under their spell in the 7th and 8th centuries. Generally, the aubergines of the region are purple, or almost black in colour, and range from large, bulbous ones to small, teardrop-shaped ones that are lovely when smoked. In Syria, dried aubergines are reconstituted in water, stuffed with an aromatic pilaff, or spicy bulgur, and then poached in a little olive oil and lemon juice, and throughout the region small aubergines are pickled.

Carrots | Wild red and purple carrots are believed to have originated in Afghanistan. Somewhere along the carrot's journey into Europe, 17th-century Dutch gardeners cultivated orange carrots as they were regarded as more appealing in colour and superior in taste. Nowadays,

Top left **Dried molokhia has a distinctive if acquired taste.**

Top right **Globe artichokes are sought after when in season, for stuffing.**

Bottom left **The perpetual spinach of the region has tough, tasty leaves and roots.**

Bottom right **Aubergines are fleshy and versatile.**

Top **Carrots.**

Bottom **Okra.**

we are more familiar with the orange carrot, but the red, purple and yellow varieties are still grown in Syria. Carrots contain a fair amount of natural sugar, making them both pretty to look at and sweet to taste, so they are tossed in salads, combined with yogurt, cooked in stews and pickled.

Courgettes (zucchini) | Both courgettes and marrows are believed to be cooling to the blood, and therefore require balancing with warming herbs such as dill and mint. The smallest, freshest courgettes are crisp and slightly perfumed, and taste best tossed raw in salads or cooked very lightly. Young courgettes are often sold with their papery yellow-orange flowers, which are then stuffed with aromatic rice or bulgur. Larger courgettes and marrows are stuffed with savoury mixtures of aromatic rice or minced lamb, and marrow seeds are roasted to nibble on.

Cucumber | These are perhaps one of the oldest cultivated vegetables in the region and have been utilised throughout the centuries for their refreshing qualities. Generally, the cucumbers of the region are much the same size as courgettes – short and stubby, and almost seedless. The skin is quite bitter, so they are usually peeled or partially peeled before eating. Strips of peeled cucumber sprinkled with salt are enjoyed as a refreshing snack, and finely sliced or chopped cucumber is often mixed with yogurt and garlic to make a salad or dip. In Lebanon cucumber and yogurt are also combined in a cold soup, *shorbet khyar bi laban*.

Globe artichokes | These regal-looking vegetables were once regarded as luxury foods, but in fact, globe artichokes are simply glorious thistles, a cultivated version of the ancient cardoon, which has grown wild in the eastern Mediterranean for centuries. Fresh artichokes are sold on their long stems in the markets so that they can be kept in a bucket of water at home, like a bunch of flowers. In Lebanon, where they are particularly popular, ready-prepared artichokes can be bought at the markets to poach in olive oil or stuff with broad (fava) beans or minced lamb.

Molokhia | The leaves of the molokhia (or melokhia) plant are particularly popular in Egypt, Jordan and Lebanon. It is a member of the mallow family. The leaves are sold in the markets fresh or dried and taste a little bit like sorrel. Generally cooked like spinach in soups and stews it is perhaps an acquired taste, partly because of its mucilaginous texture.

Okra | This is another member of the mallow family. Each pod contains compartments filled with seeds, and a gummy substance that gives okra its mucilaginous character when cooked. Immature okra is picked while still small and hung on strings to dry. The dried pods are first rubbed in a cloth to remove the hairs before being added to soups and stews for their tart flavour. Mature pods should be bought when they are fresh, firm and bright green in colour. If you like your okra crunchy you need to slice them at the last minute and cook quickly.

Onion | All types of onion are available in the markets, from round and bulbous varieties in their varying shades of red, purple, and gold to pearly white small onions, pink shallots and long green spring onions (scallions). Large onions are often hollowed out and stuffed with an aromatic rice and minced lamb filling, while smaller purple and red onions are particularly favoured for salads and mezze dishes as they are slightly sweet. Shallots are used in stews or threaded on to kebab skewers. Long onion tops are chopped and sautéed in butter with a squeeze of lemon, as a topping for an omelette.

Peppers | The bell-shaped capsicum pepper is thought to have arrived in the eastern Mediterranean from the New World in the 16th century. The most common (bell) peppers are small and green, the immature fruit of capsicum pepper plants. These firm slightly tart peppers are favoured for stuffing with rice or meat or for adding to salads. More mature, long, sweet red peppers are used in stews or grilled, skinned and marinated in olive oil. They are also dried in the sun and then ground into fruity paprika powder, or pounded into a paste.

Pumpkin | This is another vegetable that came to the eastern Mediterranean from the New World. The pumpkin is particularly linked to the cuisines of the Armenians and the Kurds, who prepare a variety of sweet dishes with them, such as baked pumpkin with honey and spices, or a sweet rice dish with cinnamon. Other pumpkin dishes include soups, stews, pilaffs, savoury pastries, jam and baklava, and the seeds are roasted and eaten as a snack.

Spinach | Originally from Persia, where it was considered a herb rather than a vegetable, spinach is regarded by Arabs as the 'prince of vegetables'. There are even medieval Arab recipes for spinach to be used in sweet dishes, combined with honey, spices and nuts. Spinach is rich in vitamins and minerals and grows all year round in the temperate climate of the Fertile Crescent.

Tomatoes | These are another 16th-century import, yet tomatoes are so entwined in the cuisine that it is difficult to imagine how the people of the eastern Mediterranean ever managed without them. Tomato harvests are abundant, and the bright red, flavoursome fruits come in a variety of shapes and sizes. Ripe tomatoes are crushed to a pulp, then poured into trays and thickened in the sun to make a paste that is used in soups and stews. The unripe green fruit is often pickled.

Top **Pumpkin.**

Bottom **Red peppers.**

# Fruit

The market stalls are piled high with seasonal fruit – juicy peaches, grapes, pomegranates, mulberries, apples, oranges, melons, green plums, apricots, dates, figs, quinces and lemons. Although ripe fruits are mainly enjoyed fresh and uncooked, several favourite puddings feature poached fruit, and cherries, grapes, plums, figs and apricots are added to savoury stews and roasted meats in their fresh or dried forms. Fruit syrups and sherbet drinks are also popular.

Apricots | These little fruits come in varying colours and sizes, although the most common is orange-yellow with a velvety skin. When harvested, soft, sun-ripened fresh apricots are eaten fresh as a snack, but in rural areas many are set aside to be dried on the flat roofs so that they can be consumed throughout the year. Small unripe apricots are added to mixed pickles along with green almonds.

Cherries | Both sweet and sour cherries are native to the eastern Mediterranean. Most of the cherries in the region are deep red in colour, although there are also black ones in Syria. Sweet, juicy cherries are devoured in quantities but sour cherries are poached with sugar to make jam or a refreshing sherbet drink. They are also puréed and dried for adding to pilaffs and to stews.

Dates | These have long been a staple food in desert regions of the Middle East and, at times, the only source of food for nomadic herdsmen and the Bedouin, who can thrive on a diet of dates and fermented milk for long periods. In the eastern Mediterranean, dates fall into three main categories: the soft, juicy ones which are eaten fresh or dried and compressed into blocks or date paste – this is the main type for export; the dry, fibrous fruit known as 'camel' dates, which are one of the staple foods of the nomads; and semi-dry dates, which are slightly tart.

Most of the dates in the regional markets come from Syria, Jordan, Iraq, Saudi Arabia and Egypt. They are often sold stuffed, or pounded with rose water and cinnamon to form a paste. Dried dates are also added to savoury dishes, such as fruity pilaff prepared with nuts and apricots or vegetables and meat.

Figs | Muhammad is reputed to have adored figs and commented that they must be heaven-sent. Fresh figs really need to mature on the tree under a hot sun to be at their moist, ultra-sweet best. They are generally eaten as a snack and sometimes cooked in desserts, whereas the dried fruits find their way into compotes, jams, savoury stews and roasts. Unripe green figs are picked for a delectable honey-flavoured jam.

Top **Oranges ripening.**

Bottom **Fresh date fruits at a market in the West Bank.**

Grapes | There are paintings of vines on the walls of early Egyptian tombs, and Noah was reputed to have planted vines in the foothills of Mount Ararat when the Great Flood subsided. The Phoenicians spread the vine wherever they settled and the Romans cultivated it. Today in the eastern Mediterranean there are many varieties of grape grown for the table and for wine, with some specially grown to dry. Fresh grapes are also puréed and dried flat to make a fruit leather, or boiled down to form a useful fruit molasses. Tart green grapes are sometimes added to savoury stews, and the dried fruits are used in sweet and savoury dishes.

Lemons and limes | Before the cultivation of lemons and limes in the eastern Mediterranean began in Roman times, sour pomegranate molasses, fermented grape juice and sumac were used as souring agents. Today, lemons are grown and harvested all year round, and appear in some form at almost every meal. Fresh limes are not as common, but dried limes from Oman are popular in Jordan.

Oranges | Seafaring Arabs brought sour oranges to the eastern Mediterranean from China and India, but the sweet orange did not arrive there until the 15th century. Oranges of both kinds are used in sweet and savoury dishes. Orange peel is preserved in syrup, and the blossoms of the bitter orange are distilled to make a fragrant essence, which in its diluted form is sold as orange blossom water.

Melon | Not of the same family, watermelons thrived in the region long before the other types of melon, which were only cultivated after the fall of the Roman Empire. Both kinds of melon grow at speed, like weeds, providing plenty of fruit in both summer and winter. Unripe melons and watermelons are pickled in vinegar or poached with sugar for a conserve.

Pomegranates | This fruit has a rich and ancient history. Both sweet and sour pomegranates were cultivated during the Ottoman period. The sour variety was valued for its juice, which was used to make a refreshing drink and served as a souring agent before the arrival of lemons in the region. The juice of sour pomegranates is also boiled down to make the ubiquitous molasses, dibs, and to make fruit leathers. The seeds of the sweet pomegranate are sometimes sprinkled with a little rose water and served as a dessert, and vividly garnish both savoury and sweet dishes.

Quinces | Related to the apple and the pear, the quince is similar in appearance, although larger and pale yellow in colour. The fruit and seeds are both extremely high in pectin, and transform their poaching juices to a jelly. The fresh fruit is firm, mildly perfumed, and slightly tart. However, the fruit really comes to life when cooked, as it emits a delightful floral fragrance and lends a honeyed taste to any dish.

Top left **Apricots.**

Top right **Lemons.**

Bottom left **Pomegranates.**

Bottom right **Figs.**

# Fish and shellfish

Lebanon and Syria are in the enviable position of having a regular supply of fish on their Mediterranean doorstep, and Jordan has a gateway to the Red Sea. In the early cooking manuals of the eastern Mediterranean, recipes rarely specified the type of fish to be used. This was probably because people tended to use whatever fish was available and, in the case of Jordan and Iraq, that was more likely to be of the inland freshwater variety. The most popular fish caught off the coast of Lebanon and Syria, as well as in the Gulf of Aqaba off the Jordanian coast, include sea bass, red snapper, garfish, grouper, sardines, swordfish, tuna, grey mullet, red mullet and sole.

Most firm-fleshed fish are interchangeable in soups, kibbeh and stews, and are equally ideal for barbecuing and baking. A popular Arab speciality is *sayadieh samak*, a dish of sea fish combined with walnuts and pomegranate seeds. The most common way of cooking fish is to grill it whole over charcoal. Alternatively it can be baked in the oven and served with a tahini sauce, lemon wedges or herbs. However, fish is rarely cooked with milk or served with yogurt or any kind of cheeses.

Sole | Favoured by the Romans, sole is named after Moses (samak Moussa), as it is believed that when he divided the Red Sea, this particular fish was cut in half and remained thin and flat ever after. In Lebanon, sole is cooked French-style, fried quickly with almonds, and is at its best when lightly cooked. It is often rubbed with garlic and ground sumac, salt and pepper, briefly grilled and served with a wedge of lemon.

Red mullet | This is a prized fish in Lebanon, where it is generally grilled or fried whole so that its pink, dappled skin and juicy flesh can be enjoyed in its full glory. It is often served with strips of fried pitta bread and a bowl of tahini sauce.

Grey mullet | This is an expensive fish, highly prized in the eastern Mediterranean for its roe – almost as valuable as caviar from the Caspian Sea. Arab cooks make a traditional delicacy called *batarekh*, which involves salting, pressing and drying the roe, and encasing it in beeswax to preserve it. The Lebanese, in particular, enjoy the roe preserved in this manner, and serve it cut into very thin slices, drizzled with a little olive oil and lemon juice.

Sea bass | With its firm flesh and subtle flavour, sea bass is an incredibly versatile fish employed in all sorts of dishes that call for firm chunks and fillets. It is also large enough for stuffing, and fleshy enough for flaking to make kibbeh.

Top left **Sea bass.**

Top right **Prawns.**

Bottom left **Red mullet.**

Bottom right **Salt-cured fish.**

**Mackerel** | The oily, richly flavoured flesh of mackerel is also ideally suited to kibbeh. Another speciality, from Ottoman tradition, is *uskumru dolmas*, a whole mackerel stuffed with a filling of nuts and spices combined with its own cooked flesh.

**Freshwater fish** | The fish from the rivers and inland waters, such as trout, eel, carp and barbell, end up in the rural markets, or are sold by lone fishermen standing by the roadside. In Lebanon there is a leaping carp with a pale pink flesh, just like the leaping salmon of other countries, which is highly prized when available.

**Shellfish** | These are mainly enjoyed by people in the coastal regions, although many Muslims will not eat anything with a shell. Squid, mussels and lobster are consumed in some parts of Lebanon and the Gulf of Aqaba in Jordan. There is one intriguing species of crab which has a penchant for white mulberries and can be caught while climbing mulberry trees to devour the fruit; these were considered a great delicacy by the French and other Europeans during their occupation of Lebanon. The crabs are often steamed and served during Lent in the Christian communities.

Prawns (shrimp) are perhaps the most common of all shellfish and are generally baked, sautéed, or threaded onto kebab skewers with pieces of bell pepper and cherry tomatoes. They also blend very well with rice dishes and salads.

**Frogs and snails** | These are also eaten to some extent in parts of the Levant, particularly in Lebanon and Syria, where the French have left their mark on the cuisine. Most Muslims will not touch these creatures for religious reasons, but a number of Christians do eat them. It is not uncommon to come across recipes in the Christian communities for fried frogs' legs cooked with rice, or simmered in a tomato-based ragout. Snails were often regarded as the food of the poor and were sold in the markets at a low price; nowadays, though, they are back on some restaurant menus, often served with a garlicky nut sauce, a tahini sauce or, as in France, with garlic butter.

**Preserving fish** | Drying and salting fish is an ancient tradition in the eastern Mediterranean and a very practical one, enabling it to be transported inland and cooked out of season. Whole fish or boned fillets are hung up on makeshift lines to dry, like socks hanging on a washing line, and then rubbed in salt to preserve them. The Orontes River in Lebanon made a name for itself during the Ottoman Empire as the place to buy the best salt-cured fish, which was in demand throughout the eastern Mediterranean. Nowadays, salted fish is a delicacy rather than a necessity, and is often consumed with bread for a delicious snack.

Top **The harbour in Byblos.**

Bottom **Sheep and rams grazing on the green hills in Lebanon.**

# Meat and poultry

Above **Skewered lamb cooked on hot coals is universally popular.**

Throughout the history of the eastern Mediterranean, the preferred meat for everyday meals has been mutton or lamb. Pork is never eaten by Muslims and is practically unknown in this region, and the addition of beef and veal to the diet is relatively recent, as traditionally cows and oxen were valued solely for their milk and their labour in the fields. Beef is used in some stews and meatballs, but lamb remains the preferred choice for celebrations.

Ever since the early nomads herded their sheep for sale into the villages and towns, lamb and mutton have been included in the daily diet, although still somewhat sparingly by the majority of the population. The wealthy have always indulged in huge portions of meat, often roasting a whole sheep for banquets, but the poorer communities have had to rely on devising recipes that enable small quantities of meat to go far. Three of the most popular meat dishes are *kibbeh*, *shawarma* and *mansaf*.

Lamb and mutton | A whole lamb roasted on a spit is the festive dish most commonly prepared for special occasions, such as weddings, family gatherings, the visit of an important guest, and religious feasts. (In some rural regions, a whole goat or camel may be roasted for special occasions.) More daily fare includes a variety of lamb and mutton stews, kibbeh and shawarma, the Arab equivalent of Turkish döner kebabs. The most highly prized lamb and mutton comes from the hardy Awassi breed of sheep, as it produces a strong-tasting meat, and every part of the animal is used – head, eyes, brain, tongue, lungs, heart, stomach, intestines, testicles, feet and the podgy tail. The fat in this tail is rendered to produce a primitive cooking oil which has provided a unique flavour to dishes since ancient times. Lamb cut into cubes and fried before being stored in its own rendered fat is a traditonal method of preservation.

Poultry | The delicate meat of chickens and other poultry was so highly regarded in the medieval Arab kitchen that numerous chicken recipes, flavoured with rhubarb, mulberries, almonds, walnuts and pomegranates, were recorded. During the Ottoman period, more exotic and interesting poultry recipes were created, resulting in a vast choice of chicken dishes in the eastern Mediterranean. Chicken, turkey duck, pigeon, pheasant, partridge and quail were all used, and once the Ottomans introduced turkey from the New World, it too gained a place in the repertoire. For the most part, chickens are free range and fed on corn, so the meat is lean and tasty. Turkeys remain a popular choice for Christian religious feasts, whereas Muslim feasts invariably involve a whole ram or goat. Quail is spit-roasted at street stalls and at picnics in the countryside, and pigeon stew is popular in parts of Jordan and Lebanon.

Wild game | Rabbits, hares, gazelles, wild boars, porcupines and game birds have long been hunted in parts of Greater Syria. In the Shuf, a scenic part of the Lebanon Mountains inhabited mainly by the Druze people, the sight and aroma of small game birds such as pigeon and quail being marinated in a pomegranate sauce and then grilled over charcoal is just as common now as it was in medieval times.

Cured meat | There are two main types of cured meat – *basterma*, beef fillet encased in a pungent paste of fenugreek, garlic and red pepper, and *maqaniq*, a spicy sausage made from lamb, or beef. These sausages are usually simply grilled and enjoyed as mezze, or added to bean and pulse dishes for the subtle spicy flavour they impart to the dish.

Kibbeh | Popular throughout the eastern Mediterranean, kibbeh are often regarded as the national dish of Lebanon. It is a dish of hospitality, a dish of nostalgia and comfort, and a dish for special occasions. There are endless variations but all require the pounding of bulgur with meat, chicken, fish or vegetables. The most typical combines minced lamb and bulgur with grated onion and a variety of herbs and spices. The origins of kibbeh are ancient, possibly dating back to Mesopotamia. The word itself is derived from the Arabic verb meaning 'to form a lump or ball'. The pounding and shaping of this traditional dish requires practice and patience, as well as a degree of strength if using the stone mortar and heavy wooden pestle, and the procedure can be lengthy and arduous.

Shawarma | Delicious at any time of day, as a snack or a meal, shawarma is prepared on a long vertical spit which is threaded with marinated pieces of lamb or chicken, interspersed with pieces of fat to keep the meat moist. The spit is then rotated in front of a charcoal fire, as the cook deftly slices off the meat with a very sharp knife so that the fine slices are deliciously moist and tender. The pieces of meat are packed into a pitta bread pocket, or laid on top of flatbread, and smothered in tahini or yogurt. The whole mixture is topped with onions, tomatoes, pickles and leafy herbs, such as coriander, parsley and mint.

Mansaf | The Bedouin prepare their own festive dish, mansaf, meaning 'big dish'. This consists of a large tray, sometimes as large as 1.8 metres (6 feet) in diameter, lined with flatbread and a layer of rice, on top of which sit chunks of lamb, though other meats can be used. The dish is flavoured with a traditional sauce, *jameed*, prepared from the juices of the lamb thickened with the dried curds of sheep or goat's milk yogurt. The dish, prepared for wedding feasts, state banquets and distinguished guests, can reach mammoth proportions – it is not unusual for a young camel to be stuffed with a sheep, then a turkey, and then a chicken, like a Russian doll. Also enjoyed in Syra, this is the national dish of Jordan.

Top **Lamb shawarma cooking on its spit in front of the flames.**

Bottom **Pigeon is a favourite game bird in Lebanon and Syria.**

# Wheat, lentils, beans and rice

No household in the eastern Mediterranean is complete without a little grain in the kitchen. There will always be enough wheat to grind for bread, enough bulgur to prepare some delicious kibbeh, or enough pulses to prepare a stew.

With these ingredients alone a meal will appear on the table. The most ancient crop of all, wheat is at the root of many classic dishes, such as flatbread, pastry-based snacks, bulgur salads and pilaffs, and, of course, the much-loved kibbeh. The Bekaa Valley, which acted as an important granary for ancient Rome, still provides Lebanon with most of its grain, and the plains of Syria are major producers of wheat for the whole region. Lentils, beans and chickpeas have long been associated with the diet of the poor and peasant population as, although they are filling and nutritious, they are also cheap. Tables have turned, however, and pulses are now part of everyone's daily fare.

Bulgur | This is a staple food of many rural folk and a great favourite among the Druze and Maronite communities of Mount Lebanon and the peasant communities of Syria. When wheat is harvested some of it is parboiled, drained, and then dried and rubbed to remove the bran before crushing it into the grains known as bulgur. Traditionally, this was achieved by laboriously boiling the wholewheat grains first, then spreading them on trays which were placed on the flat roofs of houses to dry in the sun, and finally crushing them. Nowadays, bulgur is prepared commercially for sale.

The bulgur grains can be coarse, medium or fine, and vary in colour from light to dark brown. They require soaking or boiling in water before eating, and the resulting taste is nutty, with a springy texture. Bulgur is highly nutritious and performs much the same role in a dish as rice. Its primary role in Lebanon, Jordan and Syria is as the base for kibbeh.

Freekeh (freek, frkkeh) | Popular since medieval times, this is the immature wheat grain that is still green in colour. When cooked it has a delicious nutty taste and texture, which is enjoyed in several pilaffs, and served with meat and poultry.

Kishk | In the wheat-growing areas of Lebanon and Syria, bulgur is mixed with yogurt and spread out on clean cloths on trays to dry in the sun. As the bulgur grains soak up the moisture, they are rubbed between the palms to break them up until they resemble fine breadcrumbs. Known as kishk in Arabic, this dried, fermented powder is used to flavour and thicken soups and stews, or to make a kind of porridge, which is often enjoyed for breakfast.

Top left **Bulgur grains, or cracked wheat.**

Top right **Kishk is made by fermenting bulgur with yogurt.**

Bottom left **Filo pastry is made from ground wheat flour and water.**

Bottom right **Freekeh are the unripe grains of wheat.**

Semolina | The harvested wheat grain can also be coarsely milled to produce the brittle grains of semolina which, when cooked, have a light, slightly gritty texture. These grains are popular in some breads, cakes and puddings, such as the Syrian *mamounia*, a sweet porridge-like dish. They can be ground to an even finer texture to produce a superfine flour used to make best-quality couscous and noodles. Couscous is associated with North African cuisine so any dish it appears in is called *mughrabiyya*, meaning 'from the Maghreb' – Morocco, Tunisia and Algeria.

Lentils | These are the best-known legumes of antiquity. Lentils have been endowed with various characteristics throughout history. The Egyptians, who were the first to cultivate them, believed they could cheer up children; the Persians thought they had a calming effect on the mind and metabolism; and the Romans maintained that they reduced rage and encouraged mildness. In fact, one Roman general blamed a defeat by the Persians on these pulses as his troops, who had run out of wheat, had survived on a diet of lentils, and he was sure that this had resulted in slow reactions and sluggishness. Crossing all classes of society, lentils form part of the daily diet of the poor because they are cheap, but are also enjoyed in a variety of family and festive dishes. The most common lentils are the tiny reddish-orange ones, sometimes referred to as Egyptian lentils, but the pale yellow, brown and larger green varieties are enjoyed too. Two of the most popular lentil dishes are *moujadara* (or *mdardara*), a rice pilaff with brown lentils and crispy onions, and *imjadra*, a spicy bulgur pilaff with red or green lentils.

Beans and Chickpeas | There are so many types of legume to discover – black-eyed beans, haricot beans, soya beans, speckled borlotti beans, broad beans, long green beans and Egyptian brown beans. Another staple food of the rural population of this region, chickpeas were first grown in ancient Egypt and the Fertile Crescent. The small bushy plants bear pods that are dried and threshed to release the two or three seeds – the chickpeas – that are contained inside. These freshly harvested chickpeas are then dried in the sun to rid them of moisture. Before being cooked, chickpeas need to be soaked in plenty of water for at least six hours to absorb liquid and increase in size. The Arabic word for chickpea, hummus, is also the name of one of the most famous mezze dishes.

Rice | The ancient Greeks and Romans first brought rice to the eastern Mediterranean region from China, but as it was such an expensive commodity, it was enjoyed exclusively by the wealthy. Now that rice is cultivated in the region, it is affordable and readily available but wheat is still the cheaper and more accessible grain in the rural areas. White rice can also be ground to a fine powder, or flour, which is employed in numerous milk puddings to thicken and give them body.

Top **Stone-grinding grains into flour.**

Bottom **Sacks of pulses, legumes and grains at the souk.**

# Bread

A meal without bread in Lebanon, Jordan and Syria is almost unthinkable. An essential component of every meal, leavened or unleavened bread is employed as a scoop to raise and transport tasty morsels to the mouth, as a mop for soaking up the divine oily cooking juices on the plate, as a dipper to sink into a puréed, garlicky mezze dish, or as an all-round table companion to munch on throughout the meal.

Since medieval times, bread has been prepared with barley, millet and wheat, but corn was introduced from the New World during the Ottoman era and became a common ingredient in loaves made in the rural areas. The industrious bread-making and amazingly diverse recipes of the Ottoman Empire were remarked upon in the diaries and letters of a number of travellers who passed through the Fertile Crescent. From the middle of the 17th century until the occupation of the French after World War I, Armenians monopolised the bread-making industry in Lebanon and Syria. Under the influence of the French, soft white baguettes and some of the delicious specialities of French patisserie also made an appearance in the cafés and cosmopolitan homes of Beirut.

Bread does not come in one simple form in the Levant. The dough is used to make tasty snacks such as the famous Arab pizza, *lahm bi ajeen*, so popular in Lebanon and Syria that both claim it as their own, and *manakakeish bil zahtar*, little flatbreads smeared with a herby paste made from thyme and sumac. A favourite street snack in Lebanon is *kahk*, tiny sesame-covered rolls, which are shaped either like thick bracelets or like bags with a little handle. Trays piled high with kahk are carried proudly on the heads of vendors as they walk through the streets.

The most common bread in the eastern Mediterranean is called *khubz arabi*, or simply khubz. This is a round, flat, slightly leavened loaf that comes in different sizes, sometimes with a hollow pouch. It is the ubiquitous everyday loaf. On the other hand, the bread of the mountain regions, *markouk*, is much thinner and is generally prepared in a saaj, a slightly curved griddle pan. This is the loaf that the Lebanese and the Syrians are most proud of and see as part of their food heritage. The Jordanians and Palestinians produce a similar thin loaf called *shrak*.

In rural areas the wide, flat, thin sheets of bread known as *khubz markouk* are used to make quick, impromptu snacks. Farmers and shepherds often carry leather bags over their shoulders containing several sheets of this flatbread, some crumbled cheese and a few olives, which they put together to make a good meal whenever they get peckish. Raw or cooked vegetables are sometimes included, or jam and honey. Another popular snack prepared with this flatbread is *arus*, 'the bride', which consists of a sheet of bread spread with yogurt cheese, drizzled with olive oil, sprinkled with zahtar and rolled up to eat.

Top **A small traditional bakery making flatbread, in Safi, Jordan.**

Bottom **Preparing sesame breads in a Tripoli bakery.**

Above **Flatbread, spread with yogurt cheese and a scattering of zahtar.**

Traditionally bread was baked at the communal oven, the *furn*, or on a domed oven made out of clay, called a *tanur*. In some rural areas, a small pit dug in the ground was used as the oven and flatbreads were cooked over the fire on the *saaj*, a type of griddle pan. The communal baking at the village furn was often a social outing for the women of the village, who gathered around the oven preparing bread loaves of different proportions and shapes, while they chatted and sang.

All of these methods of baking bread are still in use today, particularly in the rural areas, but in the towns most neighbourhoods are blessed with a local bakery that produces batches of freshly baked bread several times a day. Even in the busiest modern cities, most people buy their bread every day, freshly made and still warm, from their neighbourhood baker. Furthermore, they often buy fresh bread two or three times a day, so that each meal is graced with a fresh loaf.

In the Arab world, bread is regarded as a gift from God, and should be broken by hand, as to cut it with a knife would be like raising a sword, and if a piece of bread should fall to the ground, it is picked up and symbolically pressed to the lips and forehead as a mark of respect.

Leftover bread is never thrown away; that would be a waste of this precious food. Instead it is used up in a number of sweet and savoury dishes. The famous salad *fattoush*, and tasty *fatta* dishes, are delicious ways of using up stale bread. The word fatta describes bread broken into pieces, which are toasted and soaked in broth to form the basis of this all-in-one recipe. The next step is to add meat, vegetables or pulses to the bread base, and then yogurt and nuts are spooned over the top.

# Traditional drinks

Lebanon, Syria and Jordan all share similar traditions of hospitality when it comes to offering drinks. For example, it is usual to give a cup of coffee or tea to a guest to welcome them into a home. On a hot day, the drink might be a cold sherbet. It is polite to accept the drink, otherwise it looks as if the guest is rejecting the host's kind offer of refreshment.

Coffee | The introduction of coffee from Yemen to the eastern Mediterranean in the 15th and 16th centuries made a significant impact on the social life of the region. Coffee-drinking became primarily a male pastime in the men-only coffee houses, although women who could afford it enjoyed coffee in their own homes. Some coffee houses were set up as luxurious establishments, private meeting places for the noble and rich; others were less sophisticated but no less pleasing, as locations were selected for their small yet scented gardens, or for the shade of several large trees. In the evenings some coffee houses provided entertainment with dancers, singers, musicians and storytellers.

There are two styles of coffee served: Turkish and Arabic. Turkish coffee is very finely ground, thick and grainy – it is prepared sweet (*hilweh*), medium-sweet (*wassat*), and without sugar (*murra*). Cloves, cardamom pods, cinnamon sticks and orange flower water or rose water are often added to enhance the flavour of Arabic coffee. Coffee is always served in tiny ornate cups; the most decorative are inlaid with real strands of gold or silver, and they may have both handles and saucers. It is the custom to serve a glass of water with the thick, strong brew. Among the Bedouin, strong bitter coffee flows freely, and if your cup is empty, it will always be filled up.

Tea | Although it is surrounded by fewer customs, tea holds its own significance in the culture of the region. Generally, tea is made strong and black, and is sweetened with sugar, either by stirring it into the hot liquid, or by holding a sugar lump between the teeth and sipping the tea through it. In Jordan and Lebanon, herbs and spices are added, and there are numerous herb and floral teas, such as thyme, lemon verbena, hibiscus, jasmine and camomile. Some teas are medicinal, thought to be good for colds or to aid digestion, or to increase fertility.

Sherbet drinks | Some sherbets are served on specific occasions, but all are popular as welcoming drinks for guests, or simply as a refreshing interlude in the day. One of the most unusual sherbet drinks in the region, a recipe known to be hundreds of years old, is prepared from a syrup of mint and vinegar, but the more common sherbets are made from the infinite variety of seasonal fruits, nuts, pods and blossoms. These include lemons, sour cherries, pomegranates, mulberries, rose and orange blossom waters, almond milk and tamarind pods.

Alcoholic drinks | Although wine was enjoyed by the ancient Egyptians, Phoenicians and Romans, and by the Arabs, its consumption was curtailed by the introduction of Islam and its religious prohibitions. Lebanon was regarded as one of the prime producers of arak, the local spirit, although excessive drunkenness and gambling led to prohibition in the early 20th century. The production of wine continued in the region, however, within the Christian and Jewish communities. Naturally, when the French occupied Lebanon after World War I, they took advantage of the fertile soil and wonderful climate of the Bekaa Valley, and set about producing wines there. Lebanon is admired to this day for its quality wines and flourishing grape vines, and wines are still made in private homes and Christian monasteries. Other alcoholic beverages made today include beer and arak, a clear spirit distilled from grapes and flavoured with aniseed, which turns cloudy when water is added, just like the raki of Turkey and the ouzo of Greece.

Top **Believed to aid digestion, mint infusion makes a refreshing drink. Hot water is poured over sprigs of fresh mint in a glass or a teapot, and sugar added to taste. Steep for at least 5 minutes before drinking.**

Bottom **Rose sherbert is typically offered to guests. Water and sugar are simmered for 5–10 minutes until the syrup coats the back of the spoon. A few tablespoons of rose water is added and boiled for a few more minutes, then the syrup is left to cool. To serve, a spoon of the rose syrup is diluted with water, and with ice, if you like.**

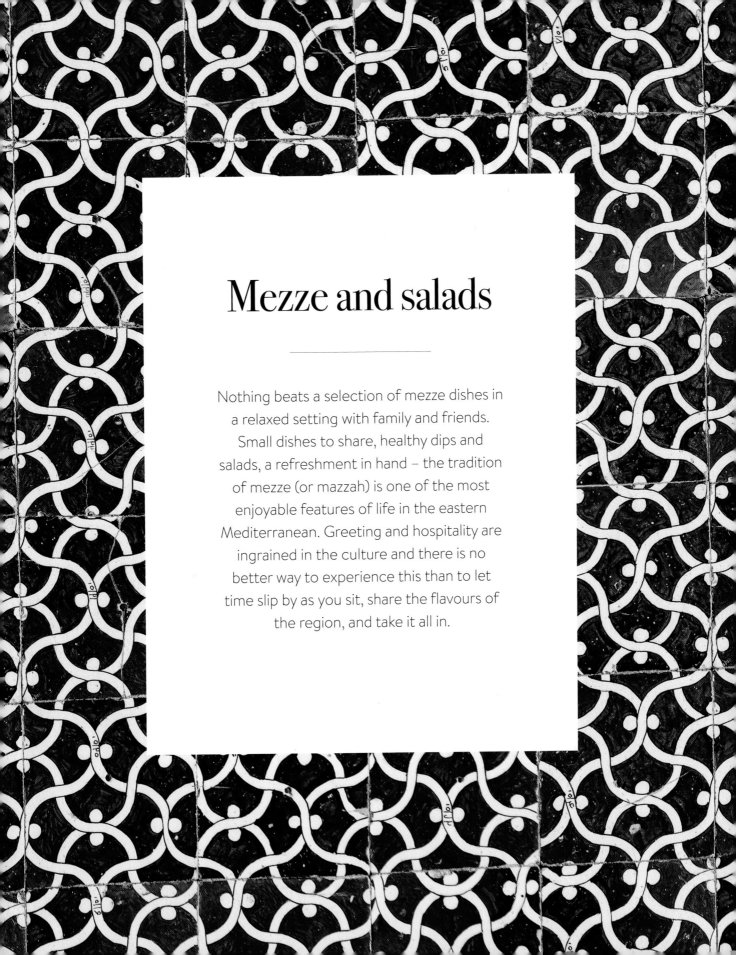

# Mezze and salads

Nothing beats a selection of mezze dishes in a relaxed setting with family and friends. Small dishes to share, healthy dips and salads, a refreshment in hand – the tradition of mezze (or mazzah) is one of the most enjoyable features of life in the eastern Mediterranean. Greeting and hospitality are ingrained in the culture and there is no better way to experience this than to let time slip by as you sit, share the flavours of the region, and take it all in.

# Yogurt cheese balls in olive oil

Straining yogurt to make labneh is a daily occurrence in almost every kitchen, as it is so delicious and versatile. But, if you extend the straining for 2–3 days it becomes firmer and a little dry, and you can make these little yogurt cheese balls, *labneh bi zeit*, which can be stored in oil in a jar and brought out to sprinkle with herbs or spice and share with friends whenever you like.

 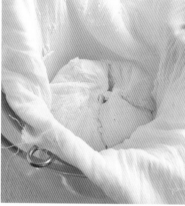 

## Serves six

**1kg/2¼lb thick, creamy Greek-style (strained plain) yogurt**

**5ml/1 tsp sea salt**

**olive oil**

**ground paprika, to serve**

In a bowl, stir the yogurt with the salt, then pour the yogurt into a piece of muslin suspended above a bowl, or lining a colander set over a bowl. Fold or tie the cloth over the yogurt and leave it to drain in the refrigerator for 36–48 hours (48 ideally), pouring off the whey as needed. The yogurt will reduce by half in this time.

When the straining is complete, remove the drained yogurt from the cloth, stand it on a plate and leave to dry out for about 6 hours. Then lightly dampen or oil your fingers and palms and divide the cheese into small pieces.

Roll the pieces into 2cm/¾inch balls. Place on a tray, cover with a clean dishtowel and and leave in a cool place for 6–12 hours, until they are quite dry and firm. Pack the balls into a sterilised jar and pour in enough olive oil to cover.

Store in a cool place for 2–3 weeks and serve sprinkled with paprika, Aleppo pepper, zahtar, chopped fresh herbs or flaked chillies.

Left **Olives with chillies and thyme**  Right **Fried halloumi with zahtar**

# Olives with chillies and thyme

Olives are never far from the table at any time of day – great for breakfast with salty cheese and bread, delicious popped into salads, and as here, *zaytun*, bathed in fruity olive oil and lightly spiced with chilli, fresh herbs, zahtar, or dukkah spice. A perfect mezze nibble.

## Serves four

250g/9oz fleshy green olives, soaked in water for 24 hours

1 fresh hot red chilli, seeded and finely chopped

15ml/1 tbsp fresh thyme leaves

100ml/3½fl oz olive oil

juice of ½ lemon

sea salt

Drain the olives, pat dry with kitchen towel and, using a sharp knife, cut 3 slits in each one, placing them in a large bowl as you work.

Add the chopped chilli and thyme leaves to the bowl, and toss in the olive oil and lemon juice. Season with salt and stir well so that all the olives are coated in the oil and flavourings.

Cover the bowl and leave the olives to marinate for 1–2 hours before serving as needed. These olives will keep in a jar, refrigerated, for 3–4 weeks.

# Fried halloumi with zahtar

Halloumi is a fabulous invention – a cheese that can be fried without melting and combined with a whole range of spices and condiments, both sweet and savoury. Traditionally made from cow's milk and matured in whey, you can find plain or flavoured halloumi in most supermarkets. The key is to serve it hot, no matter what you are doing with it, as it becomes rubbery in texture when it cools.

## Serves two to four

250g/9oz plain halloumi cheese

45–60ml/3–4 tbsp olive oil

15ml/1 tbsp zahtar (more if you like)

honey, to drizzle

lemon wedges, to squeeze

Rinse the block of halloumi under cold running water and pat dry with kitchen paper. Using a sharp knife, cut the halloumi into thin slices.

Heat the oil in a heavy pan. Fry the halloumi slices for 2 minutes until golden, then flip over and fry the other side. Drain on kitchen paper.

Transfer the hot halloumi on to a serving dish and sprinkle with zahtar. Eat immediately with a drizzle of honey or a squeeze of lemon.

# Aubergines with pomegranate molasses

Smoked, grilled, fried, baked and pickled – there are so many delicious ways to enjoy aubergines. Sweet and sour, this is a medieval Arab dish (*batinjan bil rumman*) which you can serve warm with yogurt or at room temperature as part of a spread of mezze dishes.

## Serves four

**1 large aubergine (eggplant), peeled, cut in half lengthways and sliced into half-moons**

**sea salt**

**45–60ml/3–4 tbsp olive oil**

**1 red onion, cut in half lengthways and finely sliced with the grain**

**15–30ml/1–2 tbsp sultanas (golden raisins)**

**15–30ml/1–2 tbsp pomegranate molasses**

**juice of ½ lemon**

**10ml/2 tsp fragrant, runny honey**

**150ml/5fl oz/½ cup boiling water**

**a bunch of flat leaf parsley, and a few mint leaves, chopped, to garnish**

Sprinkle the aubergine slices with salt and leave them to weep for about 15 minutes. Drain, then rinse off the salt and pat the slices dry.

Heat the oil in a heavy pan and lightly fry the aubergine slices until golden brown – you can do this in batches. Add the sliced onions to the pan to soften (drizzle in a little extra oil if you need to). Toss in the sultanas to heat and plump them up.

In a small bowl, mix together the pomegranate molasses, lemon juice, honey and a little salt. Add the boiling water to the bowl and mix. Pour the mixture into the pan and cook gently for 10–15 minutes until the aubergine is tender.

Garnish with the parsley and mint and serve warm, or at room temperature, perhaps with dollops of garlicky yogurt.

# Spicy bean balls

Everyone knows *falafel* – the tasty, spicy, broad bean balls from Egypt and the eastern Mediterranean. Popular street food, they are often tucked into toasted pitta breads with sliced onion and parsley, but also delicious served with a tahini sauce or with garlic-flavoured yogurt.

## Serves four to six

- 250g/9oz/1 cup dried broad (fava) beans, soaked overnight
- 115g/4oz/½ cup chickpeas, soaked overnight
- 10–15ml/2–3 tsp ground cumin
- 10ml/2 tsp ground coriander
- 1 red chilli, seeded and chopped
- ½ onion, chopped
- 1 red or green (bell) pepper, chopped
- 4 cloves of garlic, crushed
- a small bunch of fresh coriander (cilantro), chopped
- a bunch of fresh flat leaf parsley, chopped
- 5ml/1 tsp bicarbonate of soda (baking soda)
- sunflower oil, for deep-frying
- sea salt and ground black pepper
- lemon wedges and yogurt, to serve

Drain the beans and chickpeas and place in a blender with the dried spices. Blend to a paste, then add the chilli, onion, pepper, garlic and herbs. Season well, then whizz until smooth. Transfer to a bowl, beat in the bicarbonate of soda, cover, and leave for 15 minutes.

With wet hands, mould the mixture into small, tight balls. Heat enough oil for deep-frying in a pan and when it is hot enough, fry the balls in batches until golden brown.

Drain the falafel on kitchen paper and serve them warm or at room temperature, with lemon wedges to squeeze over them, and a dollop of yogurt flavoured with garlic and chopped fresh mint if you like.

# Spicy tartare balls

Perhaps not for everyone, because they are prepared with raw meat, *kibbeh naye* (*çi köfte* in Syria) are enduringly popular in the eastern Mediterranean. Flavoured with a multitude of spices, the raw meat and bulgur balls are often served with sprigs of parsley to chew on, lettuce leaves to fold around them and wedges of lemon to refresh them.

## Serves four to six

225g/8oz lean minced (ground) lamb or beef

125g/4½oz fine bulgur, soaked in boiling water for 20 minutes

2 small onions, finely chopped

4 cloves of garlic, finely chopped

1 red chilli, seeded and finely chopped

10ml/2 tsp tomato purée or paste

5ml/1 tsp ground paprika

5ml/1 tsp ground coriander

2.5ml/½ tsp ground cumin

2.5ml/½ tsp ground cinnamon

2.5ml/½ tsp ground allspice

2.5ml/½ tsp ground fenugreek

sea salt and freshly ground black pepper

a bunch of fresh flat leaf parsley, chopped

roughly 12 small lettuce leaves

flat leaf parsley sprigs and lemon wedges, to serve

Put the minced meat into a bowl. Knead it and slap it down into the base of the bowl to knock out the air. Squeeze out the bulgur and add it to the meat with the onions, garlic and chilli. Knead well.

Add the tomato purée and spices to the meat mixture, and knead well again. Season with salt and pepper and add the chopped parsley, and knead once more until everything is mixed together.

Moisten your fingers and the palms of your hands with water, and roll small portions of the mixture into balls. Make a small indentation with your finger in each ball.

Arrange them on a plate with lettuce leaves and parsley sprigs, and serve with wedges of lemon to squeeze into the little well you've made with your finger.

# Smoked aubergine dip

The flavour of smoked aubergine is unique and the soft flesh lends itself to numerous dips and salads. To get the required flavour you need to place the aubergines directly on the gas flame or over a charcoal burner – you don't get the flavour by baking or grilling them. This classic smoked aubergine and tahini dish, *baba ghanoush*, also known as *moutabal*, is one of my absolute favourites – I could eat it every day.

## Serves four to six

**3 large aubergines (eggplants)**

**30–45ml/2–3 tbsp creamy tahini**

**juice of 1 lemon**

**15ml/1 tbsp pomegranate molasses**

**a little cold water**

**2–3 cloves of garlic, crushed**

**a bunch of fresh flat leaf parsley, finely chopped**

**sea salt and ground black pepper**

**olive oil, for drizzling**

Place the aubergines directly over a gas flame or on a charcoal grill, turning them from time to time, until they are soft to touch and the skin is charred and flaky.

Place the aubergines in a plastic bag for a few minutes to sweat. When cool enough to handle, hold them by the stems under cold running water and peel off and discard the skin. Squeeze out the excess water and then chop the flesh to a pulp.

Place the pulp in a bowl and beat in the tahini, lemon juice and pomegranate molasses. Thin with a little water and beat until creamy. Beat in the garlic and most of the parsley and season well with salt and pepper. Add more lemon juice, pomegranate molasses or tahini to suit your taste.

Transfer the mixture to a serving dish, drizzle a little olive oil over the top, sprinkle with the reserved parsley and serve with toasted flatbreads or chunks of crusty loaf.

# Spicy walnut and yogurt dip

A dish of friendship and hospitality, *muhammara* is a medieval Arab dish, also enjoyed in Turkey. Everyone has their own recipe but the principal ingredients include walnuts and hot red pepper paste, or roasted red peppers pounded with chillies. Whenever I visited Syria I always asked for this version, *muhammara labneh*, a creamy combination of the classic muhammara with strained yogurt – delicious with toasted flatbread. Allow time to make the labneh, or buy it ready-made.

## Serves six

For the labneh

**450g/1lb thick, creamy Greek-style (strained plain) yogurt**

**2.5ml/½ tsp sea salt**

For the muhammara

**225g/8oz/2 cups walnuts, roughly chopped**

**2 cloves of garlic, crushed**

**5–10ml/1–2 tsp ground cumin**

**30–45ml/2–3 tbsp hot red pepper paste, or 2 roasted red (bell) peppers pounded to a paste with 1 roasted red chilli**

**5–10ml/1–2 tsp tomato paste**

**3 slices of bread, soaked in water and squeezed**

**15ml/1 tbsp pomegranate molasses**

**45ml/3 tbsp olive oil, plus extra for drizzling**

**sea salt and ground black pepper**

To prepare the labneh, beat the yogurt with the salt and tip it into a piece of muslin lining a colander, suspended above a bowl. Fold or tie the cloth over the yogurt and leave it to drain in a cool place or the refrigerator for about 12 hours. Pour off the whey that collects in the bowl. The yogurt will reduce to half the original amount (roughly 225g/8oz) and be the consistency of cream cheese.

Using an electric blender, whizz together the walnuts, garlic, cumin, red pepper paste (or pounded roasted peppers), and tomato paste. Add the soaked and squeezed bread and pomegranate molasses, and drizzle in the olive oil, whizzing the mixture to a smooth paste.

Tip the mixture into a bowl and beat in 2–3 tablespoons of the labneh. Season well with salt and pepper and add the rest of the labneh if you like. Spoon the mixture into a serving bowl and drizzle with more olive oil. Enjoy with vegetable crudités and toasted flatbreads.

# Village cheese and labneh dip with zahtar

*Jibne wa labneh* is thick, creamy and slightly sour, a combination of local cheese and labneh. If you want to make your own labneh you just need to tip full-fat yogurt into a piece of muslin, tie the ends and suspend it over the tap in the kitchen sink for 12 hours so that it drains and reduces in quantity by half. In the villages of the eastern Mediterranean region people do this every day, then use it in different ways, like this dip made with the village feta-style cheese.

## Serves six

250g/9oz feta cheese, or other soft, salty cheese

250g/9oz labneh (made from strained thick yogurt, see page 82)

30ml/2 tbsp olive oil

15ml/1 tbsp zahtar

Drain and rinse the feta cheese and pat dry with kitchen paper. Place the feta in a bowl and mash it well with a fork. Using a wooden spoon, beat the strained yogurt (labneh) into the mashed feta to form a thick paste.

Spread the mixture in a shallow dish and drizzle the olive oil over the top. Sprinkle the zahtar over the top and serve with toasted bread.

# Tahini dip with parsley

Fabulously quick and simple, *tarator bi tahini* is a great little dip as well as a tangy sauce to drizzle over falafel. Make sure you buy a loose, creamy tahini.

## Serves three to four

150ml/5fl oz tahini

2 cloves of garlic, crushed

juice of 1–2 lemons

cold water

a small bunch of fresh flat leaf parsley, finely chopped

sea salt and ground black pepper

Beat the tahini in a bowl with the crushed garlic until smooth. Gradually beat in the lemon juice – the mixture will thicken at first, then loosen.

Add several teaspoonfuls of cold water to lighten, until thick and creamy. Season well and adjust the lemon to suit your palate.

Stir in most of the parsley, then spoon the mixture into a serving bowl and garnish with the rest of the parsley.

Left **Village cheese and labneh dip with zahtar**  Right **Tahini dip with parsley**

# Cheese and cucumber dip

This is one of those dips that is great on its own with bread but also works well as an accompaniment. Thought to be Egyptian in origin, *michotet* is often served with the national bean dish, *ful medames* – both the dip and the beans are a great favourite in Lebanon and Jordan too.

## Serves three to four

**1 small cucumber, or ½ large one, partially peeled**

**225g/8oz feta cheese, rinsed and drained**

**30ml/2 tbsp olive oil**

**juice of 1 lemon**

**2 spring onions (scallions), white and green parts finely chopped**

**a small bunch of fresh dill, finely chopped**

**a small bunch of fresh mint, finely chopped**

**sea salt and ground black pepper**

Finely dice the partially peeled cucumber, and place on a plate. Sprinkle with a little salt. Leave to weep for about 15 minutes, then squeeze out the excess water with your hands and place on kitchen paper.

In a bowl, mash the cheese well with a fork and then, with a wooden spoon, beat in the olive oil and lemon juice.

Add the spring onion and cucumber to the beaten cheese, and season to taste with salt and black pepper. Fold in the herbs and serve with warm pitta bread or a selection of crudités.

# Lebanese hummus with orange

Nowadays everyone is familiar with hummus but it is important to remember that the word is Arabic for chickpeas as well as the dip made with them – it is not a generic word for every purée! Although a very traditional dish, the basic *hummus bi tahina* can exhibit subtle changes in flavour from region to region. I only ever had this version in Lebanon.

## Serves four to six

225g/8oz dried chickpeas, soaked overnight or for at least 8 hours

1–2 cloves of garlic, crushed

juice of 1 lemon

juice and zest of 1 Seville orange

30–45ml/2–3 tbsp tahini

60ml/4 tbsp olive oil, plus a little for drizzling

a small bunch of fresh coriander (cilantro), roughly chopped

sea salt and ground black pepper

Drain the chickpeas and bring to the boil in a pan with plenty of water, and simmer for about 1½ hours until very soft. Drain.

Put the chickpeas into an electric blender with the garlic, lemon juice and orange zest and juice. Whizz to a thick paste. Add the tahini and continue to whizz.

Gradually, pour in the olive oil, whizzing all the time, until it reaches a smooth, dipping consistency. Season well with salt and pepper.

Transfer the hummus to a serving bowl and drizzle a little oil over the top. Sprinkle with a little coriander and serve with warm pitta bread or crudités.

Cook's tip | **If you prefer to use canned chickpeas, use 2 x 400g/14oz cans and rinse and drain before blending.**

# Toasted bread salad with sumac

A classic Lebanese dish that is enjoyed all over the eastern Mediterranean, *fattoush* is such a creative way of using day-old bread. With the delightful tang of sour pomegranate molasses and ground sumac berries, the salad is both substantial and refreshing.

## Serves four to six

**2–3 day-old flatbreads**

**½ cos or romaine lettuce**

**2–3 tomatoes, skinned**

**1 carrot, peeled**

**5–6 small radishes, trimmed**

**1 red or green (bell) pepper**

**4–5 spring onions (scallions)**

**45–60ml/3–4 tbsp olive oil**

**juice of 1 lemon**

**15ml/1 tbsp pomegranate molasses**

**1–2 cloves of garlic, crushed**

**5–10ml/1–2 tsp honey**

**a small bunch of fresh flat leaf parsley**

**10ml/2 tsp sumac**

**sea salt**

Toast or griddle the breads and break into pieces.

Trim and chop the lettuce leaves and arrange them in a bowl. Seed and chop the skinned tomatoes, thinly shred the carrot and slice the radishes, seed and chop the pepper, and trim and slice the spring onions. Place all the vegetables with the lettuce leaves in the bowl.

Whisk the olive oil with the lemon juice, pomegranate molasses, garlic and honey to make the dressing. Add the parsley to the bowl, together with the pieces of bread, then pour the dressing over the salad. Sprinkle the sumac over the top and season with salt.

Just before serving, toss the salad well, making sure the bread is well coated. Serve immediately as part of a mezze spread, or on its own as a snack or light lunch.

# Fresh broad bean salad

When broad beans are in season local people rush to the markets to fill their baskets. There are traditional dishes to make, friends and family to invite round, and the fresh season is short. This incredibly simple salad, *foul moukala*, is hugely popular all over the eastern Mediterranean. It is generally served cold but is also good eaten while the beans are still warm. In this case, simply drain them without refreshing under cold water, toss the beans in the oil, then add the other ingredients and serve immediately.

## Serves four to six

**500g/1¼lb/2 cups shelled broad (fava) beans**

**5ml/1 tsp sugar**

**30–45ml/2–3 tbsp olive oil**

**juice of ½ lemon**

**1–2 cloves of garlic, crushed**

**a small bunch of fresh coriander (cilantro), finely chopped**

**sea salt and ground black pepper**

Put the shelled beans in a pan with just enough water to cover. Stir in the sugar to preserve the colour of the beans, and bring the water to the boil. Reduce the heat and simmer, uncovered, for about 15 minutes, until the beans are cooked but remain al dente.

Drain the beans and refresh them under running cold water, then drain again and put them in a bowl. Toss the beans in the oil, lemon juice and garlic. Season well with salt and pepper to taste, and stir in the chopped coriander, reserving a little to sprinkle over before serving.

# Aubergine with pomegranate seeds

Smoked aubergine is one of the most versatile vegetables, the texture and flavour combining so well with all kinds of other ingredients. Here the subtle, smoky flesh blends with walnuts and crunchy pomegranate seeds. Variations of this salad, *batinjan rahib*, can be found throughout the eastern Mediterranean.

## Serves four to six

**2 aubergines (eggplants)**

**2 tomatoes, skinned, seeded and chopped**

**1 green (bell) pepper, chopped**

**1 red onion, finely chopped**

**a bunch of fresh flat leaf parsley, finely chopped**

**2 cloves of garlic, crushed**

**30–45ml/2–3 tbsp olive oil**

**juice of 1 lemon**

**15–30ml/1–2 tbsp walnuts, finely chopped**

**15–30ml/1–2 tbsp pomegranate seeds**

**sea salt and ground black pepper**

Place the aubergines directly over a gas flame, or over a charcoal grill, and leave to char until soft, turning occasionally. Hold the aubergines by their stems under running cold water and peel off the charred skins, or slit open the skins and scoop out the flesh.

Squeeze out the excess water from the aubergine flesh then chop it to a pulp and place it in a bowl with the tomatoes, pepper, onion, parsley and garlic. Add the olive oil and lemon juice and toss thoroughly. Season to taste with salt and pepper, then stir in half the walnuts and pomegranate seeds.

Turn the salad into a serving dish and garnish with the remaining walnuts and pomegranate seeds. It is best served warm or at room temperature.

# Parsley and bulgur salad

Although this salad, *tabbouleh*, is very well known, it is often misunderstood. It is essentially a parsley salad with fine bulgur grains running through it, not the other way around – tiny gems in a sea of green. A real Lebanese classic, it is a palate stabiliser on a mezze table full of flavour, and it is a perfect accompaniment to grilled meats.

## Serves four to six

65g/2½oz/½ cup fine bulgur

juice of 2 lemons

a large bunch of fresh flat leaf parsley (about 225g/8oz)

a handful of fresh mint leaves

2–3 tomatoes, skinned, seeded and finely diced

4 spring onions (scallions), trimmed and finely sliced

60ml/4 tbsp olive oil

sea salt and ground black pepper

1 cos or romaine lettuce, trimmed and split into leaves, to serve, optional

Rinse the bulgur in cold water and drain well. Place it in a bowl and pour over the lemon juice. Leave to soften for 10 minutes while you prepare the salad.

With the parsley tightly bunched, slice the leaves as finely as you can with a sharp knife. Transfer to a bowl. Slice the mint leaves and add them to the bowl together with the tomatoes, spring onions and the soaked bulgur. Pour in the oil, season with salt and pepper and toss the salad gently.

Serve immediately, so that the herbs do not get the chance to soften. If you like, arrange lettuce leaves around the salad and use them to scoop up mouthfuls of tabbouleh.

Cook's tip | The trick when preparing the parsley is to make sure it is sliced rather than chopped, with a very sharp knife; this means the herb stays dry and fresh rather than mushy, giving the salad its distinctive appearance and texture.

# Olive and pepper salad

Almost every hillside in the eastern Mediterranean is dotted with olive trees, and most villages have a communal olive press where the harvest can be crushed for its valuable, fruity oil. Olives appear on most mezze tables, marinated in oil and herbs or spices, or tossed with sun-ripened red peppers in this refreshing salad, *salatet zaytoon*.

## Serves four to six

2 long red Mediterranean peppers, or red or orange (bell) peppers

30–45ml/2–3 tbsp kalamata or other fleshy black olives

30–45ml/2–3 tbsp fleshy green olives

1 large tomato, skinned, seeded and diced

2 spring onions (scallions), trimmed and finely sliced

a handful of fresh mint leaves, roughly chopped

a small bunch of fresh coriander (cilantro), roughly chopped

30ml/2 tbsp olive oil

juice of 1 lemon

sea salt and ground black pepper

Place the peppers on a hot griddle, or directly over a gas flame, turning until the skin is evenly charred. Place in a plastic bag for a few minutes to sweat, then hold each one under cold running water and peel off the skin. Remove the stalks and seeds, dice the flesh and place in a bowl.

Pit the olives and slice them in half lengthways. Add to the bowl with the chopped peppers. Add the tomato, spring onions and herbs, and pour in the oil and lemon juice. Season and toss well.

Serve with warm pitta bread.

# Chickpea and bulgur salad with mint

Grains and pulses are the staple of every region and taste so delightfully fresh when combined in salad. This particular salad, *safsouf*, is also used as a filling for vine leaves or to stuff peppers and aubergines.

## Serves four to six

**150g/5oz/scant 1 cup fine bulgur, rinsed**

**400g/14oz can of chickpeas, drained and rinsed**

**1 red onion, finely chopped**

**15–30ml/1–2 tbsp toasted sesame seeds**

**2–3 cloves of garlic, crushed**

**60–75ml/4–5 tbsp olive oil**

**juice of 1–2 lemons**

**a bunch of fresh flat leaf parsley, finely chopped**

**a large bunch of fresh mint, coarsely chopped**

**sea salt and ground black pepper**

**5ml/1 tsp ground paprika, to garnish**

Place the bulgur in a bowl and pour over boiling water to cover. Leave to soak for 10–15 minutes, until it has doubled in volume.

Meanwhile, place the chickpeas in a bowl with the onion, sesame seeds and garlic, and bind with the olive oil and lemon juice. When cool enough to handle, squeeze the bulgur to remove any excess water and add it to the chickpeas. Add the chopped parsley and mint to the bowl.

Toss well, season with salt and pepper to taste, and sprinkle the paprika over the top before serving.

Cook's tip | To toast sesame seeds, heat a frying pan, pour in enough seeds to just cover the bottom of the pan, then dry-fry over a low heat, stirring constantly, until the seeds turn golden brown. Remove from the pan immediately, and leave to cool. Alternatively, roast in a medium oven for a few minutes until golden brown.

# Orange, lemon and onion salad

Tart, fruity salads are quite common accompaniments to spicy dishes. It's all about balance of flavours and textures and refreshing the palate. Some versions of this salad omit the lemons or use the salty, preserved ones instead but I have fond memories of *salata narani* as served on the spicy mezze table of my friends in Aleppo.

## Serves four

**3 sweet, juicy oranges, peeled with pith and pips removed**

**1 juicy lemon, peeled with pith and pips removed**

**1 red onion, finely sliced in rounds**

**8–12 kalamata or other black olives, pitted if preferred**

**5ml/1 tsp cumin seeds, crushed**

**30ml/2 tbsp olive oil**

**a small bunch of fresh mint, finely chopped**

**a small bunch of fresh coriander (cilantro), roughly chopped**

**sea salt**

Carefully slice the oranges and lemons into neat rounds on a plate to catch the juice. Place the orange slices into a bowl with the reserved juice and toss in the sliced onion. Add the olives, the cumin seeds and salt to taste, and drizzle with olive oil.

Chill the salad in the refrigerator for about 30 minutes, then stir in the chopped herbs before serving.

# White cabbage salad

White cabbage is a great favourite as a dressed salad or as a tart pickle, particularly in meat restaurants and kebab houses. This simple white cabbage salad, *salatat malfouf abiad*, is often served as an appetiser or as a palate cleanser.

## Serves four

1 small white cabbage, trimmed and rinsed

30ml/2 tbsp olive oil

juice of 1 lemon

1 clove of garlic, crushed

sea salt

Cut the cabbage into quarters and then slice these into very thin strips. Place the strips in a large serving bowl and sprinkle with salt.

Whisk together the olive oil, lemon juice and garlic in a small bowl. Pour the dressing over the cabbage and toss well. Leave the salad to sit for about 30 minutes and serve to whet the appetite, or as part of a mezze spread.

# Lebanese country salad

Each region has its own 'country' or 'peasant' salad – similar ones can be attributed to gypsies and monks too. This one, *salatah Lebanieh*, is a typical Lebanese version that appears on mezze and kebab tables.

## Serves four to six

1 cos or romaine lettuce

1 cucumber

2 tomatoes

2–3 spring onions (scallions)

a bunch of fresh mint

a bunch of fresh flat leaf parsley

30ml/2 tbsp olive oil

juice of ½ lemon

sea salt

Cut or tear the lettuce leaves into bite-size pieces and place in a bowl. Partially peel the cucumber and cut into small chunks, and add to the lettuce. Skin the tomatoes and dice the flesh, and add to the cucumber. Trim and slice the spring onions and add them to the bowl too.

Wash and chop the mint and parsley, discarding the stalks, and add to the vegetables.

Toss in the olive oil and lemon juice. Season with salt, and serve straight away before the lettuce and herbs wilt.

Left **White cabbage salad**  Right **Lebanese country salad**

# Potato salad with nigella and lime

This *salatat batata* holds fond memories for me as it was prepared by a Palestinian group of friends who are no longer with us. I always think about them when I make this, or any, potato salad. Nigella is a common spice to sprinkle on to breads and savoury pastries but it is not so common to find in a salad.

## Serves four

8–12 medium new potatoes

45–60ml/3–4 tbsp olive oil

2 red onions, halved lengthways and finely sliced

2–3 cloves of garlic, finely chopped

1 red chilli, seeded and finely shredded

10ml/2 tsp nigella seeds

5ml/1 tsp coriander seeds

5ml/1 tsp cumin seeds

5–10ml/1–2 tsp ground turmeric

sea salt and ground black pepper

juice of 1 lime

lime wedges, to serve

Wash the potatoes, place in a pot of water and boil until tender but still firm. When the potatoes are cooked, drain and refresh under running cold water, then peel off the skins. Cut them into bite-size chunks.

Heat the oil in a pan and stir in the onions for 1–2 minutes to soften. Add the garlic, chilli and nigella seeds for 2–3 minutes. Add the coriander seeds, cumin seeds and the turmeric to the pan, then toss in the potato chunks, stir to coat them with the seasoned mixture, and cook to heat through.

Add salt and pepper to taste. Squeeze in the lime juice, then leave the mixture to cool in the pan before transferring to a serving dish. Serve at room temperature with lime wedges to squeeze over.

# Egg and onion salad

This is a lovely egg dish, *beid bi basal*, ideal for a snack or as part of the mezze table. In one simple dish it represents so many of the flavours of eastern Mediterranean cuisine – salty olives, toasted sesame seeds, tangy sumac, Middle Eastern red pepper, and parsley.

## Serves four

4–6 eggs

1 red onion, halved lengthways and sliced

60ml/4 tbsp fleshy black or green olives, pitted and quartered

30ml/2 tbsp pine nuts, toasted

45ml/3 tbsp sesame seeds, toasted

10ml/2 tsp Middle Eastern red pepper, or 1 red chilli, seeded and finely chopped

10ml/2 tsp sumac

30–45ml/2–3 tbsp olive oil

juice of 1 lemon

1–2 cloves of garlic, crushed to a paste with salt

a small bunch of fresh flat leaf parsley, finely chopped

ground black pepper

Put the eggs into a pan of water and bring to the boil for 4–5 minutes. Refresh the eggs under running cold water and shell them. Cut the peeled eggs into quarters and place into a bowl. Add the onion, olives, pine nuts, sesame seeds, Middle Eastern red pepper, and sumac.

In a small bowl, whisk the olive oil and lemon juice together with the garlic paste and seasoning, and pour the dressing over the eggs. Add the parsley.

Toss the salad lightly, so that the eggs don't break up, then garnish with a little more sumac. Serve at room temperature with crusty bread.

# Tomato salad with chilli and coriander

This refreshing, fiery salad reminds me of North African dishes so it was no surprise to enjoy it in Jordan. Ripe, juicy tomatoes are piled high in the markets and end up in salads every day but the combination of chilli and coriander is the attraction of this dish, *banadura salata bil kizbara*, which is just as delicious on a mezze table as it is with grilled meats, poultry and fish.

## Serves four

**6 plump, fresh tomatoes**

**1 hot green chilli, seeded and finely shredded**

**2 cloves of garlic, finely chopped**

**5ml/1 tsp ground fenugreek**

**2.5ml/½ tsp sugar**

**30ml/2 tbsp olive oil**

**juice of ½ lemon**

**a bunch of fresh coriander (cilantro), roughly chopped**

**sea salt**

Prick the tomatoes with a fork, and place in a large bowl. Pour just-boiled water from the kettle over the tomatoes and leave until the skins start to peel. Drain the tomatoes, and leave to cool. When they are cool enough to handle, peel off and discard the skin.

Cut the tomatoes in half, use a teaspoon to remove and discard the seeds, then chop the flesh finely and place in a bowl. Toss in the shredded chilli and garlic along with the fenugreek and sugar. Season with salt and pepper, and add the olive oil and lemon juice. Finally, toss in the chopped coriander and serve the salad straight away, with other mezze dishes.

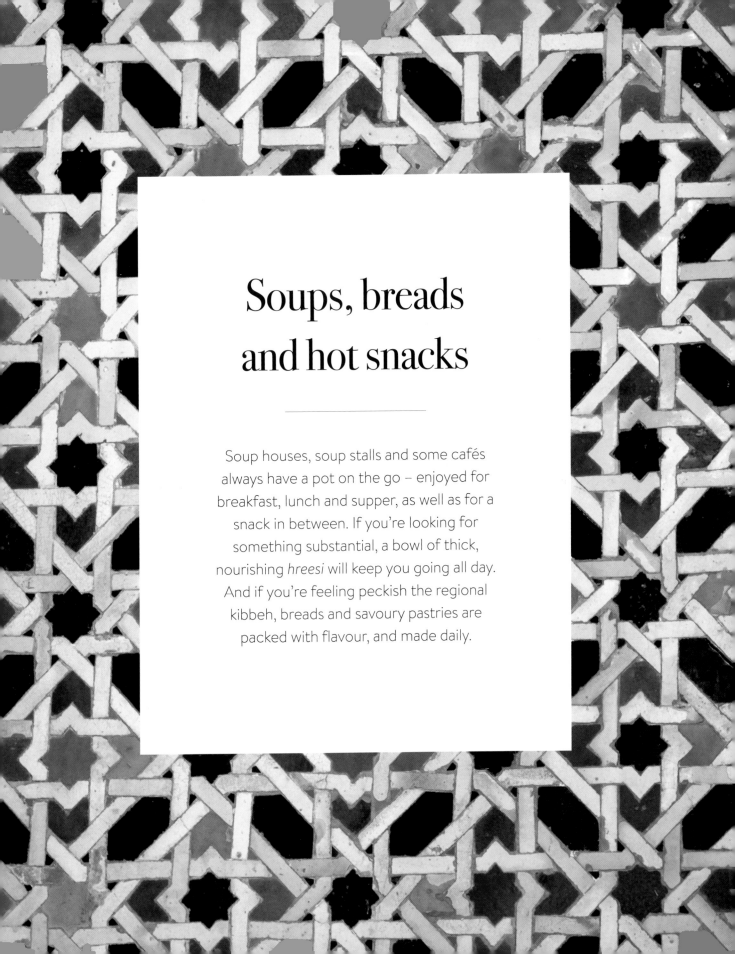

# Soups, breads and hot snacks

Soup houses, soup stalls and some cafés always have a pot on the go – enjoyed for breakfast, lunch and supper, as well as for a snack in between. If you're looking for something substantial, a bowl of thick, nourishing *hreesi* will keep you going all day. And if you're feeling peckish the regional kibbeh, breads and savoury pastries are packed with flavour, and made daily.

# Saffron broth with chicken and noodles

Delicate broths are often served as appetisers or palate cleansers whereas more substantial soups incorporating grains and pulses might be served as a meal on their own. Probably a legacy of the French culinary influence this Lebanese broth, *shorbet al dajaj*, has floral notes of saffron.

## Serves six to eight

**2 celery stalks, with leaves, roughly chopped**

**2 carrots, peeled and roughly chopped**

**1 onion, roughly chopped**

**1 lean, organic chicken, about 1.5kg/3¼lb, cleaned and trimmed**

**a small bunch of fresh flat leaf parsley, roughly chopped**

**6 peppercorns**

**6 allspice berries**

**a generous pinch of saffron fronds**

**115g/4oz vermicelli, or other noodles, broken into pieces**

**sea salt and ground black pepper**

**extra fresh flat leaf parsley or mint, roughly chopped, to garnish**

To make the stock, place all the chopped vegetables in a large pan. Put the chicken on top and add the parsley, peppercorns and allspice berries. Pour in enough water to cover. Bring the water to the boil, then reduce the heat, cover the pan and simmer gently for about 1½ hours, until the chicken starts to fall off the bones.

Lift the chicken out of the pan and set aside. Strain the stock into a fresh pan and discard the vegetables and spices. When the chicken is cool enough to handle, pull the meat off the carcass. Discard the bones and reserve the dark meat for another dish. Use your fingers to tear the breast meat into thin strips, cover and keep warm.

Reheat the broth and stir in the saffron fronds. Bring the broth to the boil and add the noodles. Reduce the heat and boil gently for about 10 minutes, until the noodles are cooked. Add the chicken strips to the soup and heat through.

Check the seasoning and add salt and pepper to taste. Pour the hot soup into individual bowls and sprinkle with parsley or mint.

Cook's tip | Chicken stock will remain clear if the water is simmered gently rather than boiled, but if it does become cloudy don't worry, the flavour is not impaired, and some say that the stock becomes more nutritious if it is boiled rather than simmered.

# Lamb and wheat soup

With a consistency of porridge, this traditional wheat soup is similar to Scotch Broth. *Hreesi* is a peasant soup found all over the region and beyond – there are versions of it throughout the Middle East, right across North Africa and in Turkey and the Black Sea countries. It is also prepared by Christian communities for the Feast of the Assumption, and Muslims traditionally eat it to break their fast at Ramadan.

## Serves four to six

900g/2lb lamb shanks

225g/8oz/1 cup wholegrain wheat, soaked in water overnight

10–15ml/2–3 tsp cumin seeds

30–45ml/2–3 tbsp ghee or butter

10ml/2 tsp ground cinnamon

sea salt and ground black pepper

Place the lamb in a large pan and pour in enough water to cover. Bring the water to the boil and skim off any foam. Drain the wheat and add it to the pan. Season with salt and lots of pepper, reduce the heat, cover and simmer for 1½–2 hours, until the meat is tender. Top up with extra water, if necessary.

Lift out the lamb and remove the meat from the bones. Shred the meat into fine strands, using your fingers, or two forks, and return it to the pan. Continue to simmer the meat with the wheat, beating the mixture with a wooden spoon until it has reached the consistency of thick porridge. Adjust the seasoning, if necessary, turn off the heat, and cover with a lid to keep warm.

Heat a small frying pan and dry-fry the cumin seeds until they begin to release their fragrance – be careful not to let them scorch. Add the ghee or butter and allow it to melt, then stir in the cinnamon.

Ladle the steaming hreesi into warmed bowls and press the back of a spoon into the middle of each bowlful to make a hollow. Pour some of the spiced melted butter into each hollow and serve immediately.

# Fish soup with peppers and potatoes

Whether you are in Latakia in Syria or Sidon in Lebanon, the delicious fish soups and stews will be packed with the day's catch combined with seasonal vegetables, a sprinkling of spices and herbs, and served with bread. Fresh and satisfying, this version is known as *shurabat sumak*.

## Serves four to six

30–45ml/2–3 tbsp olive oil

1 onion, finely chopped

2 cloves garlic, finely chopped

1 red (bell) pepper and 1 green (bell) pepper, seeded and sliced

6–8 new potatoes, peeled and quartered

1 red or green chilli, seeded and sliced

10ml/2 tsp coriander seeds

5ml/1 tsp cumin seeds

a pinch of saffron threads

2 large tomatoes, skinned, seeded and sliced

15ml/1 tbsp tomato paste

5–10ml/1–2 tsp granulated white or palm sugar (jaggery)

850ml/1½ pints/3½ cups fish stock (or 600ml/1 pint/2½ cups stock and 300ml/½ pint/1¼ cups white wine)

12 prawns (large shrimp), shelled and deveined

450g/1lb fillets of a firm-fleshed fish, such as red snapper or sea bass, cut into bite-size chunks

a small bunch of fresh flat leaf parsley, roughly chopped

sea salt and ground black pepper

lemon wedges, to serve

Heat the oil in a large, heavy pan. Add the chopped onion, garlic, and red and green peppers to the pan and cook, stirring, until they soften. Add the potato pieces to the pan with the chilli, coriander seeds, cumin seeds and saffron, and cook for 2–3 minutes more.

Add the sliced tomatoes to the pan, and stir in the tomato paste together with the sugar. Pour the stock into the pan, and bring it to the boil. Reduce the heat and simmer for about 20 minutes, until the potatoes are tender.

Season to taste with salt and pepper. Add the prawns and fish. Simmer for a further 5 minutes, until the fish is just cooked. Stir in some of the parsley and garnish with the rest. Serve hot with the lemon wedges.

# Bedouin spinach and lentil soup

*Sharabat adas bi sabanikh*, this is a typical Bedouin soup, tangy and light, employing ingredients that the nomadic people carry with them, such as grains, pulses and simple flavourings. In Jordan, this soup is sometimes made with mucilaginous molokhia leaves. The soup is finished with *taklia*, a garlicky butter that is stirred in at the end.

## Serves four to six

30ml/2 tbsp olive oil

1 onion, finely sliced

2 cloves of garlic, finely chopped

150g/5oz/scant 1 cup brown lentils, well-rinsed and drained

850ml/1½ pints/3½ cups chicken or vegetable stock

juice of 2 lemons

300g/11oz spinach

a small bunch of fresh coriander (cilantro), a few leaves reserved for garnishing

sea salt and ground black pepper

For the taklia

30ml/2 tbsp butter or ghee

2–3 cloves of garlic, crushed to a paste with 2.5ml/½ tsp salt

5ml/1 tsp ground coriander

Heat the oil in a large heavy pan. Stir in the sliced onion and garlic until they begin to colour. Stir the lentils into the soup for a minute, then pour in the stock and bring it to the boil. Reduce the heat and simmer the soup gently for about 25 minutes, until the lentils are soft but not mushy.

Stir in the lemon juice. Add the spinach and coriander leaves to the pan. Season to taste, but do not add too much salt, as the taklia has enough. Simmer for 10 minutes, until the spinach wilts.

Meanwhile, prepare the taklia. Melt the butter or ghee in a small pan and add the crushed salty garlic. When the garlic is light golden in colour, stir in the ground coriander and cook for a minute, then turn off the heat.

Stir the taklia into the soup, garnish with the few remaining coriander leaves and ladle the soup into bowls.

# Creamy red lentil soup with cumin

Lentil soups are a great favourite in the region – every family has their own lentil soup recipe. Cumin is the common spice to add to dishes prepared with lentils and pulses as it eases the digestion, and cinnamon adds a warming touch at the end. This is *crema shorba al-adas*.

## Serves four

**225g/8oz/1 cup red lentils**

**30ml/2 tbsp olive oil**

**40g/1½oz butter**

**10ml/2 tsp cumin seeds**

**2 onions, chopped**

**1 litre/1¾ pints/4 cups chicken stock**

**5–10ml/1–2 tsp ground cinnamon**

**sea salt and ground black pepper**

**lemon wedges, to serve**

**60ml/4 tbsp thick Greek-style (strained plain) yogurt, to serve (optional)**

Rinse and drain the lentils. Heat the oil and butter in a large, heavy pan and stir in the cumin seeds. Cook, stirring, until they emit a nutty aroma. Add the onions, and fry, stirring until they begin to turn golden brown. Add the drained lentils to the onions, and stir to coat with oil.

Pour the stock into the pan and bring to the boil. Reduce the heat, cover the pan and simmer for about 30 minutes, topping up with water if necessary. Ladle the mixture into a food processor or blender and whizz to a paste.

Return the soup to the pan to reheat, season with salt and pepper and ladle it into individual bowls. Dust with a little ground cinnamon and serve with lemon wedges to squeeze over. Add a spoonful of yogurt to each bowl, if you like.

Left **Chilled cucumber and yogurt soup**  Right **Thick mung bean soup**

# Chilled cucumber and yogurt soup

Cucumber and yogurt are combined in mezze dishes and as an accompaniment to meat dishes but when the weather is stiflingly hot they are often combined in a chilled soup, *shorbet khyar bi laban*, to cool you down.

## Serves four

1 large cucumber, peeled, quartered lengthways and finely sliced

a handful of fresh mint leaves

600ml/1 pint thick yogurt

2 cloves of garlic, crushed

300ml/½ pint/1¼ cups water

sea salt

about 12 ice cubes, to serve

Place the cucumber slices on a plate and sprinkle them with salt. Leave to weep for 10–15 minutes, then gather the cucumber slices in your hands and squeeze gently to remove the salt and excess water.

Meanwhile, chop the mint, reserving a few whole small leaves for garnishing. In a bowl, beat the yogurt with the crushed garlic and chopped mint. Stir in the water to thin it down and then fold in the cucumber. Adjust the seasoning, cover and chill until completely cold for 1–2 hours.

When ready to serve, place 2 or 3 ice cubes in each bowl and ladle the chilled soup over them. Garnish with the reserved mint leaves.

# Thick mung bean soup

Although there are many pulse soups and stews in the region, mung beans, which are native to India, only grow in the south of Lebanon and the north of Syria. This thick soup, *hasa' alhindi*, is ideal for a hearty breakfast or hot snack.

## Serves four

30ml/2 tbsp olive oil

1 onion, finely chopped

2 cloves garlic, finely chopped

10ml/2 tsp cumin seeds

150g/5oz/scant 1 cup mung beans

850ml/1½ pints/3½ cups stock

25g/1oz medium or long grain rice

15ml/1 tbsp oil and a little butter

1 onion, cut in half and sliced

orange wedges, to serve

Heat the oil in a large pan, add the chopped onion and garlic with the cumin seeds and fry for 2–3 minutes. Add the mung beans and stock. Bring to a boil, reduce the heat and simmer for about 25 minutes, until the beans are soft. Stir the rice into the pan, simmer for 10 minutes, until the rice is cooked, and season.

Heat the oil with the butter in a pan and stir in the sliced onion until it begins to crisp and turn a deep brown.

Blend the soup until smooth, reheat, and serve, garnished with the crisp onions and with orange wedges to squeeze into it.

# Fermented bulgur broth

Ancient in origin, this traditional soup, *sharabat kishk*, is an acquired taste because of the main ingredient, kishk, which is made by soaking medium or coarse grain bulgur in milk or yogurt and leaving it to ferment before spreading it out in the sun to dry. The resulting granules are ground to a powder and used to thicken sauces and soups. Kishk is available in Middle Eastern stores.

## Serves four

15–30ml/1–2 tbsp olive oil

1 onion, finely chopped

2 cloves of garlic, finely chopped

2 red chillies, seeded and sliced

5ml/1 tsp dried mint

115g/4oz/½ cup kishk

850ml/1½ pints/3½ cups chicken stock

sea salt and ground black pepper

a handful of fresh mint leaves, roughly shredded, to garnish

lemon wedges, to serve

Heat the oil in a large heavy pan and fry the onion, garlic and chillies until they begin to colour. Stir in the dried mint and kishk and heat for 1 minute.

Pour in the stock and bring to the boil, stirring. Simmer for 10 minutes, stirring from time to time, until thick.

Season, garnish with mint, and serve hot with wedges of lemon.

# Bulgur and lamb patties

You can't go to the eastern Mediterranean without trying the classic *kibbeh*, the meat and bulgur balls and patties. Both the Lebanese and the Syrians claim kibbeh as their own, and there are many versions – grilled, fried and baked – all delicious and all part of everyday culinary life.

## Serves six

225g/8oz/1¼ cups bulgur, rinsed and drained

450g/1lb lean lamb, cut into small chunks

2 onions, grated

5–10ml/1–2 tsp ground allspice

5–10ml/1–2 tsp ground paprika

10ml/2 tsp ground cumin

a small bunch of fresh flat leaf parsley, finely chopped

5–10ml/1–2 tsp sea salt

ground black pepper

sunflower oil, for frying

lemon wedges, to serve

Tip the bulgur into a bowl and pour in just enough boiling water to cover it. Cover the bowl with a clean dish towel and leave the bulgur for up to 20 minutes to swell.

Put the lamb into a food processor and blend to a paste. Turn it into a bowl and add the onions, spices and parsley, with the salt and lots of pepper.

Squeeze any excess water from the bulgur and add it to the lambz`. Use your hands to mix everything together and knead well. Process the mixture again and return it to the bowl for further kneading.

With wet hands, divide the mixture into small balls and flatten each one in the palm of your hand.

Heat enough oil for frying in a shallow pan and cook the patties in batches, about 3 minutes on each side, until nicely browned.

Drain the kibbeh on kitchen paper as you cook them, and then serve hot with lemon wedges to squeeze over.

# Little meat pastries

A legacy of the Ottoman Empire, savoury and sweet pastries crop up all over the eastern Mediterranean. With a reputation for fine cuisine, the Lebanese produce a huge variety, in different shapes and sizes. These little meat-filled ones, *sambousak lahma*, are very popular and are often prepared for family and religious feasts.

## Serves six

30ml/2 tbsp olive oil

1 onion, finely chopped

30ml/2 tbsp pine nuts

250g/9oz lean lamb, minced (ground)

10ml/2 tsp ground cinnamon

30ml/2 tbsp labneh or thick Greek-style (strained plain) yogurt

a small bunch of fresh flat leaf parsley, finely chopped

flour, for dusting

450g/1lb ready-made puff pastry, thawed if frozen

sea salt and ground black pepper

sunflower oil, for frying

Heat the oil in a heavy pan, stir in the onion and cook until transparent. Add the pine nuts and, just as they begin to colour, stir in the minced lamb. Cook for 4–5 minutes to brown the meat. Stir in the cinnamon and season well. Transfer the mixture to a large bowl, and leave to cool, then beat in the labneh or strained yogurt and chopped parsley.

On a floured work surface, roll out the pastry thinly. Cut 10cm/4in rounds or squares, depending on whether you want moon-shaped or triangular pastries. Place 10ml/2 tsp of the meat mixture on each piece of pastry, just off-centre. Dampen the edges with water and pinch together to seal. Create a pattern along the edge with a fork, if you like.

Heat enough oil in a pan and fry the pastries in batches for 5–6 minutes, until golden brown. Drain and serve warm or at room temperature.

Cook's tip | Instead of deep-frying, the pies can be baked in a preheated oven at 200°/400°/Gas 6. Arrange them on several baking trays lined with baking parchment and brush the tops with egg yolk beaten with a little water. You can also sprinkle them with sesame seeds, if you wish. Bake for 15–20 minutes, until puffed up and golden brown.

# Cheese and dill pastries

These little savoury pastries, *sambousak jibneh*, are my favourite. Filled with melted salty cheese and flavoured with dill they are perfect for a nibble with a drink, to add to a selection of mezze dishes, or simply to enjoy as a snack. Using ready-prepared puff pastry makes them extremely easy to make. You can add any combination of herbs, crushed olives, or chilli paste.

## Serves four to six

**225g/8oz feta cheese, rinsed and drained**

**225g/8oz mozzarella or halloumi cheese**

**a small bunch of fresh dill, chopped**

**2 eggs, lightly beaten**

**flour, for dusting**

**450g/1lb ready-made puff pastry, thawed if frozen**

**2 egg yolks, mixed with a little oil or water, for brushing**

**sea salt and ground black pepper**

Preheat the oven to 200°C/400°F/Gas 6. In a bowl, mash the feta with a fork. Grate the mozzarella or halloumi, or whizz to a paste in a blender or food processor, and add it to the feta. Mix in the chopped dill and beaten eggs, season with salt and pepper and mix together. Set aside while you prepare the pastry.

Dust the work surface with flour and roll out the pastry thinly. Using a round pastry cutter, or the rim of a cup, cut out 10cm/4in rounds. Gather up the pastry trimmings, re-roll and cut out further rounds. Dust the pastry circles lightly with flour and stack them as you cut them out.

Place 10ml/2 tsp of the cheese mixture just off-centre on each pastry round. Lift the other side and bring it up over the filling until the edges touch each other, to make a half-moon shape. Dampen the edges with a little water, pinch them together to seal, and use a fork to make a pattern around the edge.

Line several baking trays with baking parchment and arrange the pastries on them. Brush the top of each pastry with a little of the beaten egg yolk mixture and place the trays in the oven. Bake for about 20 minutes, until the pastries are puffed up and golden brown. Serve immediately, while the cheese filling is still soft and warm.

# Spinach pastries with pine nuts

Another tasty pastry perfect for the mezze table, or as a snack. Prepared with spinach and pine nuts these little pastries (*fatiyer bi sabanikh*) are often prepared by the Christian communities for Lent as they don't contain any meat.

## Serves six

**500g/1¼lb fresh spinach, trimmed, washed and drained**

**30ml/2 tbsp olive oil, plus extra for brushing**

**15ml/1 tbsp butter**

**2 onions, chopped**

**45ml/3 tbsp pine nuts**

**15ml/1 tbsp ground sumac, or the juice of 1 lemon**

**5ml/1 tsp ground allspice**

**450g/1lb ready-made puff pastry, thawed if frozen**

**flour, for dusting**

**sea salt and ground black pepper**

Steam the spinach until wilted, then drain, refresh under running cold water and squeeze out the excess liquid with your hands. Chop the spinach coarsely.

Preheat the oven to 180°C/350°F/Gas 4. Heat the oil and butter in a heavy pan and stir in the onion to soften. Add the pine nuts and cook for 2–3 minutes until they begin to turn golden. Stir in the spinach, sumac or lemon juice and allspice, and season. Set aside to cool.

Roll out the pastry on a lightly floured surface and cut out as many 10cm/4in rounds as you can. Spoon a little spinach mixture into the middle of each round. Pull up the sides to make a pyramid by pinching the edges with your fingertips.

Line several baking trays with baking parchment and place the pastries on them. Brush the tops with a little oil and bake the pastries for about 30 minutes, until golden brown.

Left **Garlicky chicken wings with sumac**  Right **Eggs with garlic and sumac**

# Garlicky chicken wings with sumac

The aroma of chicken grilling over charcoal is always enticing, whether it is in a busy street market or in a clearing in the countryside. These tangy chicken wings, *jawaneh*, are great street and picnic food, best eaten with your fingers, straight from the grill or barbecue.

## Serves four to six

45–60ml/3–4 tbsp olive oil

juice of 1 lemon

4–6 cloves of garlic, crushed

15ml/1 tbsp sumac

16–20 chicken wings

sea salt

In a bowl, mix together the olive oil, lemon juice, garlic and sumac.

Place the chicken wings in a shallow dish and rub the marinade all over them. Cover the dish and leave to marinate in the refrigerator for 2 hours.

Prepare the barbecue or preheat a conventional grill or broiler. Place the chicken wings in a single layer on the rack and cook for about 6–8 minutes on each side, basting them with the marinade while they cook.

When the wings are completely cooked, remove from the heat, sprinkle with salt and serve while still hot.

# Eggs with garlic and mint

Boiled, fried or scrambled with spicy sausage or tomatoes, eggs often form part of a quick snack, served with bread. This particular dish is very popular in the streets and at bus and train stations as people head to work. You can serve *beid bi tom* with garlic yogurt or a tahini sauce.

## Serves three to four

6 eggs

30ml/2 tbsp olive oil

a knob or pat of butter

2–3 cloves of garlic, crushed

5–10ml/1–2 tsp sumac

5ml/1 tsp dried mint

sea salt

garlic-spiced yogurt, to serve

Crack all the eggs into a large bowl, being very careful not to break any of the yolks as you do so.

Heat the oil in a heavy frying pan with the butter. Stir in the garlic and sumac and fry for 1–2 minutes. Slip the eggs into the pan, moving the bowl so that each one falls into its own section of the pan. Sprinkle the dried mint over the eggs and cover the pan with a lid. Reduce the heat and cook until the egg yolks are set to taste.

Sprinkle a little sea salt over the eggs and divide them into portions. Serve immediately with garlicky yogurt and an extra pinch of sumac if you like.

# Feta, pepper and olive frittata

Known as frittata in the southern Mediterranean, *Ijjit al jibne* are flat omelettes filled with herbs, cheese, cured sausage and vegetables, spiked with chillies, often cooked in large, wide pans and sliced up for customers. Simple snack food.

## Serves four to six

**30ml/2 tbsp olive oil**

**1 red onion, chopped**

**1 green or red (bell) pepper, chopped**

**1 red chilli, seeded and chopped**

**225g/8oz feta cheese, crumbled**

**12 black olives, pitted and halved**

**a small bunch of fresh flat leaf parsley, chopped**

**a small bunch of fresh mint, chopped**

**8 eggs, lightly beaten with about 50ml/2fl oz/¼ cup milk**

**ground black pepper**

Heat the oil in a heavy non-stick pan and cook the onion, pepper and chilli until they begin to soften and brown. Stir in the feta cheese, olives and herbs, and quickly add in the beaten eggs. Season with pepper.

Pull the egg mixture into the middle of the pan to help it spread and cook evenly. Reduce the heat, cover the pan with a lid, or a piece of foil, and let the omelette cook gently for 5–10 minutes until thick and solid.

At a street stall, the omelette would be served directly from the pan at this stage, but at home, you can drizzle a little extra oil over the top and brown it under a preheated grill or in a hot oven, if you like.

When cooked through, cut the omelette into portions and serve hot or at room temperature.

# Bread omelette with minty courgettes

The Arab bread omelette, *eggah bi eish wa kousa*, is similar to the traditional Spanish one as it is thick and filling and can be eaten on its own or packed between two sides of a loaf – great bus station food. You can make this omelette with potatoes or mushrooms instead of courgettes.

## Serves four to six

**2 medium courgettes (zucchini)**

**2–3 slices of bread**

**milk, for soaking**

**30ml/2 tbsp olive oil**

**15–30ml/1–2 tbsp butter**

**1 onion, sliced**

**10ml/2 tsp dried mint**

**a bunch of fresh mint, chopped, a few leaves retained to garnish**

**8–10 eggs, beaten**

**sea salt and ground black pepper**

Thinly slice the courgettes, place in a colander, and sprinkle with salt. Leave to stand for 15 minutes, rinse and dry.

Remove the crusts from the bread and soak the slices in a little milk.

Heat the oil with a tablespoon of butter in a heavy frying pan. Stir in the onion to soften, then add the courgettes. Fry until both the onion and courgette slices are golden. Stir in the dried and fresh mint, and set aside to cool.

Crack the eggs into a large bowl and beat them lightly. Squeeze the bread dry and add it to the eggs, crumbling it with your fingers. Beat well. Add the cooled courgette and onion mixture to the beaten egg and bread. Season with salt and pepper.

Heat another tablespoon of butter in the frying pan. Tip the courgette and egg mixture into the pan, cover and cook gently until the eggs have set. Sprinkle a little finely chopped mint over the top, divide into portions and serve warm or at room temperature.

# Aubergine with basterma and halloumi

Like little fried toasties, this way of cooking aubergines with halloumi and basterma – *batinjan magli* – is genuis. The melted halloumi inside the crispy fried aubergine slices is delicious; I add in basil or mint leaves for a bit of freshness. Basterma is the air-dried beef fillet cured in a garlic and fenugreek coating; the Armenians are said to be the best producers.

## Serves four

2–3 large aubergines (eggplants)

sea salt

115/4oz basterma, cut into 8 thin slices

225g/8oz halloumi, cut into 8 thin slices

a handful of fresh mint or basil leaves

30–45ml/2–3 tbsp plain (all-purpose) flour

30–45ml/2–3 tbsp breadcrumbs

5–10ml/1–2 tsp zahtar

2 eggs, lightly beaten

sunflower oil, for frying

sea salt and ground black pepper

lemon wedges, to serve

Slice the aubergines into rounds, roughly 1.5cm/½ in thick, and discard the ends – you need 16 slices in total, to make 8 patties. Sprinkle the slices with salt and leave them to weep for 15 minutes.

Rinse the aubergine slices, pat dry, and place them on a wooden board or clean work surface. Take one slice and place a slice of basterma on it, followed by a slice of halloumi, and top with a mint or basil leaf. Season with a little salt and plenty of black pepper. Place a similar-sized slice of aubergine on top, to create a sandwich.

Place the flour in a shallow dish. Dust each side of the sandwich with flour. Repeat with the remaining aubergine, halloumi and basterma slices until you have at least 8 sandwiches.

In a shallow bowl, or on a plate, mix the breadcrumbs with a little seasoning and the zahtar. Beat the eggs in another bowl with a splash of water. Place the bowl of beaten egg next to the bowl of breadcrumbs.

Carefully, dip each aubergine sandwich into the egg and then coat it in the breadcrumbs. Let the patties stand for a few minutes to allow the breadcrumbs to adhere.

Heat enough oil for frying in a heavy skillet or frying pan. Gently, place the patties in the hot oil and fry them in batches on both sides until golden brown. Remove from the pan, and drain on kitchen paper as they are cooked. Sprinkle with a little salt, and serve hot with wedges of lemon to squeeze over them. If you like, you can accompany the patties with garlic yogurt or tahini sauce.

# Syrian sausage rolls

One family I used to stay with in Aleppo always had these rolls in the fridge, ready to bake when you wanted a snack. The children used to dip their *sambousak alsuwria* in locally produced tomato ketchup but I was always given crumbly cheese and pickles to go with them.

## Serves 6

**450g/1lb lean lamb, diced**

**2 cloves of garlic, crushed**

**10ml/2 tsp ground Middle Eastern or Aleppo pepper**

**10ml/2 tsp ground cumin**

**5ml/1 tsp ground coriander**

**5ml/1 tsp ground allspice**

**5ml/1 tsp ground turmeric**

**5ml/1 tsp ground fenugreek**

**5ml/1 tsp olive oil**

**flour, for dusting**

**500g/1¼lb ready-made puff pastry, thawed if frozen**

**sea salt and ground black pepper**

Using a mortar and pestle, pound the meat with the spices, or whizz them together in a food processor. Bind with the olive oil to make a smooth paste, and season with salt and pepper.

On a lightly floured surface, roll the pastry into a long, thin rectangle. Place the meat in a sausage shape on one side and fold over to make a roll, or spread the meat in a thin layer, taking it right to the edges, and roll it all up into a spiral.

Heat the oven to 200°C/400°F/Gas 6. Slice the pastry log or spiral into roughly 2.5cm/1in pieces and place them on a lightly oiled baking sheet. Bake them in the oven for about 12 minutes, until golden brown and puffed up. Serve hot.

# Little spicy lamb pizzas

All over the eastern Mediterranean, savoury flatbreads with spicy minced meat toppings – in the style of a pizza – are baked in communal ovens, at the local bakery and in kebab houses. When freshly made, *lahm bi ajeen* really are delicious, cut into portions and rolled up with parsley and a squeeze of lemon. These home-baked mini ones are not as flexible but just as tasty and perfect for a snack. Middle Eastern pepper is a variety of local chilli, also known as Aleppo pepper.

## Serves three to four

### For the dough

**300g/11oz/2½ cups plain (all-purpose) flour, plus extra for dusting**

**2.5ml/½ tsp sea salt**

**15ml/1 tbsp dried yeast**

**5ml/1 tsp sugar**

**50ml/2fl oz/¼ cup lukewarm water**

**150g/5oz plain set yogurt**

**45ml/3 tbsp olive oil, plus extra for brushing**

### For the topping

**250g/9oz lamb, finely minced (passed through the grinder twice)**

**1 onion, finely chopped**

**1 large tomato, skinned and finely chopped**

**a small bunch of fresh flat leaf parsley, finely chopped**

**10ml/2 tsp ground Middle Eastern or Aleppo pepper, or 1 red chilli, seeded and finely chopped**

**5ml/1 tsp ground allspice**

**5–10ml/1–2 tsp pomegranate molasses**

**5–10ml/1–2 tsp sumac, to serve**

**sea salt and ground black pepper**

Sift the flour with the salt into a large bowl. In another bowl, cream the yeast with the sugar and the water until it begins to froth. In a third bowl, beat the yogurt with the olive oil until it is light and creamy.

Make a well in the centre of the flour and pour in the creamed yeast and sugar mixture. Add the yogurt mixture. With your fingers, draw in the flour from the sides to combine into a dough. Knead until you have a smooth, silky ball. Pour a few drops of oil into the base of the bowl and roll the ball of dough in it. Cover the bowl with a clean damp dish towel and leave the dough to prove for at least 2 hours, until doubled in size.

Meanwhile, place the minced lamb on a board with the onion, tomato and parsley and chop until it forms a paste. Add the Middle Eastern pepper or chilli, allspice, pomegranate molasses and seasoning, and knead well.

Preheat the oven to 230°C/450°F/Gas 8. Punch the risen dough with your fist to knock the air out of it, then knead it lightly on a floured surface. Divide the dough into roughly 12 portions and roll each one into a ball. Flatten each ball in the palm of your hand and stretch it into a mini pizza shape. Place each round on a lightly oiled baking sheet. Brush each dough round with a little olive oil and then spread a thin layer of the meat paste over the top.

Place the pizzas in the hot oven for about 5–10 minutes, until the base is lightly browned and crispy, and the meat is just cooked. Sprinkle with sumac and serve immediately.

# Feta and fig flatbreads with honey

Similar to little pizzas, the *manoushi* bread dough produces a soft, chewy base for an assortment of sweet and savoury toppings. Served for breakfast or a snack, you will come across these tasty little flatbreads all over the eastern Mediterranean.

## Serves four

**For the dough**

350g/12oz/3 cups plain (all-purpose) flour, plus extra for dusting

2.5ml/¼ tsp salt

5ml/1 tsp dried yeast

1.5ml/¼ tsp sugar

200ml/7fl oz/scant 1 cup lukewarm water

15ml/1 tbsp olive oil

**For the topping**

225g/8oz feta, rinsed and crumbled

175g/6oz moist, dried figs, chopped

honey, for drizzling

10ml/2 tsp zahtar

Sift the flour with the salt into a large bowl. In another bowl, cream the yeast with the sugar in a little of the warm water until it begins to froth.

Make a well in the centre of the flour and tip the creamed yeast into it. Add the rest of the water and, drawing the flour in from the sides, work the mixture into a sticky dough. Add the olive oil and knead until the dough is smooth and elastic. Pour a few more drops of oil into the base of the bowl and then roll the dough ball in it. Cover the bowl with a damp dish towel and prove for 2 hours, until it has doubled in size.

Punch the dough with your fist to knock out the air and transfer it to a floured surface. Divide into 12 pieces and lightly flour. Cover with a clean dish towel and leave for another 20 minutes.

Preheat the oven to 230°C/450°F/ Gas 8. Take each portion of dough and roll into a small ball. Flatten each ball and stretch out into a circle, roughly 12.5cm/5in in diameter. Place the circles of dough on to a lightly greased baking tray and bake in the oven for 4–5 minutes, until they are golden brown and crisp.

While still hot, scatter the crumbled feta and chopped figs over each one. Drizzle a little honey over the top and sprinkle with zahtar. Serve immediately while still warm.

# Zahtar flatbreads

Flavoured with the regional thyme-scented zahtar, *manakakeish bil zahtar* are popular in the streets of Beirut and at neighbourhood bakeries, where they are often chosen for breakfast or as a snack. They are great served to accompany mezze dishes.

## Serves four to six

**7g/¼oz/2¼ tsp dried yeast**

**2.5ml/½ tsp sugar**

**300ml/½ pint/1¼ cups lukewarm water**

**450g/1lb/4 cups strong white bread flour, or a mixture of strong white and wholewheat flours**

**2.5ml/½ tsp salt**

**30–45ml/2–3 tbsp olive oil, plus extra for oiling**

**45–60ml/3–4 tbsp zahtar**

**sea salt**

In a small bowl, dissolve the yeast with the sugar in a little of the water and leave to cream for about 10 minutes, until it begins to froth.

Sift the flour with the salt into a bowl and make a well in the centre. Pour the creamed yeast into the well with the rest of the water and draw the flour in from the sides to form a dough. Turn the dough on to a floured surface and knead for 10 minutes, until it is smooth and elastic. Pour a drop of oil into the base of the bowl, roll the dough in it and cover with a damp cloth. Leave to prove for about 2 hours, until it has doubled in size. Preheat the oven to 200°C/400°F/Gas 6.

In a small bowl, mix together the olive oil and the zahtar to make a paste.

Knock back (punch down) the dough, knead it lightly, then divide it into about 20 pieces. Knead each piece into a ball, flatten and stretch it, and smear with zahtar paste.

Place the breads on lightly greased baking trays and bake them in the hot oven for about 10 minutes, until slightly risen and golden brown. Sprinkle a little sea salt over the flatbreads and serve them warm on their own, or to accompany other dishes.

# Pitta bread

Plain flat pitta breads (*khubz*) come in various guises, some crispy with hollow pockets and others thick and spongy. They are delicious when freshly baked or griddled and drizzled in butter or honey and they can be used as practical scoops and mops for all the delectable dips and dressings. This is the standard dough used to make pitta breads.

## Serves six to eight

7g/¼oz/2¼ tsp dried yeast

2.5ml/½ tsp sugar

300ml/½ pint/1¼ cups lukewarm water

450g/1lb/4 cups strong white bread flour, or a mixture of strong white and wholewheat flours

2.5ml/½ tsp salt

a little sunflower oil, for greasing

In a small bowl, dissolve the yeast with the sugar in a little of the water. Leave for about 10–15 minutes, until frothy.

Sift the flour and salt into a bowl. Make a well in the centre and pour in the yeast mixture and the rest of the water. Gradually draw the flour in and knead into a pliable dough. Turn the dough on to a lightly floured surface and knead until smooth and elastic. Pour a drop of oil into the bowl and roll the dough in it to coat. Cover the bowl with a damp cloth and leave to rise in a warm place for at least 2 hours, or overnight, until it has doubled in size.

Knock back (punch down) the dough and knead lightly. Divide into tangerine-sized balls and flatten with your hand. Dust a clean cloth with flour and place the rounds of dough on it, leaving room to expand between them. Sprinkle with flour and lay another cloth on top. Leave to prove for 1–2 hours.

Preheat the oven to 230°C/450°F/Gas 8. Place several baking sheets in the oven to heat, then lightly oil them and place the bread rounds on them. Sprinkle the rounds with a little water and bake for 6–8 minutes – they should be lightly browned but not too firm, and slightly hollow inside.

Place the breads on a wire rack to cool a little before eating while warm, or wrap them in a clean, dry dish cloth to keep them soft for eating later.

# Grains and pulses

Grains and pulses are an everyday part
of the diet in the eastern Mediterranean.
Wheat has been a staple grain since ancient
times – not only in the baking of bread, but
as the root of many classic dishes – though
rice is more recent. Even if you only spend
one day in the region you will encounter
grains and pulses in some form, as it would
be unthinkable to go through the day
without a dish of hummus, pilaff, bulgur,
beans or lentils making an appearance
on the table.

# Freekeh with pistachios

Freekeh (or *frikkeh*) is immature wheat that has been roasted in the husk to produce green grains with a nutty texture and a mild smoky flavour. An ancient food in traditional Arab cuisine, freekeh is highly nutritious, very high in fibre and with a low GI rating. Once you've tasted it you will go back for more. You can find freekeh in Middle Eastern stores and online.

## Serves four to six

**30ml/2 tbsp ghee, or olive oil with a knob or pat of butter**

**1 onion, finely sliced**

**2 cloves of garlic, finely chopped**

**1–2 green chillies, seeded and finely sliced**

**115g/4oz unsalted pistachios**

**250g/9oz /1 cup freekeh, rinsed**

**900ml/1½ pints/3¾ cups well-flavoured chicken stock**

**30ml/2 tbsp pine nuts**

**sea salt and ground black pepper**

**Greek-style (strained plain) yogurt, and baby mint leaves, to serve**

Heat the ghee, or olive oil and butter mixture, in a heavy pan and stir in the sliced onion, garlic and green chillies. Cook until they begin to colour. Halve the pistachios, and add to the pan. Fry for 1 minute, stirring. Add the freekeh to the pan, and stir it well to coat the grains in the butter.

Pour in enough stock to just cover the mixture, and bring it to the boil. Add salt and pepper to taste, reduce the heat and simmer for 15–20 minutes, until all the stock has been absorbed. Turn off the heat, cover the pan with a clean dish towel, followed by the lid, and leave the grains to steam for a further 10 minutes.

Meanwhile, put the pine nuts in a frying pan and dry-roast them over a medium heat, until golden brown. Remove from the heat and transfer them to a plate to cool and crisp.

Transfer the freekeh to a warmed serving dish and sprinkle the pine nuts over the top. Serve immediately, with a dollop of creamy yogurt and garnish of mint, as an accompaniment to any roasted or barbecued meat or poultry dish.

# Bulgur with lamb and chickpeas

Bulgur is whole wheat, boiled until the grain is tender and the husk cracks open, then dried and ground, either coarsely or finely. There are many tasty peasant dishes combining this much-loved grain with meat, chicken or vegetables. This Lebanese version is called *burghul bil lahma*.

## Serves four to six

**30ml/2 tbsp ghee, or olive oil with a knob or pat of butter**

**1 onion, finely chopped**

**5ml/1 tsp ground cumin**

**5ml/1 tsp ground fenugreek**

**200g/7oz lean lamb, cut into chunks**

**200g/7oz/1⅓ cups cooked chickpeas**

**250g/9oz/1½ cups coarse bulgur, well rinsed and drained**

**900ml/1½ pints/3¾ cups of water**

**sea salt and ground black pepper**

**fresh coriander (cilantro), to garnish**

Heat the ghee, or olive oil and butter mixture, in a heavy pan and add the chopped onion. Cook, stirring, until the onion softens and begins to turn a golden brown colour. Mix the ground cumin and fenugreek into the onions, and stir through until they release their aromas.

Toss the chunks of lamb into the pan and stir to coat the meat in the buttered onion and spices. Add the chickpeas to the pan, stir to mix and cook for 1 minute, then add the bulgur. Add the water to the pan and bring it to the boil. Season with salt and pepper and stir gently. Reduce the heat and simmer for 20 minutes.

When all the water has been absorbed, turn off the heat, cover the pan with a clean dish towel, followed by the lid, and leave the bulgur to steam for a further 10 minutes.

Fork through gently, then transfer the bulgur and lamb mixture into a warmed serving dish and garnish with the coriander. Serve immediately.

# Bulgur with fruit and nuts

The tradition of combining savoury ingredients with dried and fresh fruit is attributed to the ancient Persians but was adopted by the medieval Arabs and formed the basis of many dishes including this aromatic pilaff, *burghul mufalfal*, which can be prepared with bulgur or rice.

## Serves four to six

For the bulgur

30ml/2 tbsp olive oil with a knob or pat of butter, or ghee

1 onion, finely chopped

5ml/1 tsp sugar

2–3 cardamom pods

225g/8oz/1 cup medium or coarse bulgur, well rinsed and drained

450ml/¾ pint/scant 2 cups chicken stock, or water

sea salt and ground black pepper

For the fruit and nuts

30ml/2 tbsp olive oil with a knob or pat of butter

115g/4oz blanched almonds

100g/3½oz walnuts, roughly chopped

100g/3½oz dried, ready-to-eat apricots, or fresh, thinly sliced

100g/3½oz dried, ready-to-eat figs, or fresh, thinly sliced

50g/2oz sultanas (golden raisins)

5ml/1 tsp ground cinnamon

15–30ml/1–2 tbsp pomegranate molasses

Melt the olive oil and butter, or ghee, in a heavy pan and stir in the onion with the sugar, until it turns golden. Add the cardamom pods and stir in the bulgur. Pour the stock into the pan, season with salt and pepper and bring it to the boil. Reduce the heat and simmer for 10–12 minutes, until all the water has been absorbed. Turn off the heat, cover the pan with a clean dish towel and put on the lid. Leave the bulgur to steam for a further 10 minutes.

Meanwhile, prepare the fruit and nuts. Heat the oil with the butter in a heavy pan and stir in the almonds and walnuts. Once the nuts begin to brown, stir in the sliced apricots, figs and sultanas and cook for 1–2 minutes.

Transfer the bulgur to a serving dish, creating a mound. Spoon the nuts and fruit over the bulgur, dust with cinnamon, and drizzle the pomegranate molasses over the top.

Serve the bulgur hot with grilled meats and poultry. It can also be eaten on its own with dollops of thick, creamy strained yogurt, mixed with a little lemon juice.

# Rice with lamb and chestnuts

Palestinian in origin, the tradition of *makloub* is an impressive one, as the rice dish is turned upside down and sits in a solid mound with the key ingredients resting on top – the translation from Arabic means 'turned over'. There are many variations on this theme, some extremely elaborate with several layers of vegetables and poultry or meat, others more simple with one or two layers. This one is made with lamb and chestnuts. You could add pomegranate seeds and chopped parsley for garnish to add colour if you like.

## Serves four to six

450g/1lb medium or long grain rice

15–30ml/1–2 tbsp ghee, or olive oil with a knob or pat of butter

1 onion, sliced

225g/8oz lean lamb, cut into bite-size pieces

5–10ml/1–2 tsp cumin seeds

5–10ml/1–2 tsp coriander seeds

2–3 cinnamon sticks

10ml/2 tsp allspice berries

600ml/1 pint/2½ cups water

225g/8oz cooked chestnuts, shelled then halved

sea salt and ground black pepper

Place the rice in a large bowl and cover with plenty of cold water. Leave it to soak for about 30 minutes, then drain.

Heat the ghee in a heavy-based pot, add the onion and fry until golden. Add the meat to the pot and brown it all over. Add the spices to the pot, pour in the water, and season with salt. Bring the liquid to the boil, reduce the heat and simmer for about 30 minutes.

When the meat is tender, drain it, reserving the stock. Season the stock to taste with salt and pepper. Clean the pot or use another heavy-based pot with a lid. Brush a little oil in the base and around the sides. Arrange the meat and chestnuts in a layer on the bottom of the pot. Tip the drained rice on top, making sure it pressed down, then carefully pour the stock over the top. You may need to add a little more water but don't stir.

Cover the pot with a lid, bring the liquid slowly to the boil, then reduce the heat and simmer for about 20 minutes. By this time the liquid will have been absorbed, and the rice should be almost done. Turn off the heat, cover with a clean dish towel and the lid, and leave to steam for 15 minutes, until the rice is tender.

To serve, use a spatula to loosen all the way around the edges of the pot, then place a serving dish upside down over the top of the pot, and carefully, using both hands, invert the pot so that the serving dish is on the bottom. Leave it to rest like that for a couple of minutes and then gently ease the pot away, leaving a mould of rice with a layer of chestnuts and meat on top.

# Bulgur with courgettes, mint and dill

This delightful dish, *kousa burghul*, has the definite markings of Ottoman influence with the balancing of 'cool' vegetable with 'warm' herbs. Variations of this summery bulgur recipe appear all over the region.

## Serves four to six

**225g/8oz/1¼ cups coarse bulgur, well rinsed and drained**

**30ml/2 tbsp ghee, or olive oil with a knob or pat of butter**

**1 onion, finely chopped**

**2 courgettes (zucchini), trimmed and diced**

**a pinch of saffron threads**

**a small bunch of fresh dill fronds, chopped (reserve some for garnish)**

**a good-sized bunch of fresh mint, chopped (reserve a few leaves for garnish)**

**sea salt and ground black pepper**

**lemon wedges, to serve**

Put the rinsed, drained bulgur into a bowl and pour over enough boiling water to cover by about 2cm/1in. Cover and leave to swell for about 15 minutes.

Heat the ghee or olive oil and butter in a heavy pan and stir in the onion, stirring until it begins to go golden brown. Add the courgettes with the saffron, and sauté for 2–3 minutes until the courgettes begin to turn golden.

Add in the bulgur, making sure you heat it through, but mixing gently to combine without squashing the courgettes. Season with salt and pepper. Toss in most of the herbs.

Serve hot, garnished with the reserved dill and mint, and serve with lemon wedges to squeeze over.

# Rice with aubergine

Upside down and encased in strips of aubergine, *maklubeh bajinjan* is another Palestinian dish full of surprise with its sandwiched middle of minced lamb or chicken. It is prepared for special occasions. Serve with plain yogurt.

### Serves four to six

4 medium aubergines (eggplants)

sunflower oil, for deep-frying

300g/11oz/1½ cups medium or long grain white rice, well-rinsed

30ml/2 tbsp olive oil

1 onion, finely chopped

250g/9oz minced (ground) lamb

5–10ml/1–2 tsp ground cinnamon

5ml/1 tsp ground allspice

30ml/1 tbsp blanched almonds

30ml/1 tbsp pine nuts

sea salt and ground black pepper

Heat the oven to 180°C/350°F/Gas 4. Partially peel the aubergines, leaving stripes of skin, and cut lengthways into long, thin slices. Heat sunflower oil for deep-frying in a pan and fry the aubergine in batches until golden. Drain and set aside.

Pour 850ml/1½ pints/3½ cups water into a pan and bring it to the boil. Add the rice and boil for 1–2 minutes. Season with salt and pepper, reduce the heat and simmer for 15–20 minutes, until the rice has absorbed the water.

Heat 15ml/1 tbsp of the olive oil in a frying pan. Add the onion and stir until it begins to colour. Add the minced lamb and spices to the onion, and mix well. Stir the mixture over medium heat for about 10 minutes, until the meat is cooked and dry.

Line a lightly greased dome-shaped tin or ovenproof bowl with most of the aubergine slices. Spoon some of the rice into the dome to fill it a third of the way up. Season the lamb with salt and pepper, then spoon it on top of the rice. Then spoon the rest of the rice on top of the lamb. Place the remaining aubergine slices on top of the rice to seal, and place the tin in the oven for 15–20 minutes.

Meanwhile, heat the remaining 15ml/1 tbsp olive oil in a small heavy-based pan and stir in the almonds for 1–2 minutes, until they begin to colour. Add the pine nuts. As soon as they begin to colour, transfer on to kitchen paper to drain and crisp.

Remove the tin from the oven. Place a plate on top. Using oven gloves, hold the plate with one hand and invert the dish. Ease the tin off. Garnish the dome with the toasted nuts, and serve.

Left **Saffron rice with pine nuts**  Right **Rice and mastic parcels**

# Saffron rice with pine nuts

With precious saffron providing the main flavour and colour in this dish, *ruz bi za'faran* is a noble golden pilaff from Lebanon. A lovely accompaniment to grilled fish or roasted meat, sometimes it is simply served on its own with a dollop of creamy yogurt and a drizzle of melted butter.

## Serves four

45ml/3 tbsp butter or ghee

225g/8oz/generous 1 cup long grain rice

a pinch of saffron fronds

600ml/1 pint/2½ cups chicken stock or water

30ml/2 tbsp pine nuts

sea salt and ground black pepper

Melt 30ml/2 tbsp of the butter or ghee in a heavy pan. Stir in the rice and saffron, making sure the grains are coated in butter. Pour in the stock, season with salt and pepper, and bring to the boil.

Reduce the heat and simmer for 15 minutes, until all the water has been absorbed, then turn off the heat and cover the pan with a clean dish towel, followed by the lid. Leave to steam for a further 10 minutes.

Meanwhile, melt the remaining butter in a frying pan. Stir in the pine nuts and cook until they turn golden. Drain them on kitchen paper.

Fluff up the rice with a fork and transfer to a warmed serving dish. Sprinkle the pine nuts over the top and serve immediately.

# Rice and mastic parcels

Wafer-thin sheets are used to make these little parcels, called *boerek bit roz. Khubz markouk* are the flat, paper-thin rounds sometimes referred to in Lebanon and Syria as mountain bread; it takes time and skill to prepare them, so it is easier to use filo pastry instead.

## Serves four

225g/8oz/generous 1 cup medium or long grain white rice

sea salt

1–2 mastic crystals

5ml/1 tsp sugar

4–6 sheets of filo pastry

25g/1oz butter or ghee

sunflower oil, for frying

5–10ml/1–2 tsp sumac or zahtar

Bring 600ml/1 pint/2½ cups of water to the boil with a pinch of salt. Toss in the rice and continue to boil the water for 2–3 minutes. Reduce the heat and simmer for about 10 minutes, until the water has been absorbed. Turn off the heat, cover the pan with a clean dish towel, and put on the lid. Leave to stand for about 10 minutes so the steam completes the cooking.

Using a mortar and pestle, pound the mastic crystals together with the sugar to a powder. Stir the pulverised mastic into the rice.

Place the filo sheets on a flat surface and spoon portions of the rice into the middle of each one. Dot the rice with a little butter and fold the edges of the pastry up and over the rice to form a package, tucking in the sides.

Fry the parcels in the sunflower oil for 2–3 minutes each side, until crisp and golden brown. Sprinkle with sumac or zahtar and serve as a snack, or as an accompaniment to grilled food.

# Brown rice with chickpeas and basterma

There are so many rice dishes combining pulses or lentils– all variations on a theme – and all prepared with white rice or bulgur. Brown rice is not so common but my Syrian friends used to make this with a medium brown grain and the nutty texture worked well with the walnuts and basterma. Freekeh would be a good alternative. This dish is known as *hummus burghul*.

## Serves four to six

15–30ml/1–2 tbsp ghee, or olive oil with a knob or pat of butter

2 onions, finely chopped

2 cloves of garlic, finely chopped

1 red or green chilli, seeded and chopped

10ml/2 tsp cumin seeds

5–10ml/1–2 tsp sugar

5ml/1 tsp ground cinnamon

5ml/1 tsp ground allspice

5ml/1 tsp ground fenugreek

225g/8oz/generous 1 cup medium or long grain brown rice, well rinsed and drained

850ml/1½ pints/3½ cups chicken stock, or water

14oz/400g can of chickpeas, rinsed and drained

a small bunch of fresh coriander (cilantro), finely chopped

a few mint leaves, finely chopped

sea salt and ground black pepper

For the topping

15ml/1 tbsp butter

6–8 slices of basterma, cut into thin strips

30ml/2 tbsp walnuts, roughly chopped

Heat the ghee, or olive oil and butter, in a large pan or frying pan and stir in the onions, garlic and chilli with the cumin seeds and sugar. When the onion begins to brown, stir in the spices. Add the rice to the pan, stirring to coat the grains in the spices. Pour in the stock or water, season with salt and pepper, and bring it to the boil.

Reduce the heat and simmer for about 25 minutes, until the rice is cooked but still retains a bite. Toss in the chickpeas and most of the herbs. Cover the rice with a clean dish towel and the lid, and leave to steam.

For the topping, melt the butter in a frying pan and stir in the basterma for 1 minute. Add the walnuts and stir for another minute.

Tip the rice onto a serving dish. Spoon the basterma and walnuts over the top and drizzle with the butter from the pan. Garnish with the remaining herbs and serve hot.

# Lebanese couscous with chicken

Although couscous is most closely associated with North Africa, it is also enjoyed in Lebanon and Jordan, where it is called *mograbiyeh*, meaning 'from the Maghreb'.

## Serves six

1 small organic chicken

450g/1lb/2½ cups couscous, rinsed and drained

30ml/2 tbsp ghee, or olive oil with a knob or pat of butter

1 onion, finely chopped

2–3 cloves of garlic, finely chopped

1 red or green chilli, seeded and very finely chopped

1 medium carrot, finely diced

5–10ml/1–2 tsp ground cinnamon

a small bunch of fresh coriander (cilantro), roughly chopped

sea salt and ground black pepper

For the stock

2 onions, quartered

2 cinnamon sticks

4 cardamom pods

4 cloves

2 bay leaves

Place the chicken in a deep pan with the stock ingredients and cover with water. Bring the water to the boil, reduce the heat and simmer for 1 hour, or until the chicken is tender. Transfer the chicken to a plate. Strain the stock, return it to the pan and boil it over high heat for about 30 minutes, to reduce. Set aside.

Remove and discard the skin from the chicken and tear the flesh into thin strips, or cut it into bite-size chunks. Cover the chicken and keep warm.

Tip the couscous into a shallow bowl. Stir 5ml/1 tsp salt into 500ml/17fl oz/2 cups lukewarm water until it dissolves. Pour the water over the couscous, making sure it is all submerged, cover with a clean dish towel and leave for 10–15 minutes to swell. Rake the couscous with a fork to loosen the grains and rub them gently with lightly oiled fingers to separate any lumps.

Meanwhile, heat the ghee or olive oil and butter in a frying pan and stir in the onion and garlic. Cook for a minute to soften, then add the carrot and chilli. Fry for 2–3 minutes, until softening. Stir the cinnamon and half the coriander into the onion mixture, then add the couscous, forking through it to mix well and stop the grains from clumping together, until heated through.

Transfer the couscous into a warmed serving dish and arrange the shredded chicken on top. Season the reduced stock with salt and pepper, reheat if necessary, and spoon some of it over the chicken to moisten. Garnish with the remaining coriander and serve with the rest of the stock in a bowl for spooning over individual portions.

# Brown beans with feta and parsley

Traditionally a peasant dish, with its origins in ancient Egypt, this bean dish, known as *ful medames*, is a staple dish in the eastern Mediterranean. Made with the Egyptian meaty brown beans, it is generally served with freshly baked bread for breakfast, or as part of a mezze spread.

## Serves four to six

250g/9oz/1 cup dried brown beans, soaked overnight

225/8oz feta cheese

1–2 red onions

a bunch of fresh flat leaf parsley, chopped

30–45ml/2–3 tbsp olive oil

2 cloves of garlic, crushed

5–10ml/1–2 tsp cumin seeds, dry roasted and crushed

juice of 1 lemon

sea salt and ground black pepper

Drain the beans and place them in a deep pan. Cover with water, bring to the boil, reduce the heat and simmer for 1 hour, until the beans are tender.

When the beans are almost cooked, prepare the accompaniments. Using your fingers, roughly crumble the feta cheese into a small serving bowl. Finely slice the onions on the grain and place in another bowl. Place the chopped parsley in a third bowl.

Drain the beans and, while they are still warm, transfer them into a large serving bowl and add the olive oil, garlic and cumin. Squeeze in the lemon juice, season with salt and pepper, and mix.

Serve the warm beans immediately, accompanied by the bowls of red onions, feta and parsley, to which everyone helps themselves.

# Butter bean stew

For many people in the eastern Mediterranean this type of stew is real comfort food. You can use any beans but the creamy texture and meatiness of butter beans add to the satisfaction of this dish, *fassoulia baida*, which is often simply served with a dollop of yogurt and bread.

## Serves four

**450g/1lb/2¼ cups dried butter (lima) beans, soaked overnight, or use 4 x 400g/14oz cans of butter beans, rinsed and drained**

**30ml/2 tbsp ghee, or olive oil with a knob or pat of butter**

**2 onions, finely chopped**

**4 cloves of garlic, finely chopped**

**1–2 fresh chillies, seeded and finely chopped**

**10ml/2 tsp cumin seeds**

**10ml/2 tsp coriander seeds**

**2–3 pieces of cinnamon bark**

**10ml/2 tsp honey or sugar**

**2 x 400g/14oz cans of chopped tomatoes**

**a big bunch of fresh coriander (cilantro), roughly chopped**

**sea salt and ground black pepper**

If using dried and soaked beans rather than ready-cooked from a can, place in a pan of water, bring to the boil, reduce the heat and simmer for 45 minutes, until tender. Drain and remove any loose skins.

Heat the ghee or oil and butter in a heavy-based pan and cook the onions, garlic, chilli and spices for 2–3 minutes. Toss in the beans, making sure they are coated in the onion and spice mixture, and then stir in the honey, tomatoes and most of the coriander. Cook gently for about 20 minutes, then season well to taste.

Transfer to a bowl, garnish with the rest of the coriander and serve.

# Pulses in cabbage leaves

There are several ways to serve this traditional peasant dish, *makhlout*, but when I first had it in Jordan it was served in steamed cabbage leaves which you wrapped into a package, dipped into yogurt, drizzled with chilli oil and ate with your fingers. It is still my favourite way to enjoy it.

## Serves four to six

115g/4oz/½ cup brown lentils, rinsed and drained

115g/4oz bulgur, well-rinsed and drained

15–30ml/1–2 tbsp ghee, or olive oil with a knob of butter

2 onions, finely chopped

2–3 cloves of garlic, finely chopped

10ml/2 tsp cumin seeds

10ml/2 tsp coriander seeds

a small handful of dried sage leaves, crumbled

400g/14oz can of haricot or kidney beans, rinsed and drained

400g/14oz can of chickpeas, rinsed and drained

15–30ml/1–2 tbsp pomegranate molasses

5–10ml/1–2 tsp Aleppo pepper or ground paprika

12 cabbage leaves, trimmed

sea salt and ground black pepper

garlic-spiced thick Greek-style (strained plain) yogurt or tahini sauce, and lemon wedges, to serve

chilli oil, for drizzling

Put the lentils into a pan of boiling water, reduce the heat and simmer for about 20 minutes, until they are tender. Drain and refresh immediately under running cold water.

Tip the bulgur into a bowl and pour in just enough boiling water to cover the grains by about 1cm/½ in. Cover and leave to swell for about 15 minutes.

Heat the ghee or olive oil and butter in a frying pan, and stir in the onions and garlic with the spices and sage. Once the onions begin to brown, toss in the beans, chickpeas and lentils, making sure they are well coated. Add the bulgur, toss in the pomegranate molasses and Aleppo pepper, and season well. Put on the lid and keep warm.

Steam the trimmed cabbage leaves until wilting but not too soft. Drain and pat dry with kitchen paper.

Spoon portions of the mixture into the middle of each of the steamed cabbage leaves, then fold the edges in to wrap them up. Serve immediately with garlic-flavoured yogurt or tahini sauce, and a drizzle of chilli oil and squeeze of fresh lemon.

# Warm white bean purée with feta and olives

Bean purées are almost as popular as the ubiquitous chickpea one, hummus. The king of bean purées is *fava*, made with fresh green broad (fava) beans in season, but dried white broad beans, haricot (navy) and butter (lima) beans are all good substitutes in the winter. I like to serve this purée warm on its own or to accompany other vegetable dishes. Add chopped parsley if you like.

## Serves four to six

30–45ml/3–4 tbsp olive oil, plus a little extra to serve

1 onion, finely chopped

225g/8oz/scant 1 cup dried white beans, soaked in plenty of water overnight and drained

850ml/1½ pints/3½ cups chicken stock, or water

2 cloves of garlic, crushed to a paste with a little salt

5–10ml/1–2tsp cumin seeds

juice of 1 lemon

115g/4oz feta cheese, crumbled

30ml/2 tbsp green or black olives, stoned and chopped

5ml/1 tsp ground paprika, to serve

sea salt and ground black pepper

Heat 15–30ml/1–2 tbsp of the olive oil in a heavy pan. Stir in the onion and, when it begins to colour, add the beans. Pour in the stock and bring to the boil. Reduce the heat and simmer for about 40 minutes, until the beans are tender.

Drain the beans and remove any loose skins. Transfer them into an electric blender, or crush through a sieve or strainer with a fork. Combine the crushed beans with the garlic paste, cumin seeds, the remaining olive oil, and the lemon juice. Spoon the purée into a pan and heat it through.

Fold most of the feta and olives into the purée, season to taste, and transfer to a bowl. Scatter the rest of the feta and olives over the top, drizzle with a little extra olive oil, and garnish with a dusting of paprika. Serve while still warm.

# Chickpeas with toasted bread and yogurt

A number of popular dishes fall into the category known as *fatta*, an Arabic term denoting the breaking of toasted flatbread into pieces to provide a bed for other ingredients. The regional preference is for the bread to be soaked in the cooking liquid, topped with the principal ingredients and a dollop of yogurt. This particular *fattet hummus* is a classic example.

## Serves four to six

**225g/8oz/scant 1 cup chickpeas, soaked overnight**

**4 pitta breads**

**600ml/1 pint Greek-style (strained plain) yogurt**

**2–3 cloves of garlic, crushed**

**5–10ml/1–2 tsp dried mint**

**5ml/1 tsp ground paprika**

**15ml/1 tbsp butter**

**30ml/2 tbsp pine nuts**

**sea salt and ground black pepper**

Drain the chickpeas and transfer them to a pot. Cover with plenty of water and bring it to the boil. Reduce the heat and simmer the chickpeas for 1 hour, until tender. Drain, reserving the cooking liquid.

Toast the pitta breads, then break up into bite-size pieces and arrange them on a serving dish. Spread the chickpeas over the bread and moisten with a few tablespoons of the cooking liquid.

Beat the yogurt with the garlic and season with salt and pepper. Spoon the yogurt generously on top of the chickpeas and sprinkle with the dried mint and paprika.

Quickly melt the butter in a frying pan and fry the pine nuts, stirring constantly, until they turn golden. Sprinkle them over the top of the yogurt and chickpeas and serve immediately.

# Lentils and rice with onions

If you ask someone from the eastern Mediterranean what is their favourite dish from home, or what dish sums up comfort food for them, many will say *moujadara*, or *mejadra*. Popular throughout the Arab world, this is an ancient dish that crosses all divides. Christian communities often prepare it during Lent, Muslims serve it to break the fast during Ramadan, and families all over the region prepare it as a welcome dish, or a simple supper served with creamy yogurt. It is my favourite rice dish too.

## Serves four to six

**225g/8oz/scant 1 cup brown lentils, well rinsed**

**15–30ml/1–2 tbsp ghee, or olive oil with a knob or pat of butter**

**1 onion, finely chopped**

**5ml/1 tsp sugar**

**10ml/2 tsp coriander seeds**

**10ml/2 tsp cumin seeds**

**5ml/1 tsp ground allspice**

**5ml/1 tsp ground turmeric**

**225g/8oz/generous 1 cup long grain rice, well rinsed**

**sea salt**

**5ml/1 tsp ground cinnamon, to garnish**

**creamy yogurt, to serve**

For the crisped onions

**sunflower oil, for deep-frying**

**2–3 onions, halved lengthways and sliced with the grain**

**15ml/1 tbsp flour**

**5ml/1 tsp salt**

Boil the lentils in a pan of water for 10–15 minutes, until tender but firm. Drain and refresh under cold water.

Heat the ghee, or oil, in a heavy-based pan and stir in the chopped onion with the sugar, coriander and cumin seeds until they begin to colour. Add the allspice and turmeric then toss in the lentils and rice, coating the grains in the spicy onion mixture.

Add water to just cover the lentils and rice, stir in a little salt to season, and bring to the boil. Reduce the heat and simmer gently for about 15 minutes, until the water has been absorbed. Turn off the heat, cover the pan with a clean dish towel, followed by the lid, and leave the rice and lentils to steam for a further 10 minutes.

Meanwhile, prepare the crisped onions. Heat enough sunflower oil in a pan for deep-frying. Mix the flour and salt together in a small bowl. Toss the onion slices in the flour and salt mixture and fry in batches until golden brown and crispy. Transfer with a slotted spoon to drain on kitchen paper.

Using a fork, carefully toss half the onions through the cooked lentils and rice, then tip the lot onto a serving dish. Pile the remaining onions on top, dust with cinnamon and serve with yogurt.

# Green lentils with bulgur

Not as well known as *moujadara*, this is another popular lentil and grain dish served on its own, or to accompany grilled dishes. Regarded as more of a peasant dish, you come across *imjadara* in the countryside, particularly in Lebanon, where there are small cafés specialising in it.

## Serves four to six

**225g/8oz/scant 1 cup green lentils, rinsed**

**45ml/3 tbsp ghee, or olive oil with a knob or pat of butter**

**2 onions, finely chopped**

**5–10ml/1–2 tsp cumin seeds**

**5–10ml/1–2 tsp coriander seeds**

**225g/8oz/1¼ cups coarse bulgur, well rinsed and drained**

**900ml/1½ pints/3¾ cups stock**

**10ml/2 tsp crumbled dried sage, dried oregano, or dried mint**

**sumac, for sprinkling**

**sea salt and ground black pepper**

**fresh mint and flat leaf parsley, to garnish**

Bring a pan of water to the boil, add the lentils and cook for about 15 minutes, until they are tender but not soft or mushy. Drain and refresh.

Heat 30ml/2 tbsp of the ghee or butter in a heavy pan, stir in the onions with the cumin and coriander seeds and cook until they begin to colour. Toss in the bulgur, coating it in the ghee, and stir in the lentils.

Pour in the stock, season to taste with salt and pepper, and bring to the boil. Reduce the heat and simmer for 15 minutes. Turn off the heat and place a clean dish towel over the pan, followed by the lid. Leave to steam for 10 minutes.

Meanwhile, melt the remaining ghee or butter in a small pan and stir in the sage, oregano, or dried mint – or a mixture of all three. Transfer the rice and lentils into a serving dish, pour the melted butter over the top, and sprinkle with a little sumac. Garnish with fresh herbs to serve.

# Lentils with spring onions, parsley and mint

Lentils are part of the daily diet; this is a simple salad – *salata adas* – that can be served hot or cold. Be liberal with the herbs and pomegranate molasses so that it tastes fresh and zingy.

## Serves four

225g/8oz/scant 1 cup brown lentils

2–3 cloves of garlic, crushed to a paste with a little salt

45–60ml/3–4 tbsp olive oil

juice of 1 lemon

15–30ml/1–2 tbsp pomegranate molasses

2–3 spring onions (scallions), trimmed and finely chopped

a bunch of fresh flat leaf parsley, finely chopped

a bunch of fresh mint leaves, finely chopped

sea salt and ground black pepper

lemon wedges, to serve

Put the lentils in a pan with plenty of water and bring to the boil. Reduce the heat and simmer for about 25 minutes, until the lentils are tender but still retain a bite to them.

Rinse and drain the lentils and put in a bowl. Toss in the garlic paste with the olive oil, lemon juice and pomegranate molasses. Toss in the spring onions and most of the herbs. Season to taste and mix thoroughly.

Tip the lentils into a serving dish, garnish with the rest of the herbs and serve with lemon wedges to squeeze over it.

# Fish and shellfish

Sweet and sour, hot and spicy, fresh and
zingy, or simply grilled over charcoal and
slightly smoky, there are many ways to enjoy
the fish of the eastern Mediterranean and
the Red Sea. Arab traditions and influences
of the Persians, Ottomans and the French
are all evident in the dishes – stuffed and
baked, sautéed with nuts, grilled with dates,
cooked with dried limes and served with
sauces – there is something for everyone.

# Jordanian fish stew with tamarind

Variations of this sour, spicy stew can be found in Jordan, Egypt and the Arabian Gulf. The flavours of turmeric and fenugreek echo the history of trade between the Arabs and the Indians. This dish, *ghaliyeh mahi*, can be prepared with large prawns as well. Serve with rice pilaff or bread.

## Serves four to six

115g/4oz dried tamarind pulp, soaked in 350ml/12fl oz/
1½ cups water for 20 minutes

15–30ml/1–2 tbsp olive oil

1kg/2¼lb fish steaks, such as sea bream, grouper, or sea bass

1 onion, halved and sliced

4 cloves of garlic, chopped

5ml/1 tsp cumin seeds

10ml/2 tsp ground turmeric

5ml/1 tsp ground fenugreek

2.5ml/½ tsp ground chilli

about 12 small new potatoes, peeled and left whole

400g/14oz can of plum tomatoes, drained of juice

5ml/1 tsp palm sugar (jaggery), or honey

a bunch of fresh coriander (cilantro), chopped

sea salt and ground black pepper

Squeeze the tamarind pulp in your hand to separate the pulp from the seeds and stalks, then strain the pulp through a sieve or strainer. Reserve the strained pulp and liquid.

Heat the oil in a heavy pan and sear the fish steaks for 1–2 minutes on each side, then transfer them to a plate.

Add the onion, garlic and cumin seeds to the pan and cook, stirring, until they begin to colour. Add the ground spices to the pan, then toss in the potatoes and cook for 2–3 minutes.

Stir in the tomatoes and add the sugar. Pour the tamarind water into the pan and bring the liquid to the boil. Reduce the heat, cover the pan, and simmer gently for about 15 minutes, until the potatoes are tender.

When the potatoes are cooked, season with salt and pepper to taste, then slip in the seared fish steaks. Cover the pan again and cook gently for about 10 minutes, until the fish is cooked. Stir half the coriander into the stew and garnish with the rest. Serve hot.

# Saffron fish stew with couscous

This is a perfect one-pot meal for a busy weekday supper. It takes less than half an hour to prepare and is delicious on its own or with some steamed greens. Use whatever firm white-fleshed fish is available for this saffron-flavoured stew, *samak maghrebia*.

## Serves four to six

115g/4oz/½ cup couscous, washed and drained

30–45ml/2–3 tbsp olive oil

1 onion, finely chopped

2 leeks, trimmed and finely chopped

2–3 cloves of garlic, finely chopped

5ml/1 tsp cumin seeds

a pinch of saffron threads

a few sprigs of fresh thyme

a small bunch of fresh sage leaves, chopped

5ml/1 tsp Aleppo pepper, or finely chopped dried chilli

400g/14oz can of plum tomatoes, drained of juice

600ml/1 pint/2½ cups fish stock

4 fish fillets, such as sea bass, haddock, or trout, cut into bite-size chunks

a small bunch of fresh coriander (cilantro), roughly chopped, to garnish

sea salt and ground black pepper

lemon or lime wedges, to serve

Tip the couscous into a bowl and pour in just enough warm water to cover. Leave for 15 minutes to swell and double in volume.

Heat the oil in a heavy pan and stir in the onion, leeks and garlic, and cook for 2–3 minutes, until they begin to colour. Add the cumin, saffron, thyme, sage and red pepper to the pan, and stir in the tomatoes.

Pour in the stock and bring the liquid to the boil. Reduce the heat and simmer for 15 minutes, then season and stir in the couscous. Add the fish chunks to the pan and cook gently for 4–5 minutes, until the fish is just cooked.

Sprinkle the chopped coriander over the top and serve hot with lemon or lime to squeeze over it.

# Fish baked in tahini sauce

If you like the taste of creamy tahini – sesame paste - you will love this dish, *tajin samak bi tahina*. It is incredibly simple, garlicky and lemony - a delicious way to enjoy any firm-fleshed fish. Tahini is found in many dishes, blended into dressings, dips and sauces.

## Serves four to six

**300ml/½ pint tahini
(light or dark)**

**150ml/5fl oz/¾ cup lemon juice**

**150ml/5fl oz/¾ cup water**

**2 cloves of garlic, crushed**

**15–30ml/1–2 tbsp olive oil**

**2 onions, halved and sliced**

**5–10ml/1–2 tsp cumin seeds**

**500g/1¼lb fish fillets, such as sea
bass, haddock or trout, cut in half**

**sea salt and ground black pepper**

**a bunch of fresh flat leaf parsley,
finely chopped, to garnish**

Preheat the oven to 160°C/325°F/Gas 3. In a bowl, beat the tahini with the lemon juice and water to form a smooth, creamy sauce – it will thicken with the lemon juice at first but then thin down with the water. Beat in the garlic and season to taste.

Heat the oil in a heavy frying pan and sauté the onions with the cumin seeds, until they begin to turn golden brown.

Spread half of the onion mixture in the base of an ovenproof dish, lay the fish fillets on top, then spread the rest of the onion mixture over the fish. Pour the tahini sauce over the fish and bake in the oven for 25–30 minutes, until the fish is cooked.

Sprinkle the dish with the chopped parsley, and serve immediately, with a salad and chunks of bread to mop up the sauce.

# Fried red mullet with pitta bread

Splendidly pink and succulent, red mullet are my favourite fish from this region. Regarded as a fish of distinction in Lebanon, they are caught daily and invariably grilled or fried. In this classic dish, *Sultan Ibrahim mikli*, the fried fish is served with crisp, golden pieces of pitta bread and generously drizzled in a garlicky tahini sauce.

## Serves four

**4 red mullet, about 250g/9oz each, gutted, scaled and cleaned**

**15–30ml/1–2 tbsp flour**

**olive, sunflower, or groundnut (peanut) oil, for frying**

**2 pitta breads, cut into thin strips or bite-size pieces**

**sea salt and ground black pepper**

**lemon wedges, to serve**

For the tahini sauce

**1–2 cloves of garlic**

**150ml/5fl oz smooth tahini**

**juice of 1 lemon**

**juice of 1 small orange**

**sea salt and ground black pepper**

First prepare the tahini sauce. Pound the garlic cloves in a mortar and pestle with a little salt, until you have a paste. Beat the tahini in a bowl with the lemon and orange juices, until thick and smooth. Beat in the garlic paste, and season to taste. Set aside.

Rinse the mullet under cold running water and pat dry inside and out with kitchen paper. Using a sharp knife, slash each fish with three diagonal cuts on each side. Sprinkle with salt and pepper and toss them in flour so that they are lightly coated.

Heat enough oil for frying in a heavy pan and cook the fish, two at a time, for about 3 minutes on each side, until they are crisp and golden. Drain on kitchen paper and keep warm.

Toss the strips of pitta in the same oil, until they too are crisp and golden, and drain them on kitchen paper.

Arrange the fish on a serving dish, drizzle some of the tahini sauce over them, and scatter the crispy pitta around them. Serve immediately, with lemon wedges to squeeze over, and the rest of the tahini sauce.

# Fish sautéed with almonds

This dish definitely has a French air about it, which is not surprising as it is most often found in the coastal towns of Lebanon. *Samak bi loz* only takes a couple of minutes to prepare and, served with fresh bread and a salad, makes a very quick and easy meal.

## Serves four

30ml/2 tbsp olive oil

50g/2oz blanched almonds, halved

15g/½oz/1 tbsp butter

2 cloves of garlic, finely sliced

4 fish fillets, such as trout, sea bass or sole, divided in half

5–10ml/1–2 tsp sumac

sea salt

lemon wedges, to serve

Heat the oil in a heavy pan and stir in the almonds, until they turn golden. Remove them from the oil with a slotted spoon and set aside.

Add the butter to the same pan and stir in the garlic. Add the fish fillets and sauté for 2–3 minutes on each side. Return the almonds to the pan and sprinkle with the sumac and salt to taste.

Serve immediately, with the lemon wedges for squeezing.

# Charcoal-grilled trout with lemon

The aroma of fish grilling over charcoal or wood embers is always enticing. In the eastern Mediterranean it is the most traditional way to cook it and, to my mind, the best as the flesh retains its sweetness and juiciness and has a mild smoky flavour. This dish is called *samak mashwi*. Small whole sea bass can also be used instead of trout.

## Serves four

4 small trout or sea bass (about 300g/11oz each), gutted and cleaned

juice of 2 lemons

4 garlic cloves, crushed

10ml/2 tsp zahtar

sea salt and ground pink pepper

Using a sharp knife, score the flesh of the fish diagonally three times on each side. Rub a little salt and pink pepper into the fish, inside and out.

Prepare the barbecue or preheat a ridged griddle. In a bowl, mix together the lemon juice and crushed garlic.

Brush one side of the fish with the garlicky juice and place it, juice side down, on an oiled rack set over the glowing coals. Cook for around 4 minutes, then turn the fish over. Brush juice on the other side and cook for 4 minutes more.

Transfer to a serving dish. Sprinkle the zahtar over the top and serve.

Left **Fish sautéed with almonds**  Right **Charcoal-grilled trout with lemon**

# Poached fish with rice and pine nuts

Fish and rice both symbolise abundance and prosperity, so this classic dish, *sayadieh samak*, is often prepared to honour guests or for important occasions. In Lebanon it is prepared as a sophisticated dish in high-class restaurants.

## Serves four to six

30–45ml/2–3 tbsp olive oil

2 onions, finely sliced

1 firm-fleshed fish, such as sea bass or trout (about 900g/2lb), scaled, gutted and cleaned

a bunch of fresh flat leaf parsley

2–3 bay leaves

a cinnamon stick

6 black peppercorns

250g/9oz/1¼ cups long grain rice, well-rinsed and drained

5–10ml/1–2 tsp ground cumin

5–10ml/1–2 tsp ground cinnamon, plus extra for dusting

30ml/2 tbsp pine nuts

sea salt

lemon wedges, to serve

Heat the oil in a heavy pan and fry the onions for 5–10 minutes, until dark brown. Turn off the heat and set aside.

Rub the fish with salt inside and out. Place the parsley in the base of a pan, lay the fish on top and add the bay leaves, cinnamon stick and black peppercorns. Pour in enough water to just cover, and bring to the boil. Reduce the heat and simmer gently for about 5 minutes. Transfer the fish to a board and leave it to cool a little, remove the skin, take the flesh off the bone and pull it apart into bite-sized pieces. Cover with foil.

Return the skin, head and bones to the cooking liquid and bring to the boil. Reduce the heat and bubble for 15–20 minutes, to reduce by half. Strain the stock, return it to the pan and bring it to the boil again. Add the browned onions to the stock, and simmer for 10–15 minutes more.

With a slotted spoon, lift the onions out and press through a sieve or strainer back into the pot. Stir the stock well and add seasoning to taste. Return to the boil, add the rice, cumin and cinnamon, and simmer for 10 minutes, until the rice has absorbed the stock. Turn off the heat, cover the pan with a clean dish towel, followed by the lid, and leave to stand for 10 minutes to finish cooking.

Dry-roast the pine nuts in a pan over a medium heat until golden. Transfer the rice to a serving dish, gently toss some of the fish through it and place the rest on top. Sprinkle the roasted pine nuts on top, dust with cinnamon and serve with lemon wedges.

# Baked fish with bay, oranges and limes

Until recently many households in the villages of Lebanon, Syria and Jordan lacked ovens. Instead, once a week or so a piece of meat or a freshly caught fish might be taken along to the communal neighbourhood oven to be baked in a simple fashion. This is *tajin samak*.

## Serves four

**1 sea bass or grouper (weighing about 900g/2lb), gutted and cleaned**

**2–3 bay leaves**

**1 small orange, finely sliced**

**1 lime, finely sliced**

**15ml/1 tbsp butter**

**sea salt and ground black pepper**

For the marinade

**juice of 2 oranges**

**juice of 2 limes**

**30ml/2 tbsp olive oil**

**1 clove of garlic, crushed**

Whisk together all the ingredients for the marinade. Place the fish in a dish and pour the marinade over it. Cover and chill for 1–2 hours. Preheat the oven to 180°C/350°F/Gas 4.

Transfer the fish with its marinade to an ovenproof dish if necessary. Tuck the bay leaves underneath and arrange several slices of orange and lime alternately along the inside, and on top, of the fish.

Cover the dish with foil and bake for 15 minutes. Remove the foil, dot the fish with butter and bake uncovered for a further 10 minutes. Serve immediately.

# Roasted fish with chillies and walnuts

The Persian influence in this dish, *samak harra*, is reflected in the use of walnuts and pomegranate seeds. The dish exudes grandeur, and it is much appreciated along the coast of Lebanon. Traditionally dogfish is used but other firm white fish such as sea bass and snapper are also good.

## Serves four

1 firm-fleshed fish (weighing about 900g/2lb), gutted and cleaned

60ml/4 tbsp olive oil

2 onions, finely chopped

1 green (bell) pepper, very finely chopped

1–2 red chillies, seeded and very finely chopped

115g/4oz walnuts, finely chopped

15–30ml/1–2 tbsp pomegranate molasses

a small bunch of fresh coriander (cilantro), finely chopped

a small bunch of fresh flat leaf parsley, finely chopped

sea salt and ground black pepper

seeds of ½ pomegranate, with pith removed, to garnish

For the sauce

15ml/1 tbsp olive oil

2 cloves of garlic, finely chopped

1–2 red chillies, seeded and finely chopped

60ml/4 tbsp tahini

juice of 1 lemon

juice of 1 orange

sea salt and ground black pepper

With a sharp knife, make three or four diagonal slits on each side of the fish. Rub the cavity with salt and pepper, cover and chill for 30 minutes. Preheat the oven to 200°C/400°F/Gas 6.

Meanwhile, prepare the filling. Heat 30ml/2 tbsp of the olive oil in a heavy pan and fry the onions, pepper and chillies until lightly browned. Stir in the walnuts and pomegranate molasses, and add half the coriander and parsley. Season to taste and leave the filling to cool.

Fill the fish with the stuffing and secure the opening with a wooden skewer or cocktail sticks. Place the fish in an oiled baking dish and pour over the remaining oil. Bake in the preheated oven for about 30 minutes.

For the tahini sauce, heat the olive oil in a small pan and stir in the garlic and chillies, until they begin to colour. In a bowl, beat the tahini with the lemon and orange juice, until the mixture is smooth and creamy. Add the garlic and chilli mixture, beat to mix, then return to the pan and warm the sauce through. Season with salt and pepper and keep warm.

Transfer the cooked fish to a serving dish and drizzle some of the sauce over the top. Garnish with the pomegranate seeds and serve immediately, with the rest of the sauce served separately.

# Spicy fish with dried lime

This dish, *samak quwarmah*, is particular to the cooking of the Arabian Gulf, Egypt and Jordan. Both sweet and sour limes grow in this region but the sour ones, *limun baladi*, are dried whole and used in cooking to impart a earthy, tangy flavour to stews. Whole dried limes and powdered lime are available in Middle Eastern stores and online.

## Serves four

15–30ml/1–2 tbsp ground turmeric

15ml/1 tbsp ground coriander

500g/1lb 2oz fish steaks

15–30ml/1–2 tbsp ghee or butter

2 onions, finely sliced

1 green chilli, seeded and sliced

25g/1oz fresh ginger, peeled and grated

2 cloves of garlic, finely chopped

2 pieces of cinnamon bark

2 dried limes

5–10ml/1–2 tsp palm sugar (jaggery) or sugar

400g/14oz can of chopped tomatoes

sea salt and ground black pepper

Mix the turmeric and coriander in a dish and press the fish steaks into the spices so they are coated on both sides.

Heat the ghee in a heavy pan and brown the fish on both sides. Transfer the steaks from the pan to a plate and keep to one side.

Add the onions to the ghee and stir-fry for a few minutes. Just as it begins to soften, add in the chilli, ginger, garlic and cinnamon bark and cook for a further 1–2 minutes. Pierce the dried limes twice with a skewer and add them to the pan. Add the sugar and the chopped tomatoes, and pour in roughly 150ml/5fl oz/⅔ cup water on top. Bring the liquid to the boil then reduce the heat and simmer gently for about 15 minutes.

When the sauce has reduced and thickened, season the mixture with salt and pepper and place the fish steaks back in the pan. Cover the pan and simmer for about 8–10 minutes, until the fish is just cooked through.

Serve the fish straight from the pan, accompanied by a rice pilaff or chunks of bread.

# Grilled fish in date coating

In this Bedouin recipe, *samak mashwi bil tamr*, the coating of puréed dates seals the fish and keeps it moist while cooking, and also imparts a delicious fruity flavour to the fish. Originally it would have been cooked by simply impaling the fish on a stick through its mouth and setting it above glowing coals. If you do not want to use a barbecue, use a grill or oven.

## Serves four

**225g/8oz moist pitted dates**

**1 onion, finely chopped**

**2 cloves of garlic, crushed**

**5ml/1 tsp ground turmeric**

**5ml/1 tsp baharat spice mixture**

**1 large trout, or 2 small ones, gutted and cleaned**

**sprigs of fresh flat leaf parsley**

**sea salt**

**lemon wedges, to serve**

Put the dates in an electric blender with a tablespoon or two of water to form a smooth paste – if your dates are not moist they will need to be soaked in water for several hours first.

In a small bowl, mix the onion, garlic, turmeric, and the baharat spice mixture. Rub the mixture around the inside of the fish, sprinkle with salt and lay a sprig of parsley in the cavity too. Seal the cavity with a thin stick, or skewer, by weaving the edges together.

If roasting, preheat the oven to 180°C/ 350°F/Gas 4. Make sure the skin of the fish is dry, then rub the sticky date paste over it. Leave the fish to sit for 10–15 minutes, so that the paste firms up. If grilling, turn the grill or broiler on.

Place the fish in a roasting pan or on a rack. Grill for 6–8 minutes on each side, or bake for 15–20 minutes in a hot oven. Serve the fish while hot, with lemon wedges, a crisp salad and some bread.

# Fried sardines with lemon

This simple dish, *sardin makli*, is generally made with small sardines or sprats. Often the fish are dipped in flour and fried as soon as the catch is brought in, beside the moored fishing boats. Sometimes marinated in beer first, the small fish are fresh and juicy, and the bones become crispy; locals will buy a few on a piece of newspaper and just pop them whole into their mouths.

## Serves four

**450g/1lb fresh small sardines, gutted and cleaned**

**300ml/½ pint/1¼ cups beer (optional)**

**60–75ml/4–5 tbsp chickpea or plain (all-purpose) flour**

**olive or sunflower oil, for deep-frying**

**sea salt and ground black pepper**

**lemon halves, to serve**

If you are marinating the fish, place them in a shallow dish and pour the beer over them if using. Cover and chill for 1–2 hours, then drain and pat dry on kitchen paper.

Rub the fish with a little salt and pepper and dip them in the flour until lightly coated. Heat enough oil for deep-frying in a heavy pan.

Fry the fish in batches for 5–6 minutes, until crisp and golden. Drain them on kitchen paper and serve hot, with lemon halves to squeeze over.

# Fish with tomato and pomegranate sauce

This dish, *tajin samak bi banadura*, is a tasty method of cooking any firm-fleshed fish, such as sea bass, red snapper, grouper and trout. The pomegranate molasses adds a tangy, sour note to the sauce and enriches the colour.

## Serves four

**900g/2lb firm-fleshed fish fillets**

**45–60ml/3–4 tbsp olive oil**

**juice of 1 lemon**

**2–3 cloves of garlic, finely chopped**

**4 tomatoes, skinned, seeded, and chopped**

**15ml/1 tbsp pomegranate molasses**

**10ml/2 tsp sugar**

**sea salt and ground black pepper**

**a small bunch of fresh parsley, finely chopped, to garnish**

**lemon wedges, to serve**

Preheat the oven to 180°C/350°F/Gas 4. Arrange the fish in an ovenproof dish, and rub with salt and pepper. Pour 30ml/2 tbsp olive oil and the lemon juice over the fish. Cover with foil and bake for about 25 minutes, until the fish is cooked.

Meanwhile, heat the rest of the oil in a heavy frying pan. Fry the garlic until it begins to colour, then add the tomatoes. Cook for 5 minutes, then stir in the pomegranate molasses with the sugar. Reduce the heat and cook gently until the sauce thickens. Season with salt and pepper. Keep warm.

Arrange the fish on a serving dish, spoon the sauce over and around the fish and sprinkle with the parsley. Serve with lemon wedges to squeeze over.

# Fish kibbeh with onion and orange filling

This *kibbeh samak* is traditionally prepared in the coastal towns to mark special events. Among the Christian communities it is a dish that most families prepare for Lent. Any firm-fleshed fish, including haddock and cod, can be used for this recipe. The kibbeh can also be served as a mezze dish if you mould the mixture into tiny bite-size balls.

## Serves four

For the filling
**15–30ml/1–2 tbsp olive oil**
**2 onions, finely chopped**
**5ml/1 tsp ground cinnamon**
**grated rind of 1 orange**
**sea salt and ground black pepper**

For the kibbeh
**175g/6oz/1 cup fine bulgur, well-rinsed and drained**
**1 onion, finely chopped**
**450g/1lb boneless fish fillets**
**5–10ml/1–2 tsp ground turmeric**
**a small bunch of fresh coriander (cilantro), finely chopped**
**sunflower oil, for frying**
**flour, for dusting**
**lemon wedges, to serve**

First prepare the filling. Heat the oil in a small frying pan, stir in the onions and cook until they soften and begin to colour. Add the cinnamon and orange rind, stir through to mix together and season with salt and pepper. Set aside.

For the kibbeh, place the bulgur in a bowl and pour over enough boiling water to just cover. Place a clean dish towel over the bowl and leave the bulgur to stand for about 10 minutes, until it has absorbed the water and expanded.

Squeeze the bulgur to drain off any excess water and place it in a blender or food processor with the chopped onion, fish fillets, turmeric and coriander. Whizz the mixture to a paste and season with salt and pepper.

With wet hands, take a small portion of the kibbeh mixture and mould it into the shape of an egg. Hollow out the egg with a finger and fill the cavity with a little of the filling mixture. Pinch the edges of the kibbeh together to seal in the filling and form an egg shape once more. Repeat with the rest of the mixture.

Heat enough oil for shallow-frying in a heavy pan. Roll the kibbeh lightly in flour and fry them in batches until golden brown. Drain them on kitchen paper and serve hot with wedges of lemon to squeeze over.

# Tangy prawn and green pepper kebabs

Chargrilled prawns with green pepper, marinated in lemon and pomegranate molasses and sprinkled with salt: *kreidess kebab* leave you licking your fingers and wanting more. Tangy, salty and deliciously tender, these are a great treat in fishing village restaurants.

## Serves four

**15ml/1 tbsp pomegranate molasses**

**15ml/1 tbsp olive oil**

**juice of 1 lemon**

**2 cloves of garlic, crushed**

**10ml/2 tsp sugar**

**16 raw king prawns (jumbo shrimp), shelled and deveined**

**2 green (bell) peppers, cut into bite-size chunks**

**sea salt**

**lime or lemon wedges, to serve**

In a large bowl, mix together the pomegranate molasses, olive oil, lemon juice, garlic and sugar. Season the mixture with salt. Add the prawns to the mixture, and toss gently, making sure they are all well coated with the marinade. Cover the dish and chill for 1–2 hours.

Prepare the barbecue, if using, or preheat a griddle, grill or broiler. Thread the prawns on to four skewers, alternating with the pepper pieces.

Grill the kebabs for 2–3 minutes on each side, basting with any leftover marinade. Serve immediately.

# Sautéed prawns with coriander and lime

With just a couple of ingredients you have a simple, fresh-tasting dish – *kreidess mikli* are a perfect way to enjoy the juicy prawns of the Mediterranean. All you need is some crusty loaf to wipe around the pan. Variations of this recipe are popular all along the coast.

## Serves three to four

1 lime

2–3 cloves garlic

30–45ml/2–3 tbsp olive oil

15–16 raw king prawns (jumbo shrimp), peeled to the tails and deveined

a small bunch of fresh coriander (cilantro), roughly chopped

sea salt

lime or lemon wedges, to serve

Grate the lime skin, or use a zester to cut strips all the way around. Cut the lime in half and set aside. Using a mortar and pestle, or a large-bladed knife, crush the garlic with a little salt.

Heat the oil in a heavy pan, add the crushed garlic and cook, stirring constantly, until it just begins to turn a golden brown. Add the lime rind to the garlic, add in the prawns, and stir-fry until they begin to turn pink.

Squeeze the juice from the lime halves into the pan, add the coriander and season with salt, and let the liquid sizzle before removing from the heat. Eat immediately with your fingers, squeezing extra lime wedges over.

# Spicy grilled squid

At the busy cafés and seaside restaurants along the Mediterranean coast, you will find prawns and squid grilling all day long for lunch and supper. In *habaar mashwi*, squid is marinated in toasted spices and grilled to perfection. To toast the spices, simply toss in a heavy pan over medium heat.

## Serves four

**8 baby squid, cleaned, heads, backbone and innards removed, and rinsed**

**olive oil, for brushing**

**a few sprigs of fresh flat leaf parsley, roughly chopped, to garnish**

**lemon wedges, to serve**

For the marinade

**10ml/2 tsp cumin seeds, toasted**

**5ml/1 tsp coriander seeds, toasted**

**5ml/1 tsp black peppercorns**

**2–3 cloves of garlic, crushed**

**zest of 1 lemon**

**15ml/1 tbsp dried sage leaves, crumbled**

**30–45ml/2–3 tbsp olive oil**

**sea salt**

Make the marinade. In a mortar and pestle, pound the toasted cumin and coriander seeds with the peppercorns. Beat in the crushed garlic, lemon zest, sage leaves and a little salt. Bind with the olive oil.

Rinse the squid under cold running water and pat dry with kitchen paper. Sever the tentacles just above the eyes, so that the top of the head and the tentacles are joined together. Using a sharp knife, score the sacs in a criss-cross pattern and rub them and the tentacles with the spicy marinade. Leave to marinate for 30 minutes.

Heat a griddle pan and brush with a little oil. Place the squid sacs and tentacles on the griddle and cook for a minute on each side. Sprinkle the parsley over the squid and serve immediately with lemon wedges to squeeze.

# Langoustine shish

In the tradition of all shish kebabs, the whole languostines are threaded on to skewers interspersed with peppers and tomatoes. This is a classic way to enjoy freshly caught succulent languostines and lobster tails. You can also grill these *jambiri shish kebab* under high heat.

## Serves four

16 languoustine or Dublin Bay prawns (jumbo shrimp)

juice of 2 lemons

4 cloves of garlic, crushed

5ml/1 tsp ground cumin

5ml/1 tsp ground paprika

8–12 cherry tomatoes

1 green (bell) pepper, cut into bite-sized squares

sea salt

lemon wedges, to serve

Keep the languoustines in their shells or strip them down to the tail, leaving a little bit of shell at the end. Remove the veins then put the prawns into a shallow dish. Mix together the lemon juice, garlic, cumin, paprika and a little salt and rub it into the prawns. Leave to marinate for 30 minutes.

Light the charcoal grill. Thread the prawns on to metal skewers, alternating with the tomatoes and squares of green pepper, until all the ingredients are used up.

Place the kebabs on an oiled rack over the glowing coals and cook them for 2–3 minutes on each side, basting with any of the leftover marinade, until the prawns are tender and the tomatoes and peppers are lightly browned. Serve with lemon to squeeze over.

# Meat and poultry

Lamb and beef kebabs, stews, meatballs and kibbeh, grilled chicken and quails – all are now part of the everyday culinary scene, though there was a time when the traditional meat was only lamb or mutton, particularly from the Awassi sheep as they can thrive in arid conditions due to the fat stored in their podgy tails. This pungent, rendered fat, *aliya*, is still prized for cooking. Otherwise, Persian and Ottoman influences are evident in the fruit and meat combinations, meat-stuffed vegetables, and many meatball variations.

# Lamb kibbeh with onions and pine nuts

The tradition of kibbeh-making is part of daily life. Most households have an elected kibbeh-maker, as it is a dish of hospitality, family occasions, and religious feasts. The Lebanese regard kibbeh as a national dish and create all sorts of combinations with bulgur and meat, fish, chicken or vegetables. The most common are shaped like balls or patties but this Palestinian one, *kibbeh saniyeh*, is easy to prepare. It is delicious drizzled with tahini and served with garlicky yogurt and a tangy, crunchy salad.

### Serves four to six

**450g/1lb finely minced (ground) lean lamb**

**1 onion, grated**

**10ml/2 tsp ground cinnamon**

**5ml/1 tsp ground cumin**

**5ml/1 tsp ground allspice**

**115g/4oz/¾ cup fine bulgur, well-rinsed and drained**

**30ml/2 tbsp olive oil or ghee, plus extra for greasing**

**sea salt and ground black pepper**

For the topping

**30–45ml/2–3 tbsp olive oil**

**2–3 onions, halved and sliced with the grain**

**30–45ml/2–3 tbsp pine nuts**

**5ml/1 tsp ground cinnamon**

**15ml/1 tbsp pomegranate molasses**

**sea salt and ground black pepper**

**30ml/2 tbsp creamy tahini**

**a bunch of fresh flat leaf parsley, finely chopped, to serve**

Preheat the oven to 180°C/350°F/Gas 4 and grease a shallow ovenproof dish, such as a gratin dish or small roasting pan.

In a bowl, use a wooden spoon or your fists to pound the lamb with the onion and spices. Season with plenty of salt and pepper and knead well so the air is punched out. Add the bulgur to the lamb, and knead again for about 10 minutes, until the mixture is thoroughly blended and has a paste-like consistency. Alternatively, you can place the mixture in a blender or food processor and whizz to a rough paste. Turn the paste into the greased dish and spread it out evenly. Flatten the top with your knuckles and spread the oil or ghee over the surface.

Using a sharp knife, cut the mixture into wedges or diamond shapes and bake in the oven for about 30 minutes, until nicely browned.

Meanwhile, make the topping. Heat the oil in a frying pan and cook the onions until they begin to brown. Add the pine nuts and stir until they turn golden. Add the cinnamon and pomegranate molasses, and season with salt and pepper.

When the kibbeh is ready, spread the onion mixture over the top and return it to the oven for 5 minutes. Lift the portions on to a serving plate and drizzle tahini over each one or serve separately for people to add their own. Garnish with the parsley and serve while still warm.

# Meat patties with tahini and parsley

These beef patties are the Lebanese and Syrian answer to burgers. Often cooked by street vendors or at family barbecues, *kofta* are delicious served with tahini sauce or salads and dips, like *baba ghanoush*. The patties are small and compact but you can make them larger, more like a burger if you prefer, and serve them wrapped in flatbread, or the pocket of toasted pitta bread, with sliced onion, parsley and tahini sauce. Spicy potatoes make a good accompaniment; garnish with pomegranate seeds if you like.

## Serves four to six

For the patties

450g/1lb lean minced (ground) beef or lamb

1 onion, finely chopped

a large bunch of fresh flat leaf parsley, finely chopped

a small bunch of fresh mint leaves, finely chopped

5ml–10ml/1–2 tsp ground cinnamon

5ml/1 tsp ground allspice

5ml/1 tsp Aleppo pepper, or finely chopped dried chilli flakes

a little plain (all-purpose) flour, for coating

sunflower oil, for frying

sea salt and ground black pepper

For the tahini sauce

125ml/4fl oz creamy tahini

juice of 1–2 lemons

1–2 cloves of garlic, crushed

sea salt and ground black pepper

First make the tahini sauce. In a small bowl, beat the tahini with the lemon juice and garlic, thinning with a little water if necessary. Season to taste and put to one side.

Place the minced beef in a bowl. Add the onion, fresh herbs (reserve some for garnishing) and spices, and season. Using your hands, knead the mixture to a smooth paste and slap it down into the bowl to knock out the air.

Take apricot-sized portions of the mixture in your hands and shape them into balls. Place each ball in the palm of your hand and flatten it until it resembles a small, compact burger – if the mixture is sticky, dampen your fingers with water. Place the patties in a shallow dish or on a board or a clean surface and lightly coat them with flour.

Heat the oil in heavy pan, or smear a little of the oil over a ridged griddle pan, and cook the patties for 2–3 minutes on each side.

Garnish with the reserved herbs and serve with tahini sauce for drizzling and dipping.

# Roasted leg of lamb with lamb rice

When meat is cooked daily in the home, street or restaurant, it is usually grilled in the form of meatballs, kibbeh or kebabs, or cooked in stews, as large cuts of meat are expensive and require an oven which not everyone has. Legs, shoulders and whole beasts tend to be reserved for religious or ceremonial feasts, often cooked in a communal oven or in a pit dug in the ground. In *kharouf mahshi*, the roasted leg of lamb is served on minced lamb rice with pine nuts.

## Serves six

1kg/2¼lb leg of lamb

2 carrots, peeled and chopped

1 red (bell) pepper, chopped

6 cloves of garlic, peeled and crushed

30–45ml/2–3 tbsp olive oil

a little red wine

sea salt and ground black pepper

For the lamb rice

15ml/1 tbsp olive oil plus a knob or pat of butter

1 onion, finely chopped

30ml/2 tbsp pine nuts

10ml/2 tsp ground cinnamon

100g/3¾oz lean minced (ground) lamb

250g/9oz/1¼ cups long grain rice, well-rinsed and drained

Preheat the oven to 200°C/400°F/Gas 6. Rub the lamb with salt and pepper and place it in a roasting pan. Arrange the vegetables and garlic around the lamb and drizzle the oil over them all. Pour in about 300ml/½ pint/1¼ cups water, cover with foil and place the dish in the oven for about 50 minutes.

Meanwhile, prepare the rice. Heat the olive oil with the butter in a heavy pan and cook the onion until it begins to colour. Stir in the pine nuts, then add the cinnamon and the minced lamb. Cook over a medium heat for 2–3 minutes, then stir in the rice, coating the grains in the oil. Add 500ml/17fl oz/2 cups water to the pan, season with salt and pepper, and bring to the boil. Reduce the heat and simmer for 15 minutes, until the water has been absorbed. Turn off the heat, cover the pan with a clean dish towel, followed by the lid, and leave the rice to stand for 10–15 minutes; it will continue to cook.

Take the lamb leg out of the oven and remove the foil. Baste, then return to the oven, uncovered, for a further 15 minutes. Remove from the oven, and leave to rest. Strain the vegetables and juices to make the gravy, adding a dash of wine – you might like to whizz in a blender or food processor. Reheat in a pan and transfer to a serving jug or pitcher.

Spoon some of the lamb rice on to a serving dish. Place the roasted lamb on top and spoon the rest of the rice around it. Carve and serve with the gravy.

# Meatballs with cherries and cinnamon

Prepared with sour cherries, this medieval Arab dish is traditionally served on toasted flatbread. You can use sweet cherries instead but if you do, add a little more of the pomegranate molasses to create the tangy, sweet-sour taste. Serve *lahma bil karaz* with yogurt and a rice dish.

## Serves six

For the meatballs

**450g/1lb lean minced (ground) lamb**

**10ml/2 tsp ground cinnamon**

**5ml/1 tsp ground cumin**

**5ml/1 tsp ground allspice**

**sunflower oil, for frying**

**a small bunch of fresh flat leaf parsley**

**a small bunch of fresh coriander (cilantro)**

**sea salt and ground black pepper**

For the sauce

**15–30ml/1–2 tbsp ghee or butter**

**225g/8oz fresh sour cherries, pitted**

**15ml/1 tbsp pomegranate molasses**

**2 pieces of cinnamon bark**

**5–10ml/1–2 tsp honey**

Put the lamb into a bowl and add the spices and seasoning. Knead thoroughly with your fingers, slapping it down into the base of the bowl to knock out the air. Take apricot-sized pieces of the mixture and mould into small balls.

Heat up enough sunflower oil to cover the base of a pan and fry the meatballs in it, until they are nicely browned. Drain the meatballs on kitchen paper.

For the sauce, melt the ghee or butter in a heavy pan and add in the cherries, pomegranate molasses and cinnamon bark, stirring for 1–2 minutes. Add roughly 125ml/4fl oz water to the pan, stir in the honey, and let it bubble up.

Add the meatballs to the pan, cover, reduce the heat and cook gently for about 15 minutes.

Lift the meatballs on to a serving dish. Boil up the sauce, check the seasoning then spoon over the meatballs. Garnish with the parsley and coriander, and serve.

# Baked lamb and potato pie

Just like shepherd's pie this is a typical home-cooked dish loved in all regions and by all ages. There are variations of *kaleb batata* in Syria and Jordan, some with crunchy nut or breadcrumb toppings, others with layered slices of potato rather than mashed, but this version sandwiches the meat filling between two layers of potato. Serve with a salad or vegetable side dish.

## Serves four to six

1kg/2¼lb potatoes, scrubbed and halved

300ml/½ pint/1¼ cups milk

100g/3¾oz butter

a pinch of freshly grated nutmeg

30ml/2 tbsp olive oil

2 onions, finely chopped

15–30ml/1–2 tbsp pine nuts

5–10ml/1–2 tsp ground cinnamon

5ml/1 tsp ground allspice

450g/1lb lean minced (ground) lamb

30ml/2 tbsp white breadcrumbs

30ml/2 tbsp finely grated Parmesan

sea salt and ground black pepper

Preheat the oven to 180°C/350°F/Gas 4. Place the potatoes in a deep pan and cover with plenty of water. Bring the water to the boil and cook the potatoes for 15–20 minutes, or until they are tender. Drain and refresh under cold running water and peel off the skins. Return the peeled potatoes to the pan and mash with a potato masher or a fork. Add the milk and butter and beat the mashed potatoes over the heat, until they are light and fluffy. Season to taste with grated nutmeg and salt and pepper, cover the pan and set aside.

To prepare the filling, heat the olive oil in a heavy-based pan and cook the onions until they begin to colour. Stir in the pine nuts until they begin to turn golden, then add the cinnamon and allspice. Add the minced lamb and cook for 3–4 minutes. Season to taste.

Lightly grease an ovenproof dish and spread a layer of the potato mixture in the base. Spread the meat filling over the top of the layer of potato and then top with another layer of potato, smoothing to the edges.

In a small bowl, mix together the breadcrumbs and grated Parmesan. Sprinkle them over the top of the pie. Place the dish in the oven and bake for 30–40 minutes, until the top is nicely browned. Serve immediately.

# Meat and bulgur balls in yogurt

This is another popular kibbeh dish, only this time they are cooked in yogurt – *kibbeh labaniyya* are real comfort food in Syria and Lebanon. Kibbeh are traditionally pounded by hand but it's easier to use a food processor if you have one.

## Serves six

### For the kibbeh

225g/8oz/1¼ cups fine bulgur, well-rinsed and squeezed dry

1 onion, cut into quarters

225g/8oz lean lamb, diced

10ml/2 tsp ground cinnamon

5ml/1 tsp ground allspice

5ml/1 tsp ground paprika

sea salt and ground black pepper

### For the sauce

850ml/1½ pints Greek-style (strained plain) yogurt

7.5ml/½ tbsp cornflour (cornstarch), mixed to a paste with a little water

15ml/1 tbsp butter, or ghee

1–2 cloves of garlic, crushed

a small handful of dried mint leaves, crushed

Place the bulgur in a large bowl. Put the onion into the food processor, whizz to a purée, and add it to the bulgur. Process the lamb in batches in the food processor and add the puréed meat to the bulgur. Add the spices and the seasoning to the meat and bulgur mixture and mix well. Blend the mixture in batches, combining it with spoonfuls of cold water to ease the process, or pound it with your fist until smooth. Knead the blended kibbeh mixture once more in the bowl, if using a processor, then cover and put aside.

Beat the yogurt until it is smooth and pour it into a heavy pan. Beat in the cornflour paste with a little salt and gently heat the yogurt, stirring all the time, until it is almost at scalding point – don't let it boil as it will curdle. Reduce the heat and simmer for about 5 minutes, until it is thick.

Take portions of the kibbeh mixture in your fingers and mould them into ovals. Gently place them in the yogurt sauce, cover, and simmer gently for about 20 minutes, until the kibbeh are cooked.

Melt the butter in a pan and stir in the crushed garlic and mint until the garlic begins to brown.

Spoon the kibbeh onto a serving dish with the yogurt sauce then drizzle the minty butter over the top. Serve immediately.

# Lamb shanks with winter vegetables

This classic winter dish, *shakriya*, also known as *laban imoo*, varies from place to place but it is a delicious way to cook lamb shanks until the meat becomes so tender it falls off the bone. It is often served on its own with chunks of bread to mop up the tasty yogurt sauce but you can serve it with a plain or saffron rice pilaff, and salad.

## Serves four

60–75ml/4–5 tbsp olive oil

10ml/2 tsp cumin seeds

2 pieces of cinnamon bark

12 shallots, peeled and left whole

3–4 sticks celery, sliced

2 carrots, peeled and cut into bite-size pieces

4 cloves garlic, finely chopped

400g/14oz can of chickpeas, well rinsed and drained

400g/14oz can of chopped tomatoes

30ml/2 tbsp plain (all-purpose) flour

15ml/1 tbsp ground ginger

15ml/1 tbsp ground cinnamon

4 lamb shanks

600ml/1 pint/2½ cups chicken stock, or stock and white wine

600ml/1 pint Greek-style (strained plain) yogurt

7.5ml/½ tbsp cornflour (cornstarch), mixed to a paste with a little water

a small bunch of fresh mint leaves, chopped

zest of 1 lemon

sea salt and ground black pepper

Heat half the oil in a heavy pan and stir in the cumin seeds and cinnamon bark. Add the shallots, celery, carrots and garlic and cook for 2–3 minutes until they soften and begin to colour. Stir the chickpeas and tomatoes into the pan, season well with salt and pepper, and set aside while you prepare the lamb shanks.

On a wooden board, or a clean surface, mix together the flour with the ginger and cinnamon, and lightly coat the lamb shanks with it.

Heat the rest of the oil in a heavy pan and brown the lamb shanks. Transfer the browned lamb shanks to the top of the vegetables. Pour the stock over the lamb, put back on the heat and bring slowly to the boil. Reduce the heat to low, cover with a lid or a double layer of foil, and cook for about 1–1½ hours.

Meanwhile, prepare the yogurt. Beat the yogurt until it is smooth and transfer it to a heavy pan. Beat in the cornflour paste with a little salt and gently heat, stirring the yogurt all the time in one direction, until it almost reaches scalding point – don't let it boil as it will separate – then reduce the heat and simmer uncovered for 5–10 minutes, until it is thick.

When the meat is cooked, and coming away from the bones, carefully stir in the yogurt. Simmer gently, uncovered, for about 15 minutes. Check the seasoning.

Sprinkle the chopped mint and strips of lemon zest over the lamb shanks, and serve hot.

# Lamb kebabs with hummus and dill

Even if you spend weeks in the region you won't be able to try all the different kebabs – there are so many of them. Served with hot hummus and lots of dill, these simple minced lamb kebabs are amongst my favourite – *kofta meshweya* are a Palestinian speciality – but there are many ways of serving grilled meat with cold or hot hummus.

## Serves four to six

**For the kebabs**

450g/1lb minced (ground) lamb

1 onion, grated

10ml/2 tsp Aleppo pepper or dried red chilli flakes

10ml/2 tsp ground cumin

5ml/1 tsp ground coriander

5ml/1 tsp salt

a small bunch of fresh flat leaf parsley, finely chopped

a small bunch of fresh coriander (cilantro), finely chopped

a bunch of fresh dill, finely chopped

sea salt and ground black pepper

lemon wedges, to serve

**For the hummus**

2 x 400g/14oz cans of chickpeas, well-rinsed and drained

100ml/3½fl oz olive oil (reserve a little for drizzling)

juice of 2 lemons

5ml/1 tsp cumin seeds

2 cloves of garlic, crushed

Heat the oven to 180°C/350°F/Gas 4 and prepare the charcoal grill, if using. Mix the minced lamb and onion with the spices, salt and herbs, and knead well in the bowl to knock out the air.

Take a piece of the mixture in your fingers and mould it tightly on to the kebab skewer like a thin sheath on a sword. Repeat with the rest of the mixture, then cover the kebabs and set aside until the grill is ready.

Prepare the hummus. Whizz the chickpeas with the olive oil, lemon juice, cumin seeds and garlic in a food processor until smooth. Season to taste, tip it into an ovenproof dish and smooth it out, then drizzle over the reserved olive oil. Cover with foil and bake in the oven for about 20 minutes. Remove from the oven.

Grill the kebabs for 3–4 minutes each side over the hot charcoal, or turn the oven up to 200°C/400°F/Gas 6 and bake for 20 minutes.

When cooked through, slide the kebabs off the skewers, and serve with the hot hummus and lemon wedges to squeeze over.

# Spicy meat dumplings with yogurt

This classic dish, *shish barak*, seems to be claimed by everyone. My Palestinian, Armenian, Jewish and Arab friends have all made it but the origins probably go back to the noodle dough of the ancient Chinese brought to Anatolia by the Mongol Turks and which spread through the eastern Mediterranean region during the Ottoman Empire. Whatever the origin, it is delicious, and easy to make if you follow the modern method of using filo pastry instead of the traditional dough. You can replace the spices with *sabaa baharat*, the Lebanese spice mix, if that is easier.

## Serves six

**For the dumplings**

**6 sheets of filo pastry, cut in half**

**30ml/2 tbsp butter, melted**

**5ml/1 tsp rice flour or cornflour (cornstarch), mixed with 10ml/2 tsp water**

**1 litre/1¾ pints Greek-style (strained plain) yogurt**

**5ml/1 tsp dried oregano**

**5ml/1 tsp dried mint**

**sea salt and ground black pepper**

**For the filling**

**30ml/2 tbsp olive oil**

**2 onions, finely chopped**

**1–2 red fresh chillies, seeded and finely chopped**

**30ml/2 tbsp pine nuts**

**10ml/2 tsp ground cinnamon**

**5ml/1 tsp ground allspice**

**5ml/1 tsp ground paprika**

**450g/1lb lean minced (ground) lamb**

**15ml/1 tbsp pomegranate molasses**

**sea salt and ground black pepper**

Make the filling. Heat the oil in a heavy pan and cook the onions and chilli until they begin to brown. Stir in the pine nuts and cook for a minute, then add the cinnamon, allspice and paprika. Add the lamb to the pan and fry for 2–3 minutes to brown the meat. Season well. Stir in the pomegranate molasses and cook for a minute, then turn off the heat and leave to cool. Preheat the oven to 180°C/ 350°F/Gas 4.

Place the halved sheets of filo in a stack on a clean surface and keep covered. Brush the first sheet with a little melted butter then spoon some of the filling in a line along one of the long edges, stopping about 1cm/½ in from each end. Roll up the pastry into a long finger, tucking in the edges as you roll, then curl it into a tight coil. Repeat with the remaining filo sheets and filling to make 12 coils.

Place the filled coils on a lightly greased baking tray and bake them in the oven for about 15 minutes, until the pastry is a light golden brown but not fully cooked.

Meanwhile, beat the rice flour and water mixture into the yogurt, and pour the mixture into a wide heavy pan. Stir over a medium heat until the yogurt is at scalding point, then season with salt and pepper and stir in the oregano.

Take the filled pastry coils out of the oven and carefully place them into the yogurt. Cook over a gentle heat for 10 minutes. Sprinkle the mint over the top and serve.

# Pasha's meatballs in tomato sauce

This famous dish of meatballs cooked in a tomato sauce is said to have been one of the favourite dishes of Dawood Pasha, the first governor of Mount Lebanon appointed by the Ottomans in 1860. The dish is named after him, *daoud pasha*. Serve it with a herby rice pilaff.

## Serves four

For the meatballs

**450g/1lb lean minced (ground) lamb**

**5–10ml/1–2 tsp ground cinnamon**

**5ml/1 tsp ground allspice**

**sunflower oil, for frying**

**flour, for coating**

**sea salt and ground black pepper**

**lemon wedges, to serve**

**herby pilaff, to serve**

For the sauce

**15ml/1 tbsp ghee, or olive oil with a knob or pat of butter**

**2 onions, halved lengthways, cut in half crossways, and sliced with the grain**

**30ml/2 tbsp pine nuts**

**5ml/1 tsp ground cinnamon**

**400g/14oz can of chopped tomatoes**

**10ml/2 tsp sugar**

**sea salt and ground black pepper**

In a bowl, mix together the minced lamb, cinnamon and allspice, and season with about 2.5ml/½ tsp salt and a good grinding of black pepper. Knead the mixture well with your hands then, with wet hands, mould it into small balls about the size of large cherries.

Heat enough sunflower oil for frying in a heavy pan. Roll the meatballs in a little flour and drop them into the oil. Fry for 4–5 minutes, turning, until they are nicely browned all over. Lift the meatballs out of the oil with a slotted spoon and drain them on kitchen paper.

To make the sauce, heat the ghee or olive oil and butter in a heavy pan and sauté the onions over a medium heat for 3–4 minutes, until golden brown. Stir in the pine nuts and cook until they begin to colour, then add the cinnamon, followed by the tomatoes and sugar. Simmer the sauce, uncovered, for about 20 minutes, until it has reduced and thickened, and season with salt and pepper.

Place the meatballs in the sauce and heat through for 10 minutes. Serve hot with lemon wedges, and a rice pilaff.

# Lamb and plum stew

Inspired by the Persian tradition of combining meat with fruit, the medieval Arabs created a number of dishes that are regarded as classics today. Common meat and fruit combinations include lamb or chicken with plums, apricots, grapes, cherries and quinces. This one is called *yakhnit al-khawkh*. Serve the stew with a buttery pilaff, perhaps flavoured with saffron or herbs.

## Serves four to six

30ml/2 tbsp ghee, or olive oil with a knob or pat of butter

2 onions, finely chopped

2–3 cloves garlic, finely chopped

5ml/1 tsp cumin seeds

5ml/1 tsp coriander seeds

500g/1¼lb lean lamb, cut into cubes

plain (all-purpose) flour, for coating

400ml/14fl oz/1⅔ cups chicken stock

350g/12oz plums, stoned (pitted) and quartered

sea salt and ground black pepper

a small bunch of fresh mint leaves, finely shredded, to garnish

pilaff, to serve

Heat the ghee in a heavy pan and cook the onions until they begin to colour, then add the garlic, cumin and coriander seeds. Coat the lamb in flour, then add to the pan to brown. Pour in the stock, bring to the boil, reduce the heat, cover the pan and simmer for about 40 minutes.

When the meat is tender, add the plums to the stew and season with salt and pepper. Cover the pan again and simmer for a further 20 minutes, until the plums are soft.

Transfer the stew to a warmed serving dish, garnish with the shredded mint, and serve. Accompany it with a buttery pilaff.

# Dervish's beads

During the Ottoman period, dervish lodges were founded up and down the eastern Mediterranean, resulting in the spread of dishes attributed to the Sufi order. Traditionally, the components of this dish, *masbahat al-derwich*, are cooked separately then assembled in layers afterwards, with an emphasis on the pearl onions representing the beads, but when I've had this dish prepared for me, all the layers have been cooked together in the oven.

## Serves four to six

60–75ml/4–5 tbsp olive oil

12–15 pearl (baby) onions, peeled

5–6 potatoes, boiled and sliced

450g/1lb lean lamb fillet, thinly sliced

1 aubergine (eggplant), thinly sliced

1 green and 1 red (bell) pepper, thinly sliced

5–6 tomatoes, thinly sliced

15ml/1 tbsp tomato purée (paste)

5–10ml/1–2 tsp ground oregano

15ml/1 tbsp butter, plus a little for greasing

10ml/2 tsp sugar

5–10ml/1–2 tsp ground cinnamon

sea salt and ground black pepper

Preheat the oven to 180°C/350°F/Gas 4. Heat 30ml/2 tbsp of the oil in a heavy pan. Add the onions to the pan and fry until golden. Drain on kitchen paper.

Lightly butter an ovenproof dish and spread a layer of sliced boiled potatoes over the base. Lay the slices of lamb fillet on top, then the fried baby onions, followed by a layer of aubergine slices, a layer of pepper strips, and a final layer of tomato slices.

Mix the remaining olive oil with the tomato purée, 150ml/5fl oz/½ cup water, the oregano and plenty of salt and pepper, and pour it over the dish. Dot the tomatoes with butter and sprinkle with the sugar and cinnamon.

Cover with foil and bake for 45 minutes, then remove the foil and return the dish to the oven for a further 15–20 minutes, until browned.

# Stuffed breast of lamb with apricots

The traditional festive dish of the Bedouin is *mansaf*, meaning 'big dish', which is exactly what it is – a huge tray, lined with flatbread covered with a layer of rice, on top of which sits a whole spit-roasted lamb or kid. Although mansaf is Jordan's national dish, it is too big to prepare at home, so *dala mahshi* using breast of lamb stuffed with mince is cooked by families to celebrate Eid el-Adha, the religious feast marking the near-sacrifice of Isma'il, or Isaac.

## Serves four to six

**1 large breast of lamb, chined and with a pouch cut between the skin and the ribs, rinsed and patted dry**

**sunflower oil, for rubbing**

**175g/6oz dried apricots, soaked overnight in just enough water to cover**

**15–30ml/1–2 tbsp sugar**

**sea salt and ground black pepper**

For the stuffing

**30ml/2 tbsp ghee, or olive oil with a knob or pat of butter**

**1 onion, finely chopped**

**5–10ml/1–2 tsp ground turmeric**

**5ml/1 tsp ground cumin**

**125g/4¼oz minced (ground) beef**

**a small bunch of fresh flat leaf parsley, finely chopped**

**250g/9oz/1¼ cups long grain rice, rinsed and drained**

**115g/4oz pine nuts**

**115g/4oz unsalted pistachios, chopped**

Preheat the oven to 200°C/400°F/Gas 6. To make the stuffing, melt the ghee in a frying pan and cook the onion until it colours. Stir in the turmeric, cumin and beef and cook until it begins to brown. Add the parsley and rice to the pan and pour in 200ml/7fl oz/scant 1 cup water. Season with salt and pepper and bring the liquid to the boil. Reduce the heat and simmer for about 15 minutes until the water has been absorbed. Remove the pan from the heat, stir in both the nuts and leave to cool.

When the filling is cool, stuff the breast pouch of the lamb. If there is any left over it can be served with the meat afterwards. Rub the lamb with a little oil and then place into the oven for about 1 hour, until the meat is well browned and tender.

Meanwhile, prepare the apricots. Transfer the apricots and their soaking water to a pan and bring the liquid to the boil. Reduce the heat, stir in the sugar, and simmer partially covered until the apricots are soft.

Just before serving, spoon off any excess fat from the roasting dish and baste the meat. Turn the oven up to 220°C/450°F/Gas 8 and spread the apricots over the lamb. Return to the oven and glaze for 5 minutes. Allow the lamb to rest for 10 minutes, then slice and serve with any leftover rice filling.

# Roasted onions stuffed with lamb

Stuffing vegetables such as aubergines, courgettes and peppers is common practice in the eastern Mediterranean but these onions are more unusual. They look impressive and are utterly delicious. You can serve them on their own with garlic yogurt or a tahini sauce, or you can serve them with roasted meat or vegetables. *Mahshi basal* may be a little fiddly to make but are well worth the effort.

## Serves four to six

2–3 large onions

250g/9oz lean minced (ground) lamb

90g/3½oz/½ cup long grain rice, rinsed and drained

15ml/1 tbsp tomato purée (paste)

10ml/2 tsp ground cinnamon

5ml/1 tsp ground allspice

5ml/1 tsp ground cumin

5ml/1 tsp ground coriander

a small bunch of fresh flat leaf parsley, finely chopped

30–45ml/2–3 tbsp olive oil

15–30ml/1–2 tbsp white wine or cider vinegar

5–10ml/1–2 tsp sugar

15ml/1 tbsp butter

sea salt and ground black pepper

lemon wedges, to serve

Bring a pan of water to the boil. Make a cut down one side of each of the onions, cutting into the centre from top to bottom; this enables the layers to divide while cooking. Cook the onions in the boiling water for about 10 minutes, until they soften and the layers begin to separate. Drain and refresh the onions under cold running water and carefully detach the layers.

In a bowl, pound the meat thoroughly with your hands. Add the rice, tomato purée, spices, parsley and seasoning, and knead well to mix.

Spread out the separated onion layers and place a spoonful of the meat mixture inside each one. Roll them up loosely, leaving room for the rice to expand as it cooks, and tuck in any open ends. Preheat the oven to 200°C/400°F/Gas 6.

Pack the stuffed onion layers close together in a heavy ovenproof pan and pour over the olive oil, vinegar and sugar. Cover and cook the onions on the stovetop over a medium heat for about 25 minutes, until the meat and rice are cooked.

Dot the stuffed onions with a little butter and place in the oven, uncovered, for 15–20 minutes, until they are nicely browned on top and slightly caramelised. Serve hot with wedges of lemon.

# Lamb-stuffed artichokes

The globe artichoke season is an exciting time – vegetable sellers in the streets and markets prepare the artichokes for you so all you have to do is go home and cook them. In the absence of these helpful vegetable sellers you can prepare them yourself: pull off the outer leaves, cut off the stalks and slice away the purple choke, the small leaves and any hard bits. Remove any fibres with the edge of a spoon and rub the artichoke bottoms with a mixture of lemon juice and salt to prevent them from discolouring, or place them in a bowl of cold salted water combined with a little lemon juice, until ready to use. *Ardishawk bil lahma* is a traditional way of serving artichokes.

## Serves four

30ml/2 tbsp olive oil

2 medium onions, finely chopped

15–30ml/1–2 tbsp pine nuts

350g/12oz lean minced (ground) lamb

5ml/1 tsp ground cinnamon

2.5ml/½ tsp ground allspice

4–6 fresh or frozen artichoke bottoms

juice of 1 lemon

200ml/7fl oz/scant 1 cup water

15ml/1 tbsp plain (all-purpose) flour

sea salt and ground black pepper

lemon wedges, to serve

Preheat the oven to 180°C/350°F/Gas 4. Heat the oil in a heavy pan and cook the onions for 2–3 minutes until they begin to colour. Stir in the pine nuts, reserving a few for garnishing, and cook for 1–2 minutes until they turn golden. Add the lamb and spices to the pan, and fry until the meat begins to brown. Season with salt and pepper.

Place the artichoke bottoms, side by side, in a shallow ovenproof dish. Using a spoon, fill the artichokes with the meat mixture.

Combine the lemon juice and water in a bowl and stir in the flour, making sure it is thoroughly blended. Pour the flour, water and lemon juice mixture over and around the artichokes.

Cover the dish with foil and place it in the oven for 25–30 minutes, until the artichokes are tender. Meanwhile, heat a frying pan and dry-roast the reserved pine nuts until golden brown.

Remove the artichokes from the oven and transfer to a warmed serving dish. Sprinkle the roasted pine nuts over the top of the artichokes and serve with wedges of lemon to squeeze over.

# Lamb and vegetable stew

This is a traditional dish, *lahm bi-khal*, dating back to a time when meat had to be preserved either by searing it in its own fat and storing underground for weeks or even months, by drying it in the sun, or by cooking it with vinegar. As it is quite light on the palate and digestion, it is now a popular summer stew, often served on its own with flatbread.

## Serves four to six

**450g/1lb lean boneless lamb, cut into bite-size chunks**

**about 12 small shallots or pearl (baby) onions, peeled and left whole**

**about 8 cloves of garlic, peeled**

**2 cinnamon sticks**

**5ml/1 tsp fennel seeds**

**5ml/1 tsp cumin seeds**

**6 peppercorns**

**60ml/4 tbsp white wine or cider vinegar**

**2 courgettes (zucchini), cut into bite-size chunks**

**2 medium aubergines (eggplants), cut into bite-size chunks**

**10ml/2 tsp dried mint**

**sea salt**

Place the meat in a deep pan with the shallots, garlic, cinnamon sticks, fennel and cumin seeds, and the peppercorns. Add water to cover and bring to the boil, skimming off any foam. Reduce the heat, cover and simmer for 35–40 minutes, until the meat is tender.

Season with salt and stir in the vinegar. Add the courgettes and aubergines to the pan and bring the liquid back to the boil. Reduce the heat, cover the pan and simmer for a further 10 minutes, until the vegetables are tender.

Transfer the stew to a serving dish, sprinkle the mint over the top and serve immediately with some flatbread.

# Lamb's liver with pomegranate molasses

Flavoured with aromatic spices and slightly tart with the lemon juice and pomegranate molasses, this medieval Arab dish, *kabid maqliya*, will change your mind if you are usually unsure about liver. Sautéed or grilled, lamb's or calf's liver is often served as part of the mezze spread or as a hot dish on its own.

## Serves four

**450g/1lb lamb's liver, cut into bite-size pieces**

**15–30ml/1–2 tbsp plain (all-purpose) flour**

**5ml/1 tsp ground cinnamon**

**2.5ml/½ tsp ground allspice**

**30ml/2 tbsp olive oil**

**2 red onions, halved and thinly sliced**

**2–3 garlic cloves, finely chopped**

**juice of 1 lemon**

**pomegranate molasses, for drizzling**

**sea salt and ground black pepper**

Pat the pieces of liver dry with kitchen towel then toss them in the flour. Once they are lightly coated, toss them in the spices to coat them lightly.

Heat the oil in a heavy-based pan and stir in the sliced onions and garlic, until they begin to colour. Toss in the liver for 2–3 minutes, until lightly browned. Add the lemon juice and season well. Drizzle the pomegranate molasses over the liver and serve immediately from the pan.

# Braised rabbit with aubergines

There was a time when the area of Greater Syria was a hunter's paradise. Boar, gazelle, porcupine, quail, partridge and pheasant as well as hare and rabbit were popular for the pot. Nowadays, game features mainly on village menus. Serve *arnab bi batinjaan* with pilaff or a rustic bread.

## Serves four

**1 rabbit, roughly 1kg/3lb, jointed**

**15–30ml/1–2 tbsp plain (all-purpose) flour**

**30ml/2 tbsp ghee, or olive oil plus a knob or pat of butter**

**10ml/2 tsp coriander seeds**

**5ml/1 tsp cumin seeds**

**1 red chilli, seeded and chopped**

**2 onions, halved and sliced**

**2–3 cloves of garlic, chopped**

**2 aubergines (eggplants), cut into bite-size pieces**

**400g/14oz can of chopped tomatoes**

**10ml/2 tsp sugar or honey**

**10–15ml/2–3 tsp pomegranate molasses**

**sea salt and ground black pepper**

**a bunch of fresh flat leaf parsley, chopped**

Toss the rabbit joints in the flour so that they are lightly coated. Heat the ghee or oil and butter in a heavy pan and brown the rabbit joints. Lift the rabbit pieces out of the pan and set aside.

Stir the coriander and cumin seeds into the oil along with the chilli, onions and garlic. Once the onions begin to colour, add the aubergine pieces to the pan and cook, stirring, until they are lightly browned. Add the tomatoes, sugar or honey, and pomegranate molasses to the pan. Cover, and bring gently to simmering point. Season with salt and pepper to taste.

Return the rabbit joints to the pan, cover, and cook gently for about 25 minutes, until the aubergine is tender but not mushy, and the rabbit is tender. You may need to add a splash of water or white wine to keep the dish moist as it cooks. Sprinkle with the parsley and serve hot.

# Spicy pigeons with olives

Pigeons used to be eaten frequently all over the eastern Mediterranean but now they are most commonly found in Jordan and neighbouring Egypt, where some families raise the birds for the pot, and street vendors grill them with lemon juice and herbs. Wild wood pigeons are best for this recipe, *hamam bi zaytun*, which is of medieval origin; they can be prepared for you by a butcher.

## Serves four

**15ml/1 tbsp tomato purée (paste)**

**10ml/2 tsp sugar**

**5ml/1 tsp ground paprika**

**5ml/1 tsp ground cinnamon**

**5ml/1 tsp ground cumin**

**5ml/1 tsp ground coriander**

**2.5ml/½ tsp ground cloves**

**a grating of nutmeg**

**30ml/2 tbsp ghee, or olive oil plus a knob or pat of butter**

**4 fresh wood pigeons, prepared, cleaned and left whole**

**2 bay leaves**

**juice of 1 lemon**

**45ml/3 tbsp cracked green olives**

**sea salt and ground black pepper**

In a bowl, mix the tomato purée with the sugar and spices.

Heat the ghee, or olive oil and butter, in a wide shallow pan and add the pigeons, breast-side down. Brown the meat and lift the pigeons out of the pan and put on a board or plate.

Add the bay leaves, spicy tomato paste, and lemon juice to the pan, together with 300ml/½ pint/1¼ cups of water, and mix together. Place the pigeons back in the pan, reduce the heat, cover the pan and simmer gently for about 1 hour, until the pigeon meat is tender. Add the olives, season to taste and simmer with the lid off for a further 15 minutes.

Serve hot, with chunks of bread to mop up the sauce.

# Aromatic chicken on pitta bread

The shawarma dishes of Lebanon, Syria and Jordan are the equivalent of the Turkish döner kebab and are the most popular type of street food. This chicken version, *shawarma dajaj*, is marinated in a delicious, aromatic combination of spices and served on pitta bread with a tahini sauce and pickles. At home, you can bake the chicken in the oven or cook it under a grill.

## Serves four

**4 chicken breasts**

**4 pitta breads**

**red onion slices and pickled vegetables, to serve**

For the marinade

**30–45ml/2–3 tbsp olive oil**

**juice of 2–3 lemons**

**10ml/2 tsp white wine or cider vinegar**

**2 cloves of garlic, crushed**

**1 cinnamon stick, broken into pieces**

**grated rind of ½ orange**

**4–6 cardamom pods, crushed**

For the tahini sauce

**100ml/3½fl oz creamy tahini**

**juice of 1 lemon**

**1–2 cloves of garlic, crushed**

**a small bunch of fresh flat leaf parsley, finely chopped**

**sea salt and ground black pepper**

Mix together all the ingredients for the marinade and toss the chicken breasts in the mixture, then cover and leave in the refrigerator for at least 6 hours.

Prepare the tahini sauce. In a small bowl, beat the tahini with the lemon juice and garlic and thin it with a little cold water to the consistency of thick cream. Stir in the parsley and season with salt and pepper.

Preheat the oven to 180°C/350°F/Gas 4. Put the chicken in an ovenproof dish, cover loosely with foil and and bake for 25–30 minutes, basting with the marinade. When cooked, lift the chicken out, shred, and return to the dish with any remaining marinade, season and return to the oven for 10 minutes.

Toast the pitta breads in the oven for 5 minutes. Serve the chicken on top of, or inside, the pitta breads, drizzle the tahini sauce over and serve with red onion slices and pickled vegetables.

# Palestinian chicken with sumac

Tangy and tasty, *musakhan* used to be one of my favourite street snacks in Jordan, where there is a huge Palestinian community fiercely proud of their own culinary traditions, such as this peasant spicy chicken dish. It is served on a thick spongy bread called *tabun*, but you can serve it inside pitta bread too. Finish off the pitta breads with a dollop of plain or garlic yogurt, tahini sauce, and some fresh sliced chillies or chilli sauce.

## Serves four

30ml/2 tbsp ghee, or olive oil with a knob or pat of butter

2 onions, sliced

2–3 cloves of garlic, crushed

450g/1lb boned chicken breasts, cut into thin strips

10–15ml/2–3 tsp sumac

5ml/2 tsp ground cinnamon

2.5ml/½ tsp ground allspice

juice of 1 lemon

4 pitta breads, halved to form 8 pockets

sea salt and ground black pepper

a small bunch of fresh flat leaf parsley, coarsely chopped

Greek-style (strained plain) yogurt, to serve

Preheat the oven to 180°C/350°F/Gas 4. Melt the ghee or olive oil and butter in a pan and stir in the onions. When they begin to soften, stir in the garlic and fry until the onions turn golden brown.

Add the chicken to the pan with the sumac and stir-fry for 2–3 minutes. Toss in the cinnamon, allspice and lemon juice and cook for another 2 minutes. Season well with salt and pepper.

Fill the pitta pouches with the chicken and place on a lightly oiled baking sheet. Pop them in the oven until for 5–6 minutes, until the pitta breads are hot but not too toasted, then add some parsley and a dollop of yogurt to the pouches. Tuck in.

# Chicken and molokhia stew with onions

The leaves of the molokhia plant are an acquired taste and texture – slightly mucilaginous- but the Jordanians and neighbouring Egyptians love them. Dried molokhia leaves are available in Middle Eastern stores and online. This traditional dish, *djaaj bi melokhia*, is half stew, half soup.

## Serves four

For the marinated onions

**1 onion, sliced**

**seeds of ½ pomegranate**

**30–45ml/2–3 tbsp white wine or cider vinegar**

**a generous pinch of salt**

For the stew

**225g/8oz dried molokhia (mallow) leaves**

**1 chicken, approximately 1kg/2lb**

**1.2 litres/2 pints/5 cups water**

**2 onions, quartered**

**2 carrots, peeled and sliced into thick lengths**

**2 cloves of garlic, smashed in their skins**

**4–5 cloves**

**3–4 cardamom pods**

**sea salt and ground black pepper**

Place the onion slices and pomegranate seeds in a bowl and toss in the vinegar and salt. Cover and set aside to marinate.

Crush the dried molokhia leaves with your hand and place them in a bowl. Pour over just enough boiling water to cover and leave them to soak until they have doubled in bulk.

For the stew, place the chicken in a deep pan and cover with the water. Add the onions, carrots, garlic, cloves, cardamom pods and seasoning. Bring the water to the boil then reduce the heat, cover, and simmer for about 25 minutes.

Stir in the soaked molokhia leaves and simmer, uncovered, for a further 25 minutes. Lift the chicken out of the pot and check the seasoning of the stock. If it lacks flavour, boil rapidly for 10 minutes to reduce. Skin the chicken, cut it into joints, and return to the stock.

Serve the chicken in shallow bowls, spooning the carrots and molokhia leaves over it. Top each bowl with a spoonful of the marinated onions and pomegranate seeds, and serve with plenty of bread.

# Quail with walnuts and lemon

There's always something irresistible about the aroma of chicken or quail grilling in the streets and markets. Somehow it manages to waft around every corner and slip through open windows, luring you to vendors roasting the birds on spits. I have fond memories of these crunchy and juicy butterflied quails at picnics in the Syrian countryside. To butterfly them, you need to split the quail down the backbone with a sharp knife, then lay skin-side up and press down hard to flatten.

## Serves four

**8 quail, cleaned and split down the backbone**

**2 cloves of garlic, crushed to a creamy paste with a little salt**

**50g/2oz walnuts, lightly toasted and chopped**

**zest and juice of 1 lemon**

**5–10ml/1–2 tsp Aleppo pepper or dried chilli flakes**

**a small bunch of fresh mint leaves, finely chopped**

**a small bunch of fresh coriander (cilantro), finely chopped**

**60ml/4 tbsp olive oil**

**sea salt and ground black pepper**

**lemon wedges, to serve**

Lay the quail flat on a clean surface and pierce a wooden or metal skewer right through them, from one side to the other, to keep them flat.

In a bowl, mix the garlic paste with the walnuts, lemon zest and juice, Aleppo pepper and the fresh herbs. Bind with the olive oil and season well. Rub the walnut and lemon mixture all over both sides of the quail and leave them to marinate in a cool place for at least 1 hour. Meanwhile, prepare the charcoal grill.

When the barbecue is glowing, place the quail, skin-side down, on an oiled rack set over it. Grill the quail for 2–3 minutes each side, until the skin is crisp and the juices run clear when pricked with a skewer. Serve with lemon wedges to squeeze over them.

# Roasted stuffed turkey with thyme

I once spent Christmas with a Christian family in Lebanon and was surprised to discover that they also roasted turkey for dinner. Somehow, I was expecting elaborate meatballs or a cut of lamb, but turkeys were shepherded through the local market several days before Christmas to remind everyone to prepare for the big celebratory meal. This is *habash mahshi*.

## Serves four to six

**1 medium turkey, approximately 2.25–2.5kg/5–5½lb**

**115g/4oz butter, softened**

**6–8 sprigs of fresh thyme**

**sea salt and ground black pepper**

For the stuffing

**30ml/2 tbsp olive oil plus a knob or pat of butter**

**2 onions, finely chopped**

**30ml/2 tbsp pine nuts**

**30ml/2 tbsp blanched almonds, chopped**

**30ml/2 tbsp currants**

**225g/8oz lean minced (ground) lamb**

**10–15ml/2–3 tsp ground cinnamon**

**250g/9oz/1¼ cups short grain rice**

**500ml/17fl oz/generous 2 cups chicken stock**

**sea salt and ground black pepper**

Preheat the oven to 200°C/400°F/Gas 6. To make the stuffing, heat the oil with the butter in a heavy pan and cook the onions until they begin to colour. Add the pine nuts, almonds and currants, and stir until the nuts begin to brown and the currants plump up.

Add the lamb and the cinnamon to the stuffing mixture, and stir until browned. Stir in the rice, coating it with the oil. Pour in the chicken stock, stir well, season with salt and pepper and bring to the boil. Reduce the heat and simmer gently for about 15 minutes, until the liquid has been absorbed. Remove from the heat and leave to cool.

Season the turkey inside and out with salt and pepper. Stuff the cavity with the rice mixture and secure the opening with a skewer. Rub the skin of the turkey with the butter and place it breast-side up in a roasting pan. Arrange half the sprigs of thyme around the turkey, place in the hot oven, and roast for about 30 minutes.

Reduce the heat to 180°C/350°F/Gas 4. Baste the turkey with the cooking juices and pour about 250ml/9fl oz/1 cup water into the dish. Roast for a further 1½–2 hours, or until the juices run clear when a thigh is pierced with a skewer.

Transfer the turkey to a serving platter and garnish with fresh sprigs of thyme. Cover with foil to keep it warm and leave it to rest for 15 minutes before carving. Reduce the cooking juices over a medium heat, skimming off the fat, and season to taste. Pour the juices into a jug and serve with the turkey.

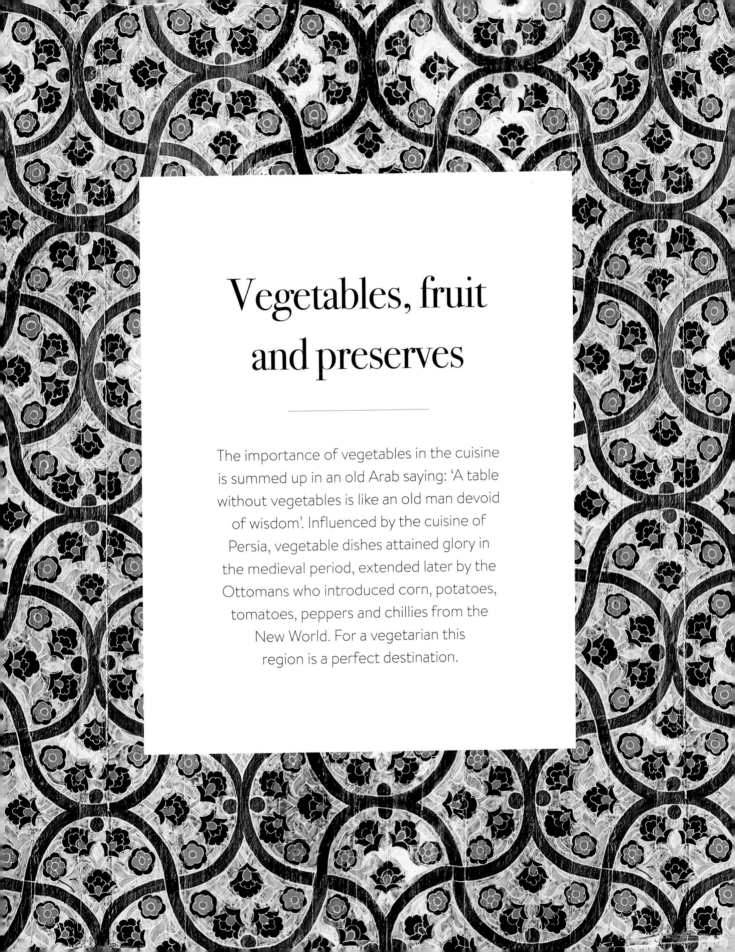

# Vegetables, fruit and preserves

The importance of vegetables in the cuisine is summed up in an old Arab saying: 'A table without vegetables is like an old man devoid of wisdom'. Influenced by the cuisine of Persia, vegetable dishes attained glory in the medieval period, extended later by the Ottomans who introduced corn, potatoes, tomatoes, peppers and chillies from the New World. For a vegetarian this region is a perfect destination.

# Potato kibbeh stuffed with spinach

The much-loved kibbeh of Jordan, Syria and Lebanon are eaten at festivals, feasts, and family celebrations. These potato kibbeh, *kibbeh batata*, are often stuffed with minced lamb, cheese, or as here, sautéed spinach with feta, and served as a mezze dish or to accompany grilled meats.

## Serves four to six

**For the kibbeh**

175g/6oz/1 cup fine or medium bulgur

500g/1¼lb potatoes, cooked

25g/1oz plain (all-purpose) flour

5ml/1 tsp ground allspice

5ml/1 tsp ground cumin

5ml/1 tsp ground coriander

sea salt and ground black pepper

sunflower oil for frying

lemon wedges and yogurt, to serve

**For the filling**

15ml/1 tbsp olive oil

1 onion, finely chopped

30ml/2 tbsp pine nuts

250g/9oz spinach, steamed and finely chopped

a pinch of nutmeg

115/4oz feta, crumbled

For the kibbeh, pour the bulgur into a bowl and pour in enough boiling water to just cover. Leave to swell for 10 minutes.

Use your hands to squeeze out any excess water. Put the cooked potatoes and bulgur in a bowl and mash together. Add the flour, spices and seasoning, and knead until smooth. Cover the bowl and chill for 30 minutes before using.

To prepare the filling, heat the oil and stir in the onion until it softens. Add the pine nuts and sauté for 1–2 minutes, until the pine nuts and the onion are golden brown. Toss in the spinach with the nutmeg and heat it through. Toss in the crumbled feta and season to taste, as feta is often quite salty.

Take an apricot-sized lump of kibbeh in your hand. Roll it into a smooth ball then, using your finger, hollow out the middle to create a shell. Fill the shell with a teaspoon of the filling, then pinch the edges together and smooth it over with a dampened finger to create a sealed mini torpedo. If not cooking them immediately, cover with cling film and keep in the refrigerator.

Heat enough oil in a wide, shallow pan for frying. Cook the kibbeh in batches until golden brown all over. Drain them on kitchen paper. Serve hot with wedges of lemon and a dollop of yogurt, if you like.

# Potatoes with walnuts and rose petals

Heavily scented with cumin, this is a delicious way to prepare potatoes. There are variations of this dish, known as *kammouneh*, throughout Lebanon, a hazelnut version in the Black Sea region, and a more fiery version in parts of Syria and Jordan.

## Serves three to four

**750g/1½lb new potatoes**

**30–45ml/2–3 tbsp olive oil**

**5ml/1 tsp sea salt**

For the kammouneh

**10–15ml/2–3 tsp cumin seeds**

**30–45ml/2–3 tbsp walnuts, finely chopped**

**1 red onion, finely chopped**

**1 red chilli, seeded and finely chopped**

**a small bunch of fresh basil, finely shredded**

**a small bunch of fresh mint, finely shredded**

**15ml/1 tbsp dried edible rose petals**

**juice of 1 lemon**

Prepare the kammouneh. Roast the cumin seeds in a heavy pan, until they give off a nutty aroma. Using a mortar and pestle, grind them a little to release the flavour, then add the walnuts and grind a little more. Add the onion, chilli, herbs and most of the dried rose petals, and pound lightly to combine the ingredients, but don't pound to a paste.

Boil the potatoes in their skins, until tender but not too soft. Drain, refresh quickly under running cold water and peel off the skins while still warm. Transfer them to a bowl and toss in the olive oil and salt, so that the potatoes absorb a little of the oil.

Bind the cumin and rose mixture with the lemon juice and spoon it over the potatoes while they are still warm. Toss well and garnish with the remaining rose petals.

# Chicory in olive oil

In Lebanon this simple dish of chicory dressed in olive oil is called *asoura*, meaning 'squeezed', as you need to squeeze the cooked vegetable by hand to get rid of all excess water. It is served as a mezze dish or as an accompaniment to meat, poultry or fish.

## Serves four

**about 350g/12oz chicory (Belgian endive)**

**45ml/3 tbsp olive oil**

**juice of 1 lemon**

**sea salt and ground black pepper**

Bring a pan of water to the boil. Drop in the chicory and boil for 10 minutes, until soft. Drain and refresh under cold running water.

Take the chicory in your hands and squeeze tightly to remove all the excess water, so that it is almost dry. Divide it into four portions and squeeze them into tight balls. Cover and leave in the refrigerator until ready to serve.

Just before serving, place each ball on a plate and flatten it out a little with the palm of your hand, or the back of a wooden spoon. Drizzle each one with olive oil and a little lemon juice and sprinkle with salt and pepper.

# Green beans with cumin and tomatoes

Cooking vegetables like beans, artichokes and aubergines in olive oil is a legacy of the Ottomans. Traditionally the olive oil dishes were created to be eaten cold, but you can serve these beans – *loubia bi zeit* – hot or cold, as a mezze dish or as an accompaniment.

## Serves four to six

- 30–45ml/2–3 tbsp olive oil
- 2 onions, finely chopped
- 2–3 cloves of garlic, finely chopped
- 10ml/2 tsp cumin seeds
- 450g/1lb green beans, trimmed and left whole
- 5ml/1 tsp ground cinnamon
- 5ml/1 tsp ground allspice
- 5ml/1 tsp sugar
- 400g/14oz can of chopped tomatoes
- sea salt and ground black pepper
- lemon wedges, to serve

Heat the oil in a heavy-based pan and stir in the onion and garlic, until they begin to colour. Stir in the cumin seeds, then toss in the green beans and cook, stirring, for 2–3 minutes.

Add the cinnamon, allspice and sugar to the pan and stir through to cover all the beans in the spice mixture.

Stir the tomatoes into the pan. Cover with a lid and cook gently for 15–20 minutes, until the beans are tender but still retain a bite to them. Season to taste with salt and pepper. Serve hot or at room temperature with wedges of lemon to squeeze over them.

# Aubergines stuffed with aromatic rice

As the aubergine is one of the most favoured vegetables there are numerous ways of cooking it. This one, *batinjan be zeit*, is stuffed with aromatic rice and is really satisfying to make and eat. In Lebanon cooks often use the local spice mix, *sabaa baharat*, a blend of seven spices, but you can use your own combination of ground cumin, coriander, cinnamon, allspice and cloves instead.

## Serves four to six

150ml/5fl oz olive oil

1 onion, finely chopped

2 tomatoes, skinned, seeded and chopped

10ml/2 tsp sabaa baharat

10ml/2 tsp dried mint

5–10ml/1–2 tsp sugar

175g/6oz/1 cup short grain rice

6 medium aubergines (eggplants)

1–2 small potatoes, sliced

juice of 1 lemon

100ml/3½fl oz/scant ½ cup water

sea salt and ground black pepper

To make the stuffing, heat 15ml/1 tbsp of the olive oil in a heavy pan and cook the onion for 2–3 minutes, until it begins to colour. Add the tomatoes, sabaa baharat, mint and sugar, and cook for 2–3 minutes.

Add the rice to the pan, coating it well in the oil, and pour in enough water to cover the rice by a finger's width. Season with salt and pepper and bring to the boil. Reduce the heat and simmer for 10 minutes, until all the water has been absorbed. Turn off the heat, cover the pan with a clean dish towel and put on the lid. Leave the rice to steam for 10 minutes.

Meanwhile, prepare the aubergines. Pull off the stalks but leave the ends intact. Cut each aubergine in half, and use an apple corer to hollow out the middle. Fill each aubergine half with the rice mixture and seal the opening with a slice of potato. (You can discard the scooped-out aubergine, or use it in another dish.)

Mix the lemon juice and remaining olive oil with the water. Stand the aubergines in a heavy pan, making sure they support each other and don't fall over. Pour the lemon, oil and water mixture in to the pan around the aubergines. Over a medium heat, bring the liquid to the boil, reduce the heat, cover the pan and simmer for about 40 minutes.

Serve the stuffed aubergines hot or at room temperature as a mezze dish, or serve as an accompaniment to roast meat dishes.

# Aubergine and chickpea moussaka

The principal idea of a moussaka is that the dish is prepared in layers – these layers can consist of vegetables alone or can be combined with meat. Perhaps the best known is the aubergine and minced lamb dish usually attributed to Greek cuisine but which is in fact found all over the eastern Mediterranean. This meatless *musaaka* is one of the dishes Christians often prepare for Good Friday. Serve with bread.

## Serves four

2 large aubergines (eggplants)

30ml/2 tbsp olive oil, plus extra for brushing

2 onions, finely chopped

2 cloves of garlic, finely chopped

2 x 400g/14oz cans of cooked chickpeas, rinsed and drained

10ml/2 tsp ground cinnamon

5ml/1 tsp ground cumin

10ml/2 tsp pomegranate molasses

a small bunch of fresh flat leaf parsley, finely chopped

15ml/1 tsp tomato purée (paste)

10ml/2 tsp sugar

4–5 large tomatoes, thinly sliced

15ml/1 tsp butter

5–10ml/1–2 tsp zahtar

sea salt and ground black pepper

Cut the aubergines into round slices, place them in a shallow bowl or colander and sprinkle with salt. Leave them to sweat for about 20 minutes, then rinse and pat dry with kitchen paper. Brush the aubergine slices with oil and griddle them on both sides so that they are lightly browned. Preheat the oven to 180°C/350°F/Gas 4.

Heat the olive oil in a heavy pan and stir in the onions and garlic, until they begin to colour. Stir in the chickpeas for 1–2 minutes then add the cinnamon and cumin. Stir in the pomegranate molasses, toss in the parsley and season with salt and pepper.

Line an ovenproof dish with half of the aubergine slices, spoon the chickpea mixture on top, and cover with another layer of aubergine.

Mix together the tomato purée and sugar and thin it with about 120ml/4fl oz/½ cup of water. Pour the mixture over the layered aubergines. Add the tomato slices, dot with butter and sprinkle with zahtar. Bake for 25–30 minutes and serve.

# Okra with tomatoes and coriander

Okra is one of those vegetables that divides opinion – some people prefer it soft and mucilaginous, others like it crunchy. I am definitely in the crunchy camp. When fresh okra are in season this is a favourite go-to dish, *bamiya bi zayt*, adapted from the Ottoman tradition.

## Serves four

450g/1lb fresh okra, left whole, washed and patted dry

juice of 1 lemon

30ml/1 tbsp olive oil

1 onion, finely chopped

2 cloves of garlic, finely chopped

5–10ml/1–2 tsp honey

4 tomatoes, skinned and chopped

a bunch of fresh coriander (cilantro), finely chopped

sea salt and ground black pepper

Place the okra in a bowl and toss in the lemon juice. Leave them to marinate for about 15 minutes then lift them out of the juice.

Heat the olive oil in a shallow, heavy pan and stir in the onion to soften. Add the garlic and toss in the okra. Fry lightly for 3–4 minutes then drizzle with the honey and toss in the chopped tomatoes. Add most of the coriander and cook for 1–2 minutes, until the okra are tender but still retain a bite. Season with salt and pepper.

Serve the okra immediately as an accompaniment to grilled or roasted meat and poultry, or leave the okra to cool and serve at room temperature as a mezze dish.

# Courgettes baked in a cheese sauce

In this typical family dish, *kousa bi gebna*, the courgettes are baked in a cheesy egg mixture which is a bit like an omelette. Home comfort food, traditionally the dish is prepared with a crumbly, tangy cheese made from ewe's milk, but a combination of mature Cheddar and Parmesan works well. You can also make it with feta and add a little mint.

## Serves four to six

**30ml/2 tbsp olive oil plus a knob or pat of butter**

**2 onions, cut in half lengthways and sliced finely with the grain**

**5–10ml/1–2 tsp caraway seeds**

**4–6 firm courgettes (zucchini), trimmed and cut into thick slices lengthways**

**8 eggs**

**125ml/4fl oz/½ cup milk**

**250g/9oz mixed Cheddar and Parmesan cheese, coarsely grated**

**2.5ml/½ tsp ground paprika**

**sea salt and ground black pepper**

Preheat the oven to 180°C/350°F/Gas 4. Heat the oil and butter in a large pan. Add the onions and cook until soft. Stir in the caraway seeds and then remove from the heat.

Place the courgette slices in a steamer and steam for about 10 minutes until tender but not mushy. Drain well, pat dry and spread half the slices in the base of an ovenproof dish. Spread the onion mixture, including the oil and butter, over the top and arrange another layer of courgettes over the onions.

Beat the eggs with the milk and then mix in the cheese and paprika. Season generously and pour the over the courgettes. Bake the dish for 20–25 minutes, until the top is golden brown. Serve immediately.

# Stuffed courgettes with apricots

Fresh and dried apricots are one of the most commonly used fruits in the cooking of the region, and they pair beautifully with courgettes, lending their natural warmth and sweetness to the 'cool' vegetable. Medieval in origin, this Arab dish, *kablama*, can be served on its own with a dollop of creamy yogurt or as an accompaniment to meat and poultry dishes.

## Serves three to four

- 45–60ml/3–4 tbsp olive oil
- 2 onions, halved and finely sliced
- 2 cloves of garlic, finely chopped
- 2–3 tomatoes, skinned, seeds removed and chopped
- 5–10ml/1–2 tsp honey
- a small bunch of fresh flat leaf parsley, chopped
- 6 small or 3 medium courgettes (zucchini), washed
- 200g/7oz ready-to-eat dried apricots, soaked overnight in just enough water to cover
- juice of 1 lemon
- 30ml/2 tbsp grape molasses
- a little butter
- sea salt and ground black pepper
- Greek-style (strained plain) yogurt, to serve

Preheat the oven to 180°C/350°F/Gas 4. To make the filling, heat 15–30ml/1–2 tbsp of the olive oil in a heavy pan and stir in the onions and garlic for 1–2 minutes to soften. Add the tomatoes, honey and parsley. Season with salt and pepper and leave to cool.

Slice off the stem end of the courgettes and, using an apple corer, scoop out the pulp without breaking the skin. Spoon the onion and tomato filling into each courgette hollow.

Drain the apricots and reserve 300ml/½ pint/1¼ cups of the soaking water. Look for the slit in each apricot and pull it open. Arrange half the apricots in the base of an ovenproof dish. Place the stuffed courgettes on top, and arrange the rest of the apricots over them.

Mix together the reserved apricot water with the lemon juice, the remaining 30ml/2 tbsp of olive oil, grape molasses and a little salt, and pour over the apricots and courgettes. Cover with foil and bake for about 40 minutes. Dot the top with a little butter and return to the oven for 10 minutes.

Serve warm with a dollop of thick yogurt.

# Roasted courgettes with vinegar

Courgettes are regarded as cooling so they are nearly always married with warming spices or herbs, such as dill and mint. In the eastern Mediterranean you will find plain and marbled green courgettes, as well as pure white and yellow (sometimes referred to as squash). You can use any for this dish, *koussa bil khal*, which is delicious served with grilled or roasted meat, poultry and fish.

## Serves four to six

4–6 courgettes (zucchini), trimmed and sliced lengthways

4 cloves of garlic, halved and lightly crushed

45–60ml/3–4 tbsp olive oil

30ml/2 tbsp cider or white wine vinegar

10ml/2 tsp dried mint

sea salt

Preheat the oven to 180°C/350°F/Gas 4. Place the courgette slices in an ovenproof dish with the crushed garlic. Pour the olive oil over the courgettes, and roast in the oven for 25–30 minutes, until softened and lightly browned.

Mix 30–45ml/2–3 tbsp of the cooking liquid with the vinegar and dried mint to make a dressing.

Lift the courgette slices out of the dish and arrange on a warmed serving plate. Drizzle the vinegar and mint dressing over the courgettes. Sprinkle generously with salt and serve warm or at room temperature.

# Spicy potatoes with coriander

Served hot or cold, *batata harra* can be served as a mezze dish or as an accompaniment to grilled and roasted meat. Slightly waxy new or Charlotte potatoes, kept whole or halved, work well. Olive oil is preferred if the dish is to be served at room temperature, and ghee if served hot.

## Serves four

350g/12oz new potatoes

60ml/4 tbsp ghee, or olive oil with a generous knob or pat of butter

3–4 cloves of garlic, finely chopped

2 red chillies, seeded and chopped

5–10ml/1–2 tsp cumin seeds

a bunch of fresh coriander (cilantro), finely chopped

sea salt and ground black pepper

lemon wedges, to serve

Halve or quarter the larger potatoes so that the majority are a similar size and then steam them with their skins on for about 10 minutes, until cooked but still firm. Drain and refresh under cold running water. Peel off the skins.

Heat the ghee, or olive oil and butter, in a heavy pan and cook the garlic, chillies and cumin seeds for 2–3 minutes, until they begin to colour.

Toss in the potatoes for 3–4 minutes, making sure they are coated in the garlic, chillies and cumin. Season with salt and pepper and toss in the coriander. Serve with lemon wedges to squeeze over them.

Left **Roasted courgettes with vinegar**  Right **Spicy potatoes with coriander**

# Sweet-sour onions with tamarind

Medieval manuscripts suggest that courgettes, leeks and onions have been cooked in tamarind juice for hundreds of years. It is one of the oldest souring agents, and its tart flavour is much enjoyed in the region. The concentrated tamarind paste employed in this recipe is available in Middle Eastern and Indian stores, as well as online. The dish is known as *basal bi tamer hindi*.

## Serves four to six

- 30–45ml/2–3 tbsp olive oil
- 450g/1lb shallots or baby onions, peeled
- 15ml/1 tbsp tamarind paste
- 15ml/1 tbsp sugar or honey
- a bunch of fresh coriander (cilantro), chopped
- sea salt and ground black pepper

Heat the oil in a shallow heavy pan and add the shallots. Sauté the shallots until they are golden brown. Stir the tamarind paste into the shallots. Add the sugar or honey and enough water to just cover the base of the pan.

Reduce the heat, cover the pan and simmer gently for about 15 minutes, until the shallots are tender and coated in the thick sauce.

Season with salt and pepper and sprinkle the chopped coriander over the top. Serve hot or at room temperature.

# Spinach with tahini yogurt

*Fattet al sabanekh* is a great mezze dish as well as an accompaniment to grilled meat and poultry, or you can serve it as a fatta dish spooned on top of pieces of toasted pitta bread. Originally, fatta dishes were probably devised as a way of using up stale bread.

## Serves four

500g/1¼lb fresh spinach, washed and drained

15–30ml/1–2 tbsp olive oil

1 onion, chopped

5ml/1 tsp Aleppo pepper or dried red chilli flakes

5ml/1 tsp ground cumin seeds

5ml/1 tsp ground coriander

a small bunch of fresh coriander (cilantro), finely chopped

15–30ml/1–2 tbsp flaked (sliced) almonds

2 pitta breads, toasted

15ml/1 tbsp butter

15–30ml/1–2 tbsp pine nuts

sea salt and ground black pepper

For the yogurt sauce

600ml/1 pint Greek-style (strained plain) yogurt

2 cloves of garlic, crushed

30ml/2 tbsp tahini

juice of ½ lemon

sea salt and ground black pepper

To prepare the tahini yogurt sauce, beat the yogurt with the garlic, tahini and lemon juice and season it to taste with salt and pepper. Set aside.

Put the washed spinach in a steamer or a large pan and cook very briefly until just wilted. Refresh under cold running water. Drain the spinach and squeeze out the excess water. Transfer to a board and chop coarsely.

Heat the oil in a heavy pan, stir in the onion and cook for 2–3 minutes. Stir in the spices and then add the spinach, making sure all the leaves are thoroughly coated with the spiced oil. Cook for a further 2–3 minutes, until the spinach is wilted. Season well with salt and pepper. Mix in the fresh coriander and flaked almonds.

Break the toasted pitta bread into bite-size pieces and arrange them in a serving dish. Spread the spinach over the top of the bread and spoon the yogurt sauce over the spinach.

Melt the butter in a frying pan and add the pine nuts. Stir-fry until the pine nuts are golden. Tip the pine nuts, with the butter, over the yogurt and serve immediately while still warm.

# Baked vegetable stew

Simple and tasty, stews of this nature are seasonal and often baked in an earthenware dish in the oven. Different spices and herbs are added according to the region and the stew is invariably served with a dollop of plain or garlic yogurt or crumbled feta and olives. This is *khudra bil furn*.

## Serves six

150ml/5fl oz olive oil

6 large tomatoes

4–6 potatoes, peeled

3 courgettes (zucchini)

2 onions

2 green and red (bell) peppers

a small bunch of fresh flat leaf parsley, chopped

a bunch of fresh mint, finely chopped

juice of 1 lemon

2 cloves of garlic, crushed

10ml/2 tsp sugar

a little butter

sea salt and ground black pepper

Preheat the oven to 200°C/400°F/Gas 6 and lightly grease a baking dish, preferably earthenware, with a little of the olive oil. Thinly slice the tomatoes and line the base of the prepared baking dish with half the slices. Finely slice the potatoes and arrange in a layer on top of the tomatoes, followed by a layer of thinly sliced courgettes.

Cut the onions in half lengthways, and slice with the grain, then thinly slice the peppers. Toss the onion and pepper slices together with the chopped parsley and mint, then scatter the mixture over the courgettes. Complete the layering with the rest of the tomato slices.

Combine the rest of the olive oil with the lemon juice, garlic and sugar. Season, and pour the mixture over the vegetables.

Cover the dish with foil and bake in the oven for about 40 minutes, then remove the foil, dot the butter over the tomatoes and return the dish to the oven to cook, uncovered, for a further 15–20 minutes.

Serve the baked vegetables straight away, as an accompaniment to any meat, poultry or fish dish, or on its own with yogurt and flatbread.

# Jerusalem artichoke and tomato stew

Jerusalem artichokes are delicious cooked this way but they can cause indigestion and flatulence so the cumin seeds are vital component of this dish, *tartoufa*. It is best served on its own with yogurt and chunks of crusty bread to mop up the garlicky tomato juices.

## Serves four

30–45ml/2–3 tbsp olive oil

2 onions, finely chopped

2 cloves of garlic, finely chopped

5–10ml/1–2 tsp cumin seeds

500g/1¼lb Jerusalem artichokes, peeled and cut into bite-size pieces

2 x 400g/14oz cans of chopped tomatoes

10–15ml/2–3 tsp honey

sea salt and ground black pepper

a small bunch of fresh coriander (cilantro), finely chopped, to garnish

lemon wedges, to serve

Heat the oil in a heavy pan, and stir in the onions, garlic and cumin seeds for 2 minutes. Toss in the pieces of artichoke, making sure they are coated in the onion and cumin.

Add the tomatoes to the pan, together with the honey. Cover the pan and cook gently for 25–30 minutes, until the artichokes are tender.

Remove the lid and bubble up the sauce over high heat to reduce it a little. Season with salt and pepper and transfer to a serving dish. Garnish with some coriander and serve with a dollop of creamy yogurt and wedges of lemon to squeeze over the dish.

# Red cabbage with quince and walnuts

Originally of Armenian origin, this dish spread throughout the eastern Mediterranean as the Armenians migrated from the Caucasus, taking with them their love of vegetables combined with fruit. Simple to prepare, this delicious dish, *koromb wa safarjal*, is best served to accompany roasted lamb, duck or chicken.

## Serves four to six

**1 red cabbage, quartered, cored and chopped into bite-size pieces**

**115g/4oz butter, melted**

**5–10ml/1–2 tsp ground cinnamon**

**juice of 1 lemon, plus extra for acidulating**

**10ml/2 tsp pomegranate molasses**

**2 quinces**

**15–30ml/1–2 tbsp sugar**

**15–30ml/1–2 tbsp walnuts, roughly chopped**

**sea salt and ground black pepper**

Preheat the oven to 180°C/350°F/Gas 4. Grease a baking dish and arrange the cabbage in it. Pour in half the melted butter and toss with half the cinnamon, and the lemon juice and pomegranate molasses. Season with salt and pepper. Cover with foil and bake for about 30 minutes.

Meanwhile, quarter and core the quinces. Cut them into thin slices and submerge them in a bowl of cold water mixed with a squeeze of lemon juice to prevent them from discolouring.

Take the cabbage out of the oven and arrange the quince slices over the top. Sprinkle them with sugar and the remaining cinnamon, and sprinkle the walnuts over the top. Pour the rest of the butter over the quinces.

Cover and bake for 20 minutes more, then remove the foil and return the dish to the oven for about 10 minutes to brown the top. Serve immediately.

# Apricots stuffed with rice

A lovely accompaniment to roasted meats and poultry, *mishmish mahshi* is best prepared with dried apricots for texture and flavour. Another sumptuous Arab dish with medieval roots of cooking with fruit, you can combine the rice with minced lamb or keep it vegetarian.

## Serves four

30ml/2 tbsp olive oil

1 onion, finely chopped

15ml/1 tbsp pine nuts

175g/6oz/1 cup short grain or pudding rice, well-rinsed and drained

5ml/1 tsp ground cinnamon

5ml/1 tsp ground allspice

5ml/1 tsp sugar

5ml/1 tsp dried mint

1 large tomato, skinned, seeded and finely chopped

16 dried ready-to-eat apricots, soaked in water to cover for 6 hours, or overnight

15ml/1 tbsp butter

sea salt and ground black pepper

For the cooking liquid

120ml/4fl oz olive oil

50ml/2fl oz/¼ cup water

juice of 1 lemon

10–15ml/2–3 tsp honey

15ml/1 tbsp pomegranate molasses

Preheat the oven to 180°C/350°F/Gas 4. Heat the oil in a heavy pan, stir in the onion and cook until it begins to colour. Add the pine nuts and cook until golden, then stir in the rice, making sure the grains are coated in the oil. Add the spices, sugar, mint and tomato to the pan, season with salt and pepper, and pour in about 350ml/12fl oz/1½ cups water to cover the rice. Bring to the boil, stir once, then reduce the heat and leave to simmer for 10–15 minutes, until all the water has been absorbed. Remove the pan from the heat.

In another pan, poach the apricots in their soaking water for 15–20 minutes, then drain. Open them up at the slit already created by removing the stone, and spoon a portion of the rice mixture into the hollow of each apricot, so that it looks plump and appetising. Place the apricots upright in a lightly greased, shallow baking dish, packing them tightly together so that they support each other during cooking.

Mix together the ingredients for the cooking liquid and pour it over and around the apricots. Cover the dish with foil and bake for about 20 minutes.

Remove the foil and baste the apricots with the cooking juices. Dot each one with a little butter and return the dish to the oven to cook, uncovered, for a further 5–10 minutes. Serve straight away.

# Stuffed prunes in a pomegranate sauce

*Khawk bil rumman*, prunes stuffed with walnuts or aromatic rice, make a lovely contribution to a mezze spread, or as an accompaniment to grilled and roasted meats and poultry. One of my Armenian friends always served these prunes as a mezze dish to better appreciate the sweet-sour taste and texture of the nut against the soft fruit, but many people serve them with roast lamb.

## Serves four

**12–16 ready-to-eat, pitted prunes**

**12–16 walnut halves**

**15–30ml/1–2 tbsp ghee, or olive oil with a knob or pat of butter**

**30–45ml/2–3 tbsp pomegranate molasses**

**30ml/2 tbsp sugar**

**1–2 cinnamon sticks**

**3–4 cardamom pods**

**2–3 cloves**

**juice of 1 lemon**

**250ml/9fl oz/1 cup red wine or water**

**a small bunch of fresh flat leaf parsley, chopped**

**sea salt and ground black pepper**

Find the opening in each pitted prune and stuff it with a walnut half.

Melt the ghee, or olive oil and butter, in a heavy pan and toss in the prunes for 2–3 minutes, turning them over from time to time. Stir in the pomegranate molasses with the sugar and spices, and add the lemon juice and wine. Season with salt and pepper and bring the liquid to the boil. Reduce the heat and simmer, uncovered, for about 15 minutes, stirring occasionally, until the prunes are tender.

Arrange the prunes on a serving dish and spoon the spicy pomegranate sauce over and around them. Garnish with the parsley and serve hot or at room temperature.

# Pickled white cabbage with walnuts

Most cabbages grown in Lebanon are white or light green with firm, tender leaves that impart a natural sweetness to dishes. When there is a glut of these cabbages the vegetables are often preserved, and *malfouf mkhalal* is one of the favourite recipes for doing it.

## Serves four

**8 large white cabbage leaves, or 16 smaller ones**

**4 cloves of garlic**

**225g/8oz shelled walnuts, coarsely chopped**

**1 fresh chilli, seeded and finely chopped**

**15ml/1 tbsp olive oil**

**300ml/½ pint/1¼ cups cider or white wine vinegar**

**sea salt**

Steam the cabbage leaves for 5–6 minutes until softened. Refresh under cold water and drain well.

Using a mortar and pestle, pound the garlic with a little salt until creamy. Add the walnuts and pound to a gritty paste. Add the chilli and bind the mixture with the oil.

Lay the leaves on a flat surface and trim the central ribs, so that they lie flat. Place a spoonful of the walnut mixture near the top of each leaf. Pull the top edge over the mixture, tuck in the sides and roll the leaf into a tight, pointed log shape.

Pack the stuffed leaves tightly into a sterilised jar and pour over the vinegar. Seal the jar, and leave the cabbage parcels to marinate for at least a week.

After opening, store in the refrigerator for 4–5 days. Serve as a mezze, drizzled in olive oil, or as accompaniment to cheese or grilled meats.

# Pickled stuffed aubergines

If you like aubergines, you will love these. You need to find the baby aubergines or small Kenyan aubergines available in Middle Eastern, Indian and African stores, as they are individually stuffed. *Batinjan makdous* can be served as a mezze dish or simply as a pickle at any of time of day. The pickling juice is also drunk to quench the thirst.

## Serves four to six

**12 baby aubergines (eggplants), stalks removed**

**1 leek, cut in half if very long**

**225g/8oz walnuts, finely chopped**

**1 red (bell) pepper, finely chopped**

**4 cloves of garlic, finely chopped**

**1 red or green chilli, seeded and finely chopped**

**5–10ml/1–2 tsp sea salt**

**15ml/1 tbsp olive oil**

**a small bunch of fresh flat leaf parsley**

**600ml/1 pint/2½ cups white wine vinegar**

Bring a pan of water to the boil and add the aubergines and leek. Cook for 10 minutes to soften, then drain and refresh under cold running water. Set aside the aubergines. Cut the leek into long thin strips and set aside also.

Mix together the walnuts, pepper, garlic, chilli and salt, and bind with the olive oil. Make a slit in the side of each aubergine and stuff the hollow with the filling. Finish with a few parsley leaves.

Carefully wind a strip of leek around each aubergine to bind it and keep it intact. Pack them all tightly into sterilised jars and pour over the vinegar.

Seal the jars and store in a cool place for 2–3 weeks. Refrigerate once opened. As long as they are kept sealed and topped up with vinegar, these pickled aubergines will keep for several months.

Left **Pickled green peppers** Right **Pickled cauliflower with chillies**

# Pickled green peppers

This, *torshi felfel*, is such a classic pickle. The long, light green, often-knobbly peppers, which have some heat to them but also a little bit of sweetness, are ideal candidates for pickling and then serving alongside kebabs. Small, thin green chilli peppers are treated in the same way.

## Makes 1 × 1 litre jar

**450g/1lb long, green peppers, washed thoroughly and patted dry**

**300ml/1 pint/1¼ cups water**

**300ml/1 pint/1¼ cups white wine vinegar**

**15ml/1 tbsp salt**

Mix the water and vinegar and salt together in a jug or pitcher. Pack the peppers tightly into a sterilised jar and pour the vinegar mixture over.

Seal the jar tightly and store for at least 2 weeks before opening. Serve sliced or whole, with kebabs or with mezze dishes.

# Pickled cauliflower with chillies

Up there with pickled peppers, pickled cauliflower (*torshi arnabeet*) is a great favourite at the kebab and soup houses of Lebanon, Syria and Jordan. It also appears as an addition to the mezze table to whet the appetite. Some jars of pickled cauliflower are tinged pink with a little beetroot, but the ones with garlic and chilli are strong in flavour and have a good nip.

## Makes 2 × 1 litre jars

**1 head of fresh cauliflower, trimmed and cut into small florets (you can include the small light green leaves)**

**8–10 cloves of garlic, peeled and left whole**

**4–6 small green or red hot chillies, left whole**

**250ml/9fl oz/1 cup white wine or apple vinegar**

**30ml/2 tbsp sea salt**

**1 litre/1¾ pints/4 cups water**

Place the cauliflower in sterilised jars, alternating with the garlic cloves and chillies. If using the cauliflower leaves, add them too.

Mix the vinegar and salt with the water. Pour over the cauliflower and seal the jars tightly. Store in a cool place for at least 1 month before using.

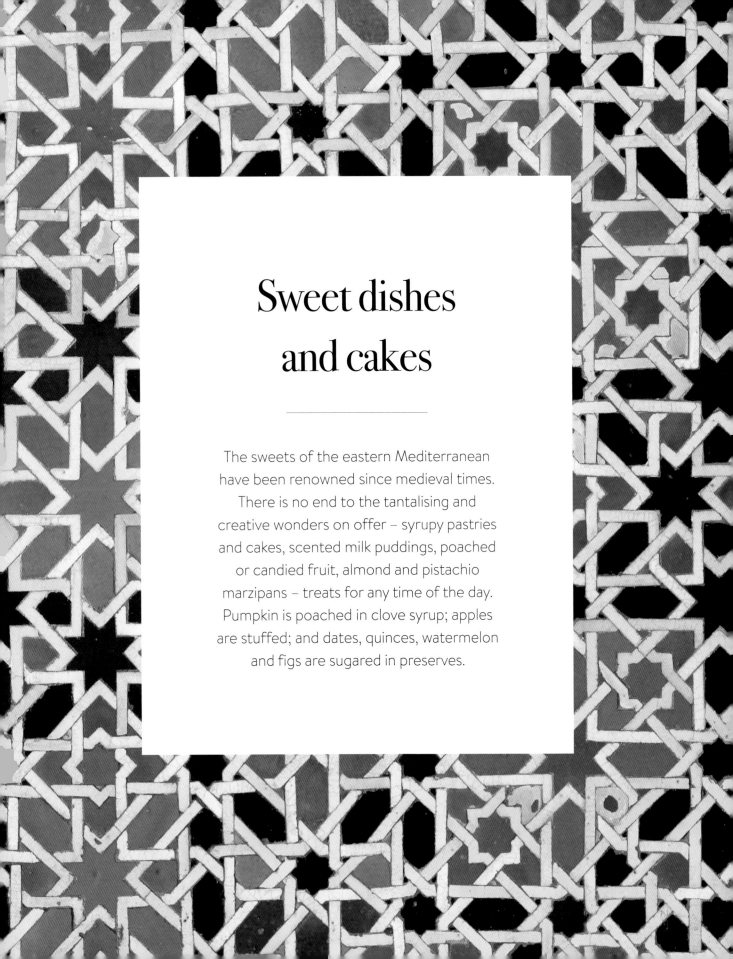

# Sweet dishes and cakes

The sweets of the eastern Mediterranean
have been renowned since medieval times.
There is no end to the tantalising and
creative wonders on offer – syrupy pastries
and cakes, scented milk puddings, poached
or candied fruit, almond and pistachio
marzipans – treats for any time of the day.
Pumpkin is poached in clove syrup; apples
are stuffed; and dates, quinces, watermelon
and figs are sugared in preserves.

# Spiced ground rice pudding

This ground rice pudding, *moughli*, is grainier than the traditional smooth milk puddings such as *ashtalieh* and *mouhalabieh*. Flavoured with cinnamon, which is regarded as beneficial to the digestive system, moughli is traditionally served in Lebanon to women who have just given birth. It is a sweet, sustaining and comforting pudding. If you like, toast the pistachios and coconut.

## Serves six

**1.2 litres/2 pints/5 cups water**

**300g/11oz/scant 2 cups ground rice**

**450g/1lb/2¼ cups sugar**

**30ml/2 tbsp ground cinnamon**

**10ml/2 tsp ground aniseed**

**30ml/2 tbsp desiccated (dry unsweetened shredded) coconut**

**15–30ml/1–2 tbsp pistachio nuts, chopped**

Pour the measured water into a heavy pan and bring it to the boil. Reduce the heat and beat in the ground rice, sugar and spices, stirring constantly to keep smooth. Simmer gently for about 15 minutes, until the mixture is very thick.

Transfer the mixture into individual serving bowls and leave to cool and set, then chill in the refrigerator.

When ready to serve, top each pudding with a sprinkling of coconut and pistachio nuts, and eat chilled or at room temperature.

# Pumpkin poached in syrup

*Shirini* is a winter classic. When the bustling markets and streets are full of pumpkins, you will always find a vendor patiently peeling and preparing them for this very dessert. Similarly, during the quince season, kitchens are filled with the sweet floral scent of fruit poaching in a clove-scented syrup. Poached pumpkin is delicious with labneh or crème fraîche.

## Serves four to six

**450g/1lb/2¼ cups sugar**

**225ml/8fl oz/scant 1 cup water**

**juice of 1 lemon**

**6 cloves**

**1kg/2¼lb peeled and deseeded pumpkin flesh, cut into cubes or rectangular blocks**

**labneh, cream or crème fraiche, to serve (optional)**

Put the sugar and water into a deep, wide heavy-based pan. Bring the liquid to the boil, stirring all the time, until the sugar has dissolved. Boil gently for 2–3 minutes, then reduce the heat and stir in the lemon juice and the cloves.

Add the pumpkin pieces to the pan and bring the liquid back to the boil. Reduce the heat, put the lid on the pan, and poach the pumpkin gently, turning the pieces over from time to time, until they are tender and gleaming. Depending on the size of your pieces, this may take 45 minutes to 1 hour. Leave the pumpkin to cool in the pan, then lift the pieces out of the syrup and place them on a serving dish.

Spoon most, or all, of the syrup over them and serve at room temperature or chilled, with labneh, cream or crème fraîche if you like.

# Baked stuffed apples

Baked apples, *tuffah bil furn*, are a home-cooked treat. Generally, they are stuffed with dried fruits and nuts, flavoured with cinnamon, and served with labneh or ice cream. Crisp and flavoursome, the apples grown in Syria and the Lebanon have been held in high esteem since medieval times.

## Serves four

**4 crisp apples, tart or sweet**

**juice of 1 lemon**

**butter, for greasing**

**300ml/½ pint/1¼ cups water**

**225g/8oz/generous 1 cup cane, palm or muscovado sugar**

**15–30ml/1–2 tbsp pomegranate or grape syrup**

**ice cream or labneh, to serve**

For the filling

**100g/3¾oz dried apricots, chopped**

**45ml/3 tbsp blanched almonds, flaked**

**30ml/2 tbsp sultanas (golden raisins)**

**30ml/2 tbsp palm sugar (jaggery) or sugar**

**5–10ml/1–2 tsp ground cinnamon**

Cut out the core of each apple to create a cavity, and peel around the top edge of the apples. Rub lemon juice over the peeled area. Preheat the oven to 180°C/350°F/Gas 4.

In a small bowl, mix together the ingredients for the filling. Place the apples side by side in a lightly buttered baking dish. Spoon the prepared filling into the apples.

Put the water, sugar and fruit syrup into a pan and bring it to the boil, stirring all the time. Reduce the heat and simmer for 10 minutes.

Pour the syrup over and around the apples and bake for 30 minutes. Baste the apples and return to the oven for 10 minutes more, until tender. Transfer to a serving dish if needed.

Bubble up the syrup in a pan to reduce and thicken, then pour over the apples. Serve with ice cream or labneh as you like.

# Sesame and pistachio biscuits

These little biscuits, called *barazek*, tend to be eaten up in a flash by hungry children at the end of a school day in Syria, Jordan and Lebanon. Sold in cake shops and by street vendors, the recipes vary from region to region but are always in demand.

  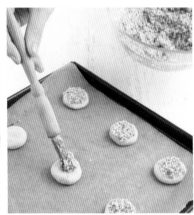

## Makes 12 to 16

**115g/4oz butter**

**115g/4oz/½ cup sugar**

**300g/11oz/2½ cups plain (all-purpose) flour**

For the topping

**115g/4oz/½ cup sesame seeds**

**30ml/1 tbsp ground pistachios**

**30ml/1 tbsp sugar**

**10ml/2 tsp ground cinnamon**

**1 egg white, lightly beaten**

In a bowl, cream the butter until soft and then beat in the sugar until the mixture is light and fluffy. Add the flour to the butter and sugar mixture, and combine with your hand to form a soft dough.

Lightly grease a baking tray and line with baking parchment. Take a cherry-sized portion of the dough in your hands and mould it into a ball. Flatten the ball in the palm of your hand and place it on the baking tray. Repeat with the rest of the dough until it is all used up.

In a small bowl, mix together the sesame seeds, ground pistachios, sugar and cinnamon and bind with the egg white. Brush a little of the mixture over each round of dough and place them in the oven for about 10 minutes, or until they begin to turn golden.

Remove the biscuits from the oven and leave to cool on the baking tray for 5 minutes. Transfer them to a wire rack to cool completely. They can be stored in an airtight container.

# Sweet pancakes with scented syrup

Pancakes are often the food of religious feasts and weddings so there can be an element of ceremony in the making and the garnishing. In this traditional dish, *qatayif*, the pancakes are dipped in syrup, sprinkled with pistachios and served with thick cream or labneh.

## Serves four to six

**15g/½oz fresh yeast**

**5ml/1 tsp sugar**

**250ml/9fl oz/1 cup lukewarm water**

**225g/8oz/2 cups plain (all-purpose) flour**

**sunflower oil, for frying**

**45ml/3 tbsp pistachios, chopped**

**a little grated lemon zest, to garnish**

**thick cream, to serve**

For the syrup

**450g/1lb/2¼ cups sugar**

**300ml/½ pint/1¼ cups water**

**juice of 1 lemon or lime**

**15–30ml/1–2 tbsp orange flower water**

In a small bowl, dissolve the yeast and the sugar in a little of the lukewarm water until it begins to froth. When the yeast and water is frothing, sift the flour into a bowl and make a well in the centre. Pour in the yeast with the rest of the water and, drawing the flour in from the sides, beat the mixture together to form a smooth batter. Cover the bowl with a cloth and leave it in a warm place for about 1 hour, until the batter rises and becomes bubbly and elastic.

Meanwhile, prepare the syrup. Heat the sugar and water together, stirring, until the sugar has dissolved. Bring to the boil, reduce the heat and simmer for 10–15 minutes. Stir in the lemon juice and orange flower water. Simmer for 5 minutes more until the syrup coats the back of the wooden spoon. Set aside to cool.

When the batter is frothy, heat a heavy frying pan with a little oil. Pour a little batter into the hot pan and roll the pan to spread to the sides. Fry for a minute, then flip over and cook the other side. Remove from the pan, fold in half and place on a serving plate.

Repeat until the batter is finished. Pour syrup over the pancakes. Sprinkle with pistachios and serve, with cream and grated lemon zest if you like.

# Dried fruit compôte with almonds

Served as a winter dessert, or at ceremonial feasts, *khushaaf* is a classic sweet dish found throughout the region. The syrup can be flavoured with rose or orange flower water, or both, but the ancient flavour of sweet scented rose is the most traditional.

## Serves six to eight

225g/8oz dried apricots

175/6oz dried prunes

120g/4¼oz sultanas (golden raisins)

120g/4¼oz blanched almonds

30ml/1 tbsp pine nuts

45–60ml/3–4 tbsp sugar

30ml/2 tbsp rose flower water

15ml/1 tbsp orange flower water

Put the dried fruit and nuts into a bowl and cover completely with water. Add the sugar, rose water and orange flower water, and gently stir until the sugar dissolves.

Cover the bowl and place it in the refrigerator. Leave the fruit and nuts to soak for 48 hours, during which time the liquid will turn syrupy and golden.

Serve this compôte chilled, on its own or with cream or ice cream, or with rice pudding. It also makes a delicious breakfast with yogurt.

# Milk pudding with mastic

The classic milk puddings of the region are absolutely delectable. Some are flavoured with orange blossom water, others with rose water, cinnamon or aniseed. Mastic, the crystallised gum of a tree from the pistachio family, gives this pudding, *mouhallabieh*, its unique resinous taste as well as its mildly chewy texture. Mastic (mastika) is available in Middle Eastern stores and online.

## Serves four to six

50g/2oz/½ cup rice flour

1 litre/1¾ pints/4 cups whole (full-fat) milk

125g/4¼oz/generous ½ cup sugar

1–2 mastic crystals, pulverised with a little sugar

15–30ml/1–2 tbsp icing (confectioner's) sugar, for dusting

Mix the rice flour with a little of the milk to form a loose paste. Pour the rest of the milk into a heavy pan and stir in the sugar. Bring the milk to boiling point, stirring all the time, until the sugar has dissolved. Reduce the heat and stir a spoonful or two of the hot milk into the rice flour paste, then transfer the mixture to the pan, stirring constantly to avoid lumps.

Bring the milk back to boiling point and stir in the ground mastic. Reduce the heat and simmer gently for 20–25 minutes, stirring from time to time, until the mixture becomes quite thick and coats the back of the spoon.

Pour the pudding mixture into serving bowls and let it cool, allowing a skin to form on top. Chill in the refrigerator and, just before serving, dust the tops with icing sugar.

Left **Dried fruit compôte with almonds**  Right **Milk pudding with mastic**

# Cream cheese pudding with syrup and nuts

This cream cheese dessert, *ashtalieh*, is similar to the classic milk pudding that pops up all over the region, but thicker and creamier so it can be cut into squares, which are then bathed in sugar syrup. The pudding is typically decorated with pistachios, almonds and pine nuts.

## Serves four to six

**1 litre/1¾ pints/4 cups whole (full-fat) milk**

**60ml/4 tbsp sugar**

**250g/9oz cream cheese**

**90ml/6 tbsp cornflour (cornstarch), slaked with a little extra milk**

**10–15ml/2–3 tsp orange flower water**

**15ml/1 tbsp pine nuts and 30ml/2 tbsp blanched, chopped almonds, soaked in cold water overnight**

**30ml/2 tbsp pistachio nuts, chopped**

For the syrup

**225g/8oz/1 generous cup sugar**

**125ml/4fl oz/½ cup water**

**juice of 1 lemon**

**rind of ½ lemon, cut into fine strips**

Heat the milk in a heavy pan with the sugar, stirring, and bring it to the boil. Reduce the heat and add the cream cheese, beating it into the milk and sugar until the mixture is smooth. Add a couple of spoonfuls of the hot mixture to the slaked cornflour, then pour it into the pan, whisking vigorously until the mixture thickens. Add the orange flower water and simmer gently for 10–15 minutes, until it is thick. Pour the mixture into a shallow dish and leave it to cool and set. Chill in the refrigerator.

To make the syrup, put the sugar in a heavy pan with the water and bring it to the boil, stirring constantly until the sugar has dissolved. Add the lemon juice and rind. Reduce the heat and simmer for 10 minutes, until the syrup is thick enough to coat the back of a spoon. Remove from the heat and set aside.

When ready to serve, cut the pudding into squares and place on individual plates. Spoon some of the syrup and rind strips over them and decorate with the nuts. Serve chilled or at room temperature.

# Creamed semolina with cinnamon

This medieval pudding, *ma'mounia*, can be served for breakfast, as a sweet snack or for a dessert. It is popular with the young and the old – general nursery and comfort food. To transform it into a dessert, serve with clotted cream or labneh and chopped nuts.

## Serves four to six

250g/9oz/1¼ cups sugar

500ml/17fl oz/generous 2 cups water

juice of 1 lemon

100g/3¾oz butter

225g/8oz fine ground semolina

5–10ml/1–2 tsp ground cinnamon

clotted or whipped cream, to serve

To make the syrup, put the sugar and water in a pan and bring to the boil, stirring. Add the lemon juice, reduce the heat and simmer for 10 minutes, until the syrup coats the back of a spoon. Turn off the heat and set aside.

Melt the butter in a heavy pan and slowly stir in the semolina. Continue to stir for 3–4 minutes, then gradually add the syrup, stirring vigorously to prevent any lumps from forming and to keep the syrup from burning.

When the pudding has thickened, take the pan off the heat and cover with a clean dish towel, followed by the lid. Leave to steam for about 15 minutes, then serve warm with a dusting of cinnamon and cream.

# Puréed apricot dessert

Dried fruit purées and compôtes are at the top of the list for winter sweet snacks. The many regional dried fruits include prunes, mulberries, grapes and apricots. This ancient dessert, *mishmishiyya*, is prepared with dried apricots.

## Serves four to six

450g/1lb dried apricots, soaked overnight in water to just cover

125g/4¼oz/generous ½ cup sugar

200ml/7fl oz/scant 1 cup double (heavy) cream

15–30ml/1–2 tbsp icing (confectioner's) sugar

15–30ml/1–2 tbsp orange flower water

15–30ml/1–2 tbsp flaked (sliced) toasted almonds

Pour the apricots, soaking water and the sugar into a pan and bring to the boil. Simmer for 10–15 minutes. When the apricots have cooled, blend them with their thin cooking syrup in a food processor to form a smooth, slightly tart, purée. Transfer the purée to a wide, shallow serving bowl or individual bowls, cover with cling film and chill until completely cold.

Just before serving, whip the cream until it begins to thicken, then add the icing sugar and orange flower water. Continue to whip until the cream forms thick peaks, and spoon it on to the apricot purée. Sprinkle the top with the nuts and serve.

Left **Creamed semolina with cinnamon**  Right **Puréed apricot dessert**

# Sweet turmeric cakes

Light and spongy with a distinctive colour and flavouring from the turmeric, these rustic cakes, called *sfouf*, are a feature of the mountain villages of Lebanon, where they are served for breakfast or to accompany a mid-morning coffee or tea.

## Makes 12 to 16

15–30ml/1–2 tbsp tahini

25g/1oz/2 tbsp butter

75ml/5 tbsp olive oil

350ml/12fl oz/1½ cups milk

250g/9oz/1¼ cups sugar

250g/9oz/1½ cups semolina

200g/7oz/1¾ cups plain (all-purpose) flour

10ml/2 tsp baking powder

30ml/2 tbsp ground turmeric

30ml/2 tbsp pine nuts

Preheat the oven to 180°C/350°F/Gas 4. Smear the tahini over the base and sides of a 25 x 20cm/10 x 8in baking tin (pan). Melt the butter with the olive oil in a small pan.

Heat the milk with the sugar in a separate heavy pan, stirring constantly, until almost boiling. Then stir the melted butter and oil into the milk.

Into a bowl, sift together the semolina, flour, baking powder and turmeric. Add the mixture to the milk and beat vigorously to make a smooth batter.

Pour the batter into the tahini-lined tin, sprinkle the surface with the pine nuts and bake the cake in the oven for about 30 minutes. Remove the cake from the oven and leave to cool, then cut it into 5cm/2in squares and serve while still warm, or at room temperature.

# Semolina cake with poppy seeds

There are many types of semolina cake, but there is something special about poppy seed cakes, *basbousa*. The Jewish community of Lebanon thinks so too as these are baked for the festival of Purim. Blue poppy seeds give a pretty speckled appearance, or you can use white poppy seeds.

## Makes 32

115g/4oz butter

175g/6oz/scant 1 cup sugar

30–45ml/2–3 tbsp white or blue poppy seeds

5–10ml/1–2 tsp vanilla extract

2 eggs

450g/1lb/scant 3 cups fine semolina

5ml/1 tsp baking powder

2.5ml/½ tsp bicarbonate of soda (baking soda)

175g/6fl oz Greek-style (strained plain) yogurt

16 blanched almonds, halved

For the syrup

250ml/9fl oz/1 cup water

450g/1lb/2¼ cups sugar

juice of 1 lemon

First make the syrup. Boil the water with the sugar, stirring constantly, until dissolved. Stir in the lemon juice, reduce the heat and simmer for 10–15 minutes, until the syrup coats the back of a wooden spoon. Leave to cool.

Preheat the oven to 180°C/350°F/Gas 4 and grease a 20 x 30cm/8 x 12in baking tin (pan). Cream the butter with the sugar, beat in the poppy seeds and vanilla, and beat in the eggs one at a time. Sift the semolina with the baking powder and bicarbonate of soda and fold it into the creamed mixture, then stir in the yogurt.

Transfer the mixture to the tin, spreading it to the edges. Arrange the almonds on top, and bake for about 30 minutes, or until firm.

Pour the syrup over the hot cake. Cut into squares or diamonds and leave to cool in the tin before lifting out.

# Little walnut cakes

These little stuffed cakes, called *ma'amoul*, are often prepared for religious festivals, such as Ramadan for the Muslims and Easter for the Christians. Traditionally they are filled with walnuts or pistachios or a date paste; if you do replace the walnuts with soft dried dates, omit the sugar.

## Makes 16 to 20

225g/8oz/2 cups plain (all-purpose) flour

115g/4oz butter, diced

115g/4oz/½ cup sugar

15ml/1 tbsp rose flower water

15–30ml/1–2 tbsp milk

15–30ml/1–2 tbsp icing (confectioner's) sugar, for dusting

For the filling

115g/4oz walnuts, finely chopped

30ml/2 tbsp sugar

15ml/1 tbsp rose flower water

In a bowl, mix together the chopped walnuts, sugar and rose water for the filling, and set aside.

Preheat the oven to 180°C/350°F/Gas 4. Sift the flour into a large bowl, add the diced butter, and rub it into the flour until the mixture resembles fine breadcrumbs. Stir in the sugar and rose water and bind the mixture together with a little milk to form a soft, malleable dough.

Take a small apricot-sized lump of dough in your fingers and mould it into a ball. Carefully, hollow out the ball to form a deep cavity into which you spoon a little of the nut filling. Fold the edges over the filling, pinch the top to seal and mould into a round ball in the palm of your hand.

Place the ball on a lightly oiled baking sheet and press it down with the palm of your hand. Repeat with the rest of the dough and the filling until you have roughly 16–20 little cakes.

Prick the tops with a fork and place them in the oven for 20–25 minutes, until pale brown but still slightly soft. Leave to cool on the baking sheet before dusting with icing sugar.

# Sesame and honey brittle

Throughout history, Arabs and Jews have had a passion for sweets of all kinds, including these little sesame snacks which children love. The little squares, *simsimiyy*, are sold by street vendors.

## Makes 16 to 20

**450g/1lb/scant 3 cups sesame seeds**

**225g/8oz blanched almonds, finely chopped**

**225g/8oz clear honey**

**225g/8oz/generous 1 cup sugar**

**5ml/1 tsp ground cinnamon**

Preheat the oven to 180°C/350°F/Gas 4. Spread the sesame seeds and almonds in a thin layer on a baking sheet and place in the oven for about 10 minutes, until lightly browned and emitting a nutty aroma.

In a heavy pan, melt the honey with the sugar, stirring all the time until it has dissolved. Stir in the cinnamon and simmer gently for about 5 minutes. Remove from the heat and stir in the roasted sesame seeds and nuts.

Lightly grease a baking tin (pan) or tray and transfer the sesame and honey mixture to it. Press the mixture down in the tin with your knuckles to compact it and spread it out evenly. Leave the mixture to cool a little and begin to set but, while it is still pliable, loosen the edge of the brittle with a sharp knife or spatula and lift the whole piece out of the dish and on to a wooden board. Using a sharp knife, cut the brittle into diamond- or square-shaped pieces.

Leave to cool completely until the pieces are hard and brittle. Serve with tea, or store them in an airtight container for several weeks.

# Pistachio baklava with orange water

I am a huge *baklava* fan. If it is made properly it can be light, melt-in-the-mouth and very tasty. Most people buy varied sweet pastries from the pastry shops to offer as gifts or to arrange on a serving dish at home but you can make a good *baklava* by yourself.

## Makes about 30

**175g/6oz clarified or plain butter**

**100ml/3½fl oz sunflower oil**

**450g/1lb filo sheets, thawed if frozen**

**450g/1lb pistachios, finely chopped**

**zest of 1 orange**

For the syrup

**450g/1lb/2¼ cups sugar**

**250ml/9fl oz/1 cup water**

**30–45ml/2–3 tbsp orange flower water**

In a small pan, melt the butter with the oil. Brush a little on the base and sides of a 12inch/30cm square cake tin (pan). Place a sheet of filo in the bottom and brush with the melted butter and oil. Continue making layers of pastry with half the quantity of filo sheets, making sure each sheet is brushed with the butter and oil. Ease the sheets into the corners of the tin and trim the edges if they flop over the rim. Preheat the oven to 325°F/160°C/Gas 3.

Once you have brushed the last of that half batch of filo sheets, mix the pistachios with the orange zest and spread them over the top. Then continue as before, layering the remaining filo sheets while brushing them with the butter and oil. Brush the final layer as well, then, using a sharp knife, cut diagonal parallel lines through all the layers to the bottom to form small diamond-shaped portions. Bake the baklava in the oven for about 1 hour, until the top is golden – if the top is still pale, turn the oven up for a few minutes at the end.

Meanwhile, make the syrup. Put the sugar and water into a heavy pan. Bring the liquid to the boil, stirring all the time, until the sugar dissolves. Reduce the heat, stir in the orange flower water and simmer for about 15 minutes, until it thickens a little. Leave the syrup to cool in the pan.

When the baklava is ready, remove it from the oven and slowly pour the cold syrup over the piping hot pastry. Put the baklava back into the oven for just 2–3 minutes – this will help it soak up the syrup – then take it out and leave it to cool in the tin. When it is completely cool, lift the baklava out of the tin, and arrange on a serving dish.

# Nights of Lebanon

This pudding is called *layali loubnan*, which literally translates as 'nights of Lebanon'. Traditionally, it is made of layers of semolina, *kashta* (a scented creamy mixture), bananas and nuts, but it can also include apricot, cherry or rose petal conserves, or even tahini.

## Serves six to eight

For the semolina

**600ml/1 pint/2½ cups whole (full-fat) milk**

**60ml/4 tbsp sugar**

**90g/3½oz/½ cup fine semolina**

**1–2 mastic crystals, pulverised with a little sugar**

For the kashta cream

**15ml/1 tbsp rice flour**

**150ml/5fl oz/⅔ cup whole (full-fat) milk**

**300ml/½ pint double (heavy) cream**

**30–45ml/2–3 tbsp sugar**

**2 slices of white bread, processed or ground into crumbs**

**15ml/1 tbsp rose flower water**

For the topping

**2 bananas, finely sliced**

**juice of ½ lemon**

**30ml/2 tbsp chopped pistachio nuts**

**30ml/2 tbsp flaked (sliced) almonds**

**45–60ml/3–4 tbsp runny honey**

**30ml/2 tbsp orange flower water**

First prepare the semolina. Heat the milk and sugar in a heavy pan, stirring until the sugar has dissolved. Bring the milk to the boil, then add in the semolina and mastic, beating vigorously. Reduce the heat and simmer, stirring from time to time, until the mixture begins to thicken. Pour it into a serving dish, level it with the back of a spoon and leave to cool.

To prepare the cream layer, mix the rice flour with a little milk. Heat the rest of the milk and cream in a heavy pan, together with the sugar, stirring constantly, until almost boiling. Stir a spoonful of the hot mixture into the rice flour mixture and then pour the rice flour mixture back into the pan. Add the breadcrumbs and rose water to the pan and stir vigorously until the mixture is thick and creamy. Leave to cool a little, then spoon it over the semolina, which should have set. Leave to cool and set, then chill the pudding.

A short time before serving, arrange the sliced bananas in a layer over the pudding. Squeeze lemon juice over the top to prevent them from turning brown. Sprinkle the nuts on top. Heat the honey with the orange blossom water and pour it over the nuts. Once the honey has cooled, chill the pudding until ready to eat.

# Puffed fritters in syrup

Lebanese Christians prepare these fritters, or *awamat*, on 6 January to celebrate the baptism of Christ. The tradition of eating fritters in syrup at religious occasions dates back to the medieval feasts of Baghdad and, later, to the lavish banquets of the Ottoman empire.

### Serves six

2.5ml/½ tsp dried yeast

2.5ml/½ tsp sugar

150ml/5fl oz/⅔ cup lukewarm water

175g/6oz/1½ cups plain (all-purpose) flour

50g/2oz/½ cup rice flour

1–2 mastic crystals, pulverised with 5ml/1 tsp sugar

pinch of salt

sunflower oil, for frying

For the syrup

225g/8oz/1 cup sugar

150ml/5fl oz/⅔ cup water

30ml/2 tbsp orange flower water

In a small bowl, cream the yeast with the sugar in the lukewarm water until frothy. Sift the flours with the mastic and salt into a bowl and make a well in the centre. Pour the creamed yeast into the well and draw in a little of the flour to form a batter. Dust the surface of the batter with a little of the remaining flour, cover the bowl with a clean, damp cloth, and leave for about 20 minutes.

Remove the cloth and draw in the rest of the flour to make a soft, sticky dough, adding a little extra water if necessary. Cover the bowl with the damp cloth again and leave the dough to prove for about 2 hours, until doubled in size.

Meanwhile, prepare the syrup. Place the sugar and water in a heavy pan and bring it to the boil, stirring constantly. Stir in the orange flower water, reduce the heat and simmer for about 10 minutes, until the syrup coats the back of a wooden spoon. Turn off the heat and leave the syrup to cool.

Heat enough sunflower oil in a pan for frying. Take a portion of the dough in your hand and squeeze it through thumb and forefinger to drop little balls of dough into the oil. Alternatively, use two teaspoons – the shapes do not need to be perfect. Fry the fritters in batches until golden brown, and drain on kitchen paper.

While still warm, soak the fritters in the cold syrup for 10–15 minutes. Scoop them out and serve at room temperature with a little of the syrup drizzled over them.

# Wheat in fragrant honey

In Lebanon, this nourishing dessert made with young wheat or barley is known as *kamhiyeh*, prepared to mark significant events. For Muslims, it's a dish for nursing mothers; Jews serve it to celebrate a baby's first tooth; for Christians, it's eaten on 4 December in honour of St Barbara.

## Serves six

**225g/8oz/1 cup whole wheat grains, soaked overnight and drained**

**1 litre/1¾ pints/4 cups water**

**60–90ml/4–6 tbsp fragrant runny honey**

**30ml/2 tbsp orange flower water**

**30ml/2 tbsp rose flower water**

**30–45ml/2–3 tbsp raisins or sultanas (golden raisins), soaked in warm water for 30 minutes and drained**

**30ml/2 tbsp pine nuts, soaked in water for 2 hours**

**30ml/2 tbsp blanched almonds, soaked in water for 2 hours**

**seeds of ½ pomegranate**

Place the soaked whole wheat grains in a heavy pan with the water and bring to the boil. Reduce the heat, cover, and simmer for 1 hour, until the wheat is tender, and most of the water is absorbed.

Meanwhile, heat the honey and stir in the orange blossom and rose waters – don't let the mixture boil. Stir in the raisins or sultanas and turn off the heat.

Transfer the wheat grains to a serving bowl, or individual bowls, and pour the honey and raisins over the top.

Garnish with the nuts and pomegranate seeds and serve while still warm, or leave to cool and chill in the refrigerator before serving.

# Pomegranate salad with pine nuts

Variations of this pretty salad, *salatet al rumman*, are prepared. It is offered as a mark of hospitality, as a palate cleanser, or just as a refreshing sweet fruit salad on a hot day.

## Serves four to six

45–60ml/3–4 tbsp pine nuts

3 ripe pomegranates

30ml/2 tbsp orange flower water

15–30ml/1–2 tbsp fragrant runny honey

a handful of small fresh mint leaves

Place the pine nuts in a bowl, cover with the water and leave for 2 hours.

Cut the pomegranates into quarters, transferring any excess juice to a bowl. Extract the seeds, taking care to discard the pith and membrane, and place in a bowl with the juice.

Drain the pine nuts and add them to the bowl. Stir in the orange blossom water and honey, cover the bowl, and chill in the refrigerator.

Serve the salad chilled, or at room temperature, decorated with a few mint leaves.

Left **Snowy white ice cream**  Right **Stuffed date fudge**

# Snowy white ice cream

Influenced by the Ottomans and their white ice cream, this traditional ice, *buza al halib*, is enjoyed throughout the Arab world. The silky ground orchid root, *sahlab*, gives the ice cream its pearly white colour as well as acting as a thickening agent.

## Serves four

1.2 litres/2 pints/5 cups whole (full-fat) milk

225g/8oz sugar

45ml/3 tbsp sahlab

30–45ml/2–3 tbsp orange flower water

Put the milk and sugar into a pan (keep a little milk back to slake the sahlab). Bring to the boil, stirring constantly, until the sugar dissolves. Reduce the heat and simmer for 10 minutes.

Put the sahlab into a small bowl. Mix it with a little cold milk, then stir in a spoonful of the hot, sweetened milk, then pour the sahlab mixture into the pan of milk, stirring all the time. Stir the orange blossom water into the pan. Beat gently and continue to simmer for 10–15 minutes more.

Pour into a freezer container, cover with a dry dish towel and leave to cool. Remove the towel, cover with foil and place in the freezer to set, beating it at intervals to disperse the ice crystals, or pour into an ice cream maker and churn according to the instructions.

# Stuffed date fudge

This is a popular Arab sweetmeat prepared for all festive occasions. As dates play an important role in the eastern Mediterranean, there is rarely a festive meal where they do not appear. This one, known as *ranginak*, is prepared as a welcoming treat for guests as dates are regarded as a gift of hospitality. Dates are stuffed with walnuts then wrapped in a fudgy covering.

## Serves four to six

500g/1¼lb moist, pitted dates

roughly 115g/4oz walnuts, enough halves to fill each date

225g/8oz butter

45–60ml/3–4 tbsp sugar

225g/8oz/2 cups plain (all-purpose) flour

15ml/1 tbsp ground almonds

15ml/1 tbsp ground pistachios

Find the opening in each date where the stone has been extracted and stuff it with a walnut half. As you work, place the stuffed dates in a lightly greased, shallow heatproof dish, packing them tightly together.

In a small pan, melt the butter with the sugar and stir in the flour. Continue to stir it over a low flame until the mixture begins to turn golden brown, then pour it over the dates.

Leave to set, then sprinkle the ground nuts over the top. Cut into little squares, each containing a stuffed date, and serve them with tea or coffee.

# Stuffed red date preserve

This is a beautiful and unusual preserve, *mrabba al-balah*, revered in Lebanon and Jordan. Dates are one of the region's most ancient staple foods, coveted for their nutritional value and their sweetness. It is said that the Bedouin are unable to sleep under fruit-laden date palms, such is their urge to pick and eat the fruit.

## Makes 2 × 450g/1lb jars

**40 fresh, ripe red dates**

**40 blanched whole almonds**

**500g/1¼lb/2½ cups sugar**

**juice and rind (cut into fine strips) of 2 clementines**

**6–8 cloves**

Place the dates in a heavy pan and just cover with water. Bring to the boil, reduce the heat and simmer for 5 minutes to soften the dates. Drain the dates, reserving the water, and carefully push the stone out of each date with a sharp knife. Stuff each date with an almond.

Pour the reserved cooking water back into the pan and add the sugar, clementine juice and rind, and cloves. Bring the water to the boil, stirring constantly until the sugar has dissolved.

Reduce the heat and drop in the stuffed dates. Simmer for 1 hour, until the syrup is fairly thick. Leave the dates to cool in the syrup, then spoon them into sterilised jars to store. Enjoy with bread, yogurt, milk puddings, or just on their own.

# Quince preserve

Many delectable jams and syrups are made in the eastern Mediterranean, but in Lebanon quince jam is particularly sought after as the fragrant fruit is associated with love and marriage. More of a conserve than a spreadable jam, this quince preserve, *mrabba al-safarjal*, is best spooned generously on to freshly baked bread, or drizzled over yogurt.

## Makes 4 × 450g/1lb jars

**1kg/2¼lb fresh quinces, peeled (optional), quartered, cored and diced**

**juice of 2 lemons**

**500g/1¼lb/2½ cups sugar**

Place the prepared fruit in a heavy pan and sprinkle with the lemon juice to prevent it from turning brown. Pour in about 600ml/1 pint/2½ cups water – just enough to surround the fruit – and add the sugar.

Bring to the boil, stirring constantly until the sugar dissolves. Reduce the heat and simmer for 1–1½ hours, until the fruit has turned a deep reddish-pink. Turn up the heat and boil vigorously for 2 minutes.

Spoon the mixture into sterilised jars. Seal and store in a cool place for 6 months, if you are not eating immediately.

Left **Lebanese coffee with cardamom**  Right **Rose water sherbert**

# Lebanese coffee with cardamom

*Kahwe Lebananieh* is very similar to the better-known Turkish version, although it is traditionally flavoured with cardamom. Very finely ground coffee is prepared in a distinctive long-handled pot known as a *rakweh*. It is generally served black, and already sweetened.

## Serves two

**20ml/4 heaped tsp finely ground coffee**

**seeds of 2–3 cardamom pods, ground**

**10ml/2 tsp sugar, or more to taste**

Put two coffee-cupfuls of water into the rakweh, or a small pot, and heap the coffee, cardamom and sugar on the surface. Place on the heat. As the water begins to boil, stir the coffee mixture into the water. Allow to bubble for 2–3 minutes, stirring constantly, then pour the coffee into the cups. Serve immediately, but let the coffee sit for a moment before drinking, so that the grounds sink to the bottom of the cup.

Cook's tip | **To grind the cardamom pods, simply crush the pods in a mortar and pestle, or on a wooden board with the flat side of a heavy-bladed knife. You want to split them rather than grind them to dust.**

# Rose water sherbert

A deliciously fragrant drink with an air of antiquity and elegance, *sharab al ward* is typically offered in sophisticated surroundings, as a drink of hospitality and celebration. The cordial is diluted to serve; with added water this makes about 900ml/1½ pints.

**500g/1¼lb/2½ cups sugar**

**250ml/9fl oz/1 cup water**

**juice of ½ lemon**

**150ml/5fl oz/⅔ cup rose flower water**

**red food colouring (optional)**

**fresh fragrant rose petals and a slice of lemon, to decorate**

Put the sugar and water into a heavy-based pan and bring it to the boil, stirring constantly until the sugar is dissolved. Stir in the lemon juice and rose water and reduce the heat. Simmer gently for 15–20 minutes, until the syrup is thick and coats the back of a wooden spoon.

If using food colouring, stir in a few drops to turn the syrup rose pink. Leave to cool in the pan, then pour it into a sterilised bottle and store in a cool place.

When ready to serve a glass of sherbert, drop several ice cubes into a stylish glass. Pour 15–30ml/1–2 tbsp (or more if you like) of the syrup into the glass, and dilute to taste with cold water. Garnish with rose petals and a slice of lemon and serve immediately.

# Nutritional notes

The nutritional analysis is calculated per serving or item, unless otherwise stated. If the recipe gives a range, such as Serves 4–6, the analysis will be for the smaller i.e. 6 servings. The analysis does not include optional ingredients, such as salt added to taste. Key: Eng = energy; Prot = protein; Carb = carbohydrates; Sug = sugars; Sat = saturates; Chol = cholesterol; Calc = calcium; Fib = fibre; Sod = sodium.

p70 | **Yogurt cheese balls with olive oil** Eng 177kcal/740kJ; Prot 10g; Carb 13g, of which sug 13g; Fat 10g, of which sats 4g; Chol 18mg; Calc 333mg; Fib 0.0 g; Sod 461mg

p73 | **Olives with chillies** Eng 291kcal/1196kJ; Prot 1g; Carb 0g; Fat 32g, of which sats 5g; Chol 0mg; Calc 44mg; Fib 1.8g; Sod 1407mg

p73 | **Fried halloumi with zahtar** Eng 328kcal/1356kJ; Prot 16.2g; Carb 1.7g, of which sug 0g; Fat 28.6g, of which sats 13.1g; Chol 48mg; Calc 311mg; Fib 0g; Sod 1331mg

p74 | **Aubergines with pomegranate molasses** Eng 228kcal/948kJ; Prot 2g; Carb 21g, of which sug 19g; Fat 16g, of which sats 2g; Chol 0mg; Calc 56mg; Fib 3.0 g; Sod 10mg

p77 | **Spicy bean balls** Eng 303kcal/1282kJ; Prot 18.5g; Carb 44.7g, of which sug 5.2g; Fat 6.9g, of which sats 1.2g; Chol 0mg; Calc 88mg; Fib 7.2g; Sod 16mg

p79 | **Spicy tartare balls** Eng 148kcal/618kJ; Prot 11g; Carb 19g, of which sug 2g; Fat 4g, of which sats 1g; Chol 28mg; Calc 40mg; Fib 0.7 g; Sod 112mg

p81 | **Smoked aubergine dip** Eng 91kcal/375kJ; Prot 1g; Carb 2.2g, of which sug 1.5g; Fat 8.8g, of which sats 1.4g; Chol 8mg; Calc 8mg; Fib 1.4g; Sod 52mg

p82 | **Spicy walnut and yogurt dip** Eng 319kcal/1327kJ; Prot 9g; Carb 17g, of which sug 13g; Fat 24g, of which sats 4g; Chol 8mg; Calc 188mg; Fib 1.8 g; Sod 332mg

p84 | **Village cheese and labneh dip** Eng 192kcal/797kJ; Prot 9.5g; Carb 2.3g, of which sug 1.5g; Fat 16.7g, of which sats 8.4g; Chol 29mg; Calc 217mg; Fib 0g; Sod 631mg

p84 | **Tahini dip with parsley** Eng 231kcal/956kJ; Prot 7g; Carb 1g, of which sug 1g; Fat 22g, of which sats 3g; Chol 0mg; Calc 258mg; Fib 3.1 g; Sod 106mg

p86 | **Cheese and cucumber dip** Eng 219kcal/907kJ; Prot 10g; Carb 2g, of which sug 2g; Fat 19g, of which sats 9g; Chol 39mg; Calc 252mg; Fib 0.5g; Sod 913mg

p89 | **Lebanese hummus with orange** Eng 265kcal/1101kJ; Prot 10g; Carb 12.6g, of which sug 0.8g; Fat 19.7g, of which sats 2.8g; Chol 0mg; Calc 210mg; Fib 4.7g; Sod 15mg

p90 | **Toasted bread salad with sumac** Eng 120kcal/499kJ; Prot 2.4g; Carb 7.7g, of which sug 7.5g; Fat 9.1g, of which sats 1.4g; Chol 0mg; Calc 54mg; Fib 3g; Sod 18mg

p93 | **Fresh broad bean salad** Eng 111kcal/464kJ; Prot 6.8g; Carb 10.7g, of which sug 2g; Fat 4.8g, of which sats 0.7g; Chol 0mg; Calc 64mg; Fib 5.8g; Sod 10mg

p95 | **Aubergine with pomegranate seeds** Eng 90kcal/374kJ; Prot 2.2g; Carb 7.3g, of which sug 6.3g; Fat 6g, of which sats 0.8g; Chol 0mg; Calc 39mg; Fib 3.1g; Sod 10mg

p96 | **Parsley and bulgur salad** Eng 232kcal/965kJ; Prot 5.2g; Carb 34.6g, of which sug 2.7g; Fat 8.4g, of which sats 1.1g; Chol 0mg; Calc 51mg; Fib 1.4g; Sod 12

p99 | **Olive and pepper salad** Eng 68kcal/283kJ; Prot 1.1g; Carb 4.6g, of which sug 4.4g; Fat 5.2g, of which sats 0.8g; Chol 0mg; Calc 30mg; Fib 1.9g; Sod 232mg

p100 | **Chickpea and bulgur salad with mint** Eng 267kcal/1116kJ; Prot 8.6g; Carb 34.1g, of which sug 3.3g; Fat 11.4g, of which sats 1.4g; Chol 0mg; Calc 89mg; Fib 4.1g; Sod 153mg

p103 | **Orange, lemon and onion salad** Eng 71kcal/298kJ; Prot 2g; Carb 14g, of which sug 13g; Fat 1g, of which sats 0g; Chol 0mg; Calc 82mg; Fib 2.9 Sod 310mg

p104 | **Cabbage salad** Eng 92kcal/381kJ; Prot 1g; Carb 5g, of which sug 4g; Fat 8g, of which sats 1g; Chol 0mg; Calc 44mg; Fib 1.9 g; Sod 104mg

p104 | **Lebanese country salad** Eng 51kcal/210kJ; Prot 1.1g; Carb 2.5g, of which sug 2.4g; Fat 4.1g, of which sats 0.6g; Chol 0mg; Calc 36mg; Fib 1.3g; Sod 8mg

p107 | **Potato salad with nigella and lime** Eng 234kcal/976kJ; Prot3; Carb 22g, of which sug 6g; Fat 16g, of which sats 2g; Chol 0mg; Calc 49mg; Fib 2.1 g; Sod 114mg

p108 | **Egg and onion salad** Eng 308kcal/1272kJ; Prot 12g; Carb 4g, of which sug 3g; Fat 27g, of which sats 5g; Chol 289mg; Calc 129mg; Fib 2.0 g; Sod 769mg

p111 | **Tomato salad** Eng 94kcal/390kJ; Prot 1g; Carb 5g, of which sug 5g; Fat 8g, of which sats 1g; Chol 0mg; Calc 15mg; Fib 1.3g; Sod 111mg

p114 | **Saffron broth with chicken noodles** Eng 260kcal/1088kJ; Prot 28.4g; Carb 11.3g, of which sug 0g; Fat 11.3g, of which sats 3.4g; Chol 86mg; Calc 17mg; Fib 0g; Sod 106mg

p117 | **Lamb and wheat soup** Eng 364kcal/1516kJ; Prot 18.8g; Carb 29.2g, of which sug 0g; Fat 19.4g, of which sats 9.8g; Chol 73mg; Calc 25mg; Fib 0g; Sod 73mg

p118 | **Fish soup with peppers and potatoes** Eng 266kcal/1118kJ; Prot 26g; Carb 20g, of which sug 9g; Fat 10g, of which sats 2g; Chol 125mg; Calc 102mg; Fib 2.5 g; Sod 438mg

p121 | **Bedouin spinach lentil soup** Eng 188kcal/786kJ; Prot 8g; Carb 16g, of which sug 3g; Fat 11g, of which sats 3g; Chol 11mg; Calc 117mg; Fib 3.7g; Sod 661mg

p122 | **Red lentil soup** Eng 235kcal/991kJ; Prot 13g; Carb 28.4g, of which sug 3.7g; Fat 8.9g, of which sats 2.2g; Chol 0mg; Calc 66mg; Fib 2.9g; Sod 40mg

p125 | **Chilled cucumber yogurt soup** Eng 77kcal/322kJ; Prot 6.9g; Carb 10.3g, of which sug 10.1g; Fat 1.3g, of which sats 0.6g; Chol 2mg; Calc 255mg; Fib 0.3g; Sod 106mg

p125 | **Thick mung bean soup** Eng 296kcal/1224kJ; Prot 12g; Carb 32g, of which sug 8g; Fat 14g, of which sats 3g; Chol 5mg; Calc 64mg; Fib 1.8g; Sod 26mg

p126 | **Fermented bulgur broth** Eng 164kcal/683kJ; Prot 4g; Carb 18g, of which sug 4g; Fat 9g, of which sats 1g; Chol 2mg; Calc 58mg; Fib 0.6 g; Sod 703mg

p128 | **Bulgur and lamb patties** Eng 407kcal/1694kJ; Prot 20.1g; Carb 35.9g, of which sug 3.9g; Fat 20.9g, of which sats 5.3g; Chol 57mg; Calc 65mg; Fib 1.4g; Sod 400mg

p130 | **Little meat pastries** Eng 555kcal/2308kJ; Prot 14.5g; Carb 34.8g, of which sug 4.4g; Fat 41.5g, of which sats 4.3g; Chol 32mg; Calc 76mg; Fib 0.9g; Sod 275mg

p133 | **Cheese and dill pastries** Eng 526kcal/2192kJ; Prot 20.6g; Carb 30.5g, of which sug 1.8g; Fat 37.4g, of which sats 11.3g; Chol 179mg; Calc 352mg; Fib 0.5g; Sod 950mg

p134 | **Spinach pastries** Eng 441kcal/1834kJ; Prot 9g; Carb 36.8g, of which sug 7.2g; Fat 30.4g, of which sats 2.3g; Chol 6mg; Calc 212mg; Fib 3.1g; Sod 371mg

p137 | **Garlicky chicken wings with sumac** Eng 272kcal/1132kJ; Prot 23g; Carb 1.4g, of which sug 0.1g; Fat 19.5g, of which sats 4.7g; Chol 98mg; Calc 12mg; Fib 0.1g; Sod 68mg

p137 | **Eggs with garlic** Eng 220kcal/911kJ; Prot 12g; Carb 0g; Fat 20g, of which sats 5g; Chol 362mg; Calc 65mg; Fib 0.1 g; Sod 243mg

p139 | **Feta, pepper and olive frittata** Eng 303kcal/1252kJ; Prot 13.8g; Carb 5.5g, of which sug 4.6g; Fat 25.4g, of which sats 8.6g; Chol 217mg; Calc 230mg; Fib 3.1g; Sod 2304mg

p140 | **Bread omelette with courgettes** Eng 230kcal/958kJ; Prot 10g; Carb 12g, of which sug 2g; Fat 16g, of which sats 5g; Chol 242mg; Calc 77mg; Fib 0.9 g; Sod 276mg

p142 | **Aubergine with basterma and halloumi** Eng 358kcal/ 1501kJ; Prot 22g; Carb 25g, of which sug 4g; Fat 19g, of which sats 8g; Chol 158mg; Calc 302mg; Fib 4.2g; Sod 622mg

p145 | **Syrian sausage rolls** Eng 449kcal/1875kJ; Prot 20g; Carb 31g, of which sug 1g; Fat 29g, of which sats 3g; Chol 56mg; Calc 70mg; Fib 0.0g; Sod 378mg

p146 | **Little spicy lamb pizzas** Eng 418kcal/1769kJ; Prot 23g; Carb 69g, of which sug 11g; Fat 7g, of which sats 3g; Chol 50mg; Calc 226mg; Fib 3.3g; Sod 231mg

p149 | **Feta breads** Eng 568/2395kJ; Prot 19g; Carb 91g, sug 24g; Fat 17g, of which sats 8g; Chol 39mg; Calc 431mg; Fib 5.7g; Sod 986mg

p151 | **Zahtar flatbreads** Eng 310kcal/1314kJ; Prot 8.2g; Carb 60.9g, of which sug 1.1g; Fat 5.6g, of which sats 0.8g; Chol 0mg; Calc 119mg; Fib 2.3g; Sod 169mg p152 | **Pitta bread** Eng 207kcal/877kJ; Prot 5.4g; Carb 44.5g, of which sug 0.9g; Fat 2g, of which sats 0.3g; Chol 0mg; Calc 80mg; Fib 1.8g; Sod 677mg

p157 | **Freekeh with pistachios** Eng 342kcal/ 1420kJ; Prot 8.7g; Carb 36.2g, of which sug 3.2g; Fat 18.6g, of which sats 2.2g; Chol 0mg; Calc 49mg; Fib 1.7g; Sod 226mg

p158 | **Bulgur with lamb and chickpeas** Eng 366kcal/1533kJ; Prot 18.5g; Carb 51.8g, of which sug 2.7g; Fat 10.3g, of which sats 2.5g; Chol 25mg; Calc 87mg; Fib 4g; Sod 46mg

p161 | **Bulgur with fruit and nuts** Eng 577kcal/ 2401kJ; Prot 12g; Carb 56g, of which sug 26g; Fat 35g, of which sats 4g; Chol 4mg; Calc 161mg; Fib 4.7g; Sod 288mg

p162 | **Rice with lamb and chestnuts** Eng 440kcal/1862kJ; Prot 14g; Carb 80g, of which sug 4g; Fat 9g, of which sats 4g; Chol 35mg; Calc 73mg; Fib 2.2g; Sod 100mg

p165 | **Bulgur with courgettes, mint and dill** Eng 216kcal/898kJ; Prot 5g; Carb 32g, of which sug 8g; Fat 5g, of which sats 19g; Chol 19mg; Calc 47mg; Fib 0.8g; Sod 85mg

p166 | **Rice with aubergine** Eng 464kcal/1946kJ; Prot 15g; Carb 50g, of which sug 6g; Fat 24g, of which sats 4g; Chol 31mg; Calc 78mg; Fib 4.8g; Sod 102mg

p169 | **Saffron rice with pine nuts** Eng 316kcal/ 1316kJ; Prot 5.5g; Carb 45.2g, of which sug 0.3g; Fat 12.5g, of which sats 5g; Chol 20mg; Calc 13mg; Fib 0.2g; Sod 246mg

p169 | **Rice and mastic parcels** Eng 356kcal/ 1459kJ; Prot 5g; Carb 57g, of which sug 2g; Fat 12g, of which sats 4g; Chol 13mg; Calc 44mg; Fib 0.5g; Sod 139mg

p171 | **Brown rice with chickpeas and basterma** Eng 337kcal/1418kJ; Prot 12g; Carb 46g, of which sug 6g; Fat 13g, of which sats 6g; Chol 27mg; Calc 73mg; Fib 3.6g; Sod 592mg

p172 | **Lebanese couscous with chicken** Eng 376kcal/1574kJ; Prot 31.9g; Carb 44.6g, of which sug 4g; Fat 8.8g, of which sats 3.5g; Chol 70mg; Calc 49mg; Fib 1.1g; Sod 128mg

p175 | **Brown beans with feta and parsley** Eng 200kcal/846kJ; Prot 13.6g; Carb 27.3g, of which sug 1.5g; Fat 4.8g, of which sats 0.7g; Chol 0mg; Calc 65mg; Fib 9.4g; Sod 12mg

p176 | **Butter bean stew** Eng 295kcal/1251kJ; Prot 18.8g; Carb 45.4g, of which sug 11.5g; Fat 5.7g, of which sats 0.9g; Chol 0mg; Calc 108mg; Fib 14.1g; Sod 29mg

p179 | **Pulses in cabbage leaves** Eng 261kcal/ 1097kJ; Prot 13g; Carb 40g, of which sug 5g; Fat 7g, of which sats 3g; Chol 14mg; Calc 104mg; Fib 5.8g; Sod 78mg

p180 | **Warm white bean purée with feta and olives** Eng 195kcal/810kJ; Prot 6g; Carb 9g, of which sug 2g; Fat 15g, of which sats 4g; Chol 13mg; Calc 105mg; Fib 2.8g; Sod 881mg

p183 | **Chickpeas with bread and yogurt** Eng 354kcal/1489kJ; Prot 21.5g; Carb 41.1g, of which

sug 13.1g; Fat 13g, of which sats 3.4g; Chol 11mg; Calc 38mg; Fib 6.5g; Sod 175mg

p184 | **Lentils and rice with onions** Eng 411kcal/1717kJ; Prot 13.7g; Carb 58.3g, of which sug 7g; Fat 14.3g, of which sats 1.8g; Chol 0mg; Calc 68mg; Fib 5g; Sod 9mg

p187 | **Green lentils with bulgur** Eng 306kcal/ 1284kJ; Prot 13.8g; Carb 52.8g, of which sug 4.2g; Fat 5.4g, of which sats 0.6g; Chol 0mg; Calc 63mg; Fib 4.3g; Sod 9mg

p188 | **Lentils with spring onions, parsley and mint** Eng 308kcal/1293kJ; Prot 14g; Carb 29g, of which sug 2g; Fat 16g, of which sats 2g; Chol 0mg; Calc 59mg; Fib 5.4g; Sod 107mg

p192 | **Jordanian fish stew with tamarind** Eng 317kcal/1337kJ; Prot 32g; Carb 26g, of which sug 5g; Fat10g, of which sats 1g; Chol 63mg; Calc 103mg; Fib 1.2g; Sod 291mg

p195 | **Saffron fish stew with couscous** Eng 348kcal/1449kJ; Prot 22g; Carb 15g, of which sug 4g; Fat 23g, of which sats 3g; Chol 80mg; Calc 166mg; Fib 1.2g; Sod 443mg

p196 | **Fish baked in tahini sauce** Eng 437kcal/ 1810kJ; Prot 25g; Carb 5g, of which sug 3g; Fat 35g, of which sats 5g; Chol 38mg; Calc 374mg; Fib 4.9g; Sod 129mg

p199 | **Fried red mullet with pitta bread** Eng 556kcal/2318kJ; Prot 35.1g; Carb 23.9g, of which sug 1.2g; Fat 36.2g, of which sats 4.4g; Chol 0mg; Calc 386mg; Fib 4.2g; Sod 329mg

p200 | **Fish sautéed with almonds** Eng 298kcal/ 1245kJ; Prot 37g; Carb 1g, of which sug 1g; Fat 16g, of which sats 2g; Chol 86mg; Calc 58mg; Fib 1.0g; Sod 214mg

p200 | **Charcoal-grilled trout with lemon** Eng 279kcal/1176kJ; Prot 47.3g; Carb 1.7g, of which sug 0.1g; Fat 9.4g, of which sats 2.2g; Chol 192mg; Calc 78mg; Fib 0.2g; Sod 175mg

p202 | **Poached fish with rice and pine nuts** Eng 385kcal/1611kJ; Prot 28.3g; Carb 40.6g, of which sug 4.9g; Fat 12.2g, of which sats 1.8g; Chol 96mg; Calc 68mg; Fib 1.3g; Sod 90mg

p205 | **Baked fish with bay, oranges and limes** Eng 257kcal/1078kJ; Prot 35g; Carb 1.1g, of which sug 1.1g; Fat 12.6g, of which sats 4g; Chol 153mg; Calc 56mg; Fib 0g; Sod 160mg

p206 | **Roasted fish with chilli** Eng 772kcal/ 3223kJ; Prot 78.8g; Carb 13.1g, of which sug 10.3g; Fat 45.3g, of which sats 6.5g; Chol 288mg; Calc 292mg; Fib 4.9g; Sod 276mg

p209 | **Spicy fish** Eng 227kcal/950kJ; Prot26; Carb 13g, of which sug 10g; Fat 9g, of which sats 5g; Chol 79mg; Calc 75mg; Fib 1.8g; Sod 218mg

p210 | **Grilled fish in date coating** Eng 335kcal/ 1415kJ; Prot 32g; Carb 41g, of which sug 40g; Fat 6g, of which sats 0g; Chol 0mg; Calc 55mg; Fib 2.8g; Sod 190mg

p213 | **Fried sardines with lemon** Eng 358kcal/1488kJ; Prot 18.7g; Carb 11.7g, of which sug 0.2g; Fat 26.5g, of which sats 4.4g; Chol 0mg; Calc 107mg; Fib 0.5g; Sod 96mg

p214 | **Fish with tomato and pomegranate sauce** Eng 284kcal/1192kJ; Prot 41.7g; Carb 6.9g, of which sug 6.9g; Fat 10.1g, of which sats 1.5g; Chol 104mg; Calc 28mg; Fib 0.8g; Sod 149mg

p217 | **Fish kibbeh with onion and orange** Eng 453kcal/1884kJ; Prot 29.7g; Carb 22.8g, of which sug 11.5g; Fat 27.7g, of which sats 9.7g; Chol 93mg; Calc 231mg; Fib 1.1g; Sod 178mg

p218 | **Tangy prawn and pepper kebabs** Eng 102kcal/427kJ; Prot 9.7g; Carb 8.6g, of which sug 8.3g; Fat 3.4g, of which sats 0.5g; Chol 98mg; Calc 48mg; Fib 1.4g; Sod 109mg

p221 | **Sautéed prawns with coriander and lime** Eng 106kcal/442kJ; Prot 11.8g; Carb 1.2g, of which sug 0.4g; Fat 6.1g, of which sats 0.9g; Chol 122mg; Calc 75mg; Fib 0.8g; Sod 123mg

p222 | **Squid** Eng 510kcal/873kJ; Prot 16g; Carb 2g, of which sug 0g; Fat 16g, of which sats 2g; Chol 225mg; Calc 43mg; Fib 0.2g; Sod 211mg

p225 | **Langoustine shish** Eng 82kcal/348kJ; Prot 15g; Carb 4g, of which sug 3g; Fat 1g, of which sats 0g; Chol 156mg; Calc 80mg; Fib 1.2g; Sod 259mg

p228 | **Lamb kibbeh with onions and pine nuts** Eng 399kcal/1659kJ; Prot 20.6g; Carb 30.4g, of which sug 9.6g; Fat 22.4g, of which sats 5.4g; Chol 57mg; Calc 69mg; Fib 2.5g; Sod 73mg

p231 | **Meat patties** Eng 176kcal/736kJ; Prot 18g; Carb 7g, of which sug 2g; Fat 8g, of which sats 2g; Chol 44mg; Calc 42mg; Fib 0.8g; Sod 50mg

p233 | **Roasted leg of lamb with lamb rice** Eng 555kcal/2312kJ; Prot 33.1g; Carb 39.6g, of which sug 4.9g; Fat 26.8g, of which sats 8.9g; Chol 115mg; Calc 36mg; Fib 1.3g; Sod 113mg

p235 | **Meatballs with cherries and cinnamon** Eng 225kcal/935kJ; Prot 16g; Carb 5g, of which sug 0g; Fat 16g, of which sats 7g; Chol 70mg; Calc 43mg; Fib 0.1g; Sod 122mg

p236 | **Baked lamb and potato pie** Eng 548kcal/2289kJ; Prot 23.3g; Carb 39.6g, of which sug 8.7g; Fat 34.2g, of which sats 16.1g; Chol 104mg; Calc 174mg; Fib 2.8g; Sod 318mg

p239 | **Meat and bulgur balls in yogurt** Eng 308kcal/1290kJ; Prot 17g; Carb 41g, of which sug 9g; Fat 9g, of which sats 4g; Chol 44mg; Calc 240mg; Fib 0.4g; Sod 192mg

p240 | **Lamb shanks with winter vegetables** Eng 620kcal/2591kJ; Prot 40g; Carbo 39g, of which sug 18g; Fat 35g, of which sats 10g; Chol 109mg; Calc 430mg; Fib 4.3g; Sod 543mg

p243 | **Lamb kebabs with hummus and dill** Eng 448kcal/1866kJ; Prot 24g; Carb 20g, of which sug 4g; Fat 31g, of which sats 9g; Chol 71mg; Calc 106mg; Fib 4.5g; Sod 507mg

p244 | **Spicy meat dumplings with yogurt** Eng 454kcal/1898kJ; Prot 27.2g; Carb 33.7g, of which sug 15.8g; Fat 24.8g, of which sats 9.3g; Chol 88mg; Calc 381mg; Fib 1.4g; Sod 237mg

p247 | **Pasha's meatballs in tomato sauce** Eng 485kcal/2014kJ; Prot 25.4g; Carb 18.1g, of which sug 11.7g; Fat 35.2g, of which sats 10.9g; Chol 95mg; Calc 66mg; Fib 2.7g; Sod 119mg p248 | **Lamb and plum stew** Eng 262kcal/1092kJ; Prot 18.4g; Carb 14.3g, of which sug 9.6g; Fat 15g, of which sats 6.7g; Chol 63mg; Calc 44mg; Fib 2.1g; Sod 212mg

p251 | **Dervish's beads** Eng 365kcal/1527kJ; Prot 18.7g; Carb 27.7g, of which sug 13.2g; Fat 20.8g, of which sats 6.8g; Chol 63mg; Calc 45mg; Fib 4.2g; Sod 111mg

p252 | **Stuffed breast of lamb with apricots** Eng 704kcal/2947kJ; Prot 31g; Carb 58g, of which sug 21g; Fat 41g, of which sats 11g; Chol 90mg; Calc 91mg; Fib 4.1g; Sod 244mg

p255 | **Roasted onions stuffed with lamb** Eng 263kcal/1094kJ; Prot 12.2g; Carb 29g, of which sug 11.4g; Fat 11.4g, of which sats 4.1g; Chol 37mg; Calc 59mg; Fib 2.4g; Sod 67mg

p256 | **Lamb-stuffed artichokes** Eng 277kcal/1153kJ; Prot 19.7g; Carb 14.3g, of which sug 7.3g; Fat 16.1g, of which sats 5.4g; Chol 67mg; Calc 61mg; Fib 2.2g; Sod 96mg

p258 | **Lamb and vegetable stew** Eng 182kcal/758kJ; Prot 17.5g; Carb 7.5g, of which sug 5.3g; Fat 9.4g, of which sats 4.1g; Chol 57mg; Calc 46mg; Fib 2.6g; Sod 69mg

p261 | **Lamb's liver with pomegranate molasses** Eng 257kcal/1074kJ; Prot 24g; Carb 8g, of which sug 6g; Fat 15g, of which sats 3g; Chol 484mg; Calc 46mg; Fib 1.2g; Sod 185mg

p262 | **Braised rabbit with aubergines** Eng 414kcal/1738kJ; Prot 38g; Carb 25g, of which sug 14g; Fat 19g, of which sats 6g; Chol 85mg; Calc 125mg; Fib 5.7g; Sod 264mg

p265 | **Spicy pigeons with olives** Eng 313kcal/1308kJ; Prot 34g; Carb 4g, of which sug 4g; Fat 19g, of which sats 5g; Chol 21mg; Calc 76mg; Fib 0.5g; Sod 501mg

p266 | **Aromatic chicken on pitta bread** Eng 408kcal/1726kJ; Prot 40.2g; Carb 44.7g, of which sug 1.8g; Fat 8.9g, of which sats 2.1g; Chol 65mg; Calc 90mg; Fib 1.7g; Sod 499mg

p269 | **Palestinian chicken with sumac** Eng 457kcal/1927kJ; Prot 39g; Carb 53g, of which sug 11g; Fat 12g, of which sats 7g; Chol 106mg; Calc 272mg; Fib 3.1g; Sod 549mg

p270 | **Chicken and molokhia stew with onions** Eng 342kcal/1441kJ; Prot 50g; Carb 21g, of which sug 16g; Fat 7g, of which sats 2g; Chol 180mg; Calc 133mg; Fib 6.3g; Sod 276mg

p273 | **Quail with walnuts and lemons** Eng 418kcal/1735kJ; Prot 32g; Carb 2g, of which sug 1g; Fat 32g, of which sats 3g; Chol 1mg; Calc 59mg; Fib 0.5g; Sod 194mg

p274 | **Roasted stuffed turkey** Eng 761kcal/3174kJ; Prot 63.9g; Carb 43.4g, of which sug 7.6g; Fat 36.9g, of which sats 12.5g; Chol 235mg; Calc 68mg; Fib 1.5g; Sod 272mg

p278 | **Potato kibbeh stuffed with spinach** Eng 345kcal/1441kJ; Prot 10g; Carb 42, of which sug 3g; Fat 16g, of which sats 4g; Chol 13mg; Calc 180mg; Fib 2.8g; Sod 411mg

p281 | **Potatoes with walnuts and rose petals** Eng 337kcal/1406kJ; Prot 6g; Carb 5g, of which sug 34g; Fat 21g, of which sats 3g; Chol 0mg; Calc 66mg; Fib 2.9g; Sod 124mg

p283 | **Chicory in olive oil** Eng 109kcal/447kJ; Prot 0.5g; Carb 2.5g, of which sug 0.7g; Fat 11.5g, of which sats 1.7g; Chol 0mg; Calc 19mg; Fib 0.8g; Sod 1mg

p284 | **Green beans with cumin and tomatoes** Eng 122kcal/507kJ; Prot 3g; Carb 10g, of which sug 8g; Fat 8g, of which sats 1g; Chol 0mg; Calc 64mg; Fib 2.9g; Sod 95mg

p287 | **Aubergines with rice** Eng 486kcal/2023kJ; Prot 10.8g; Carb 76.2g, of which sug 34.9g; Fat 16.8g, of which sats 2.3g; Chol 0mg; Calc 160mg; Fib 10.8g; Sod 26mg

p288 | **Aubergine and chickpea mousaka** Eng 467kcal/1953kJ; Prot 15g; Carb 43g, of which sug 18g; Fat 28g, of which sats 5g; Chol 8mg; Calc 112mg; Fib 6.8g; Sod 167mg

p291 | **Okra with tomatoes and coriander** Eng 143kcal/598kJ; Prot 4g; Carb 12g, of which sug 10g; Fat 9g, of which sats 1g; Chol 0mg; Calc 201mg; Fib 6.0g; Sod 117mg

p292 | **Courgettes in cheese** Eng 314kcal/1302kJ; Prot 23.3g; Carb 7.2g, of which sug 5.4g; Fat 21.6g, of which sats 10.2g; Chol 169mg; Calc 562mg; Fib 1.8g; Sod 504mg

p295 | **Stuffed courgettes with apricots** Eng 332kcal/1386kJ; Prot 7g; Carb 42g, of which sug 40g; Fat 16g, of which sats 2g; Chol 0mg; Calc 133mg; Fib 7.1g; Sod 241mg

p296 | **Roasted courgettes with vinegar** Eng 78kcal/322kJ; Prot 2.7g; Carb 3.3g, of which sug 2.1g; Fat 6g, of which sats 0.9g; Chol 0mg; Calc 36mg; Fib 1.3g; Sod 2mg

p296 | **Spicy potatoes with coriander** Eng 174kcal/723kJ; Prot 2.4g; Carb 15.5g, of which sug 1.2g; Fat 11.8g, of which sats 1.7g; Chol 0mg; Calc 16mg; Fib 0.9g; Sod 12mg

p299 | **Sweet-sour onions with tamarind** Eng 117kcal/487kJ; Prot1g; Carb 12g, of which sug 10g; Fat 8g, of which sats 1g; Chol 0mg; Calc 25mg; Fib 1.1g; Sod 69mg

p300 | **Spinach with tahini yogurt** Eng 435kcal/1818kJ; Prot 19.3g; Carb 45.1g, of which sug 20g; Fat 21.3g, of which sats 4.8g; Chol 11mg; Calc 625mg; Fib 5.9g; Sod 529mg

p303 | **Baked vegetable stew** Eng 306kcal/1280kJ; Prot 7.4g; Carb 42.7g, of which sug 16.2g; Fat 12.8g, of which sats 2g; Chol 0mg; Calc 101mg; Fib 6.3g; Sod 37mg

p304 | **Jerusalem artichoke and tomato stew** Eng 147kcal/619kJ; Prot 3.6g; Carb 19.8g, of which sug 17g; Fat 6.6g, of which sats 1g; Chol 0mg; Calc 98mg; Fib 5.1g; Sod 97mg

p307 | **Red cabbage with quince and walnuts** Eng 224kcal/927kJ; Prot 2.6g; Carb 13.5g, of which sug 12.5g; Fat 18g, of which sats 10.5g; Chol 44mg; Calc 73mg; Fib 3.6g; Sod 155mg

p308 | **Apricots with rice** Eng 449kcal/1872kJ; Prot 6.8g; Carb 54.1g, of which sug

16.3g; Fat 23.3g, of which sats 4.6g; Chol 9mg; Calc 57mg; Fib 3.8g; Sod 37mg

p311 | **Stuffed prunes in a pomegranate sauce** Eng 244kcal/1021kJ; Prot 1g; Carb 34g, of which sug 32g; Fat 8g, of which sats 5g; Chol 21mg; Calc 72mg; Fib 2.7g; Sod 116mg

p312 | **Pickled white cabbage with walnuts** Eng 440kcal/1816kJ; Prot 9.8g; Carb 7g, of which sug 6.5g; Fat 41.5g, of which sats 3.5g; Chol 0mg; Calc 110mg; Fib 4.3g; Sod 12mg

p315 | **Pickled stuffed aubergines** Eng 324kcal/1342kJ; Prot 8.4g; Carb 8.7g, of which sug 7.7g; Fat 28.7g, of which sats 2.6g; Chol 0mg; Calc 82mg; Fib 6.9g; Sod 11mg

p317 | **Pickled green peppers** (total) Eng 134kcal/560kJ; Prot 5g; Carb 14g, of which sug 13g; Fat 1g, of which sats 0g; Chol 0mg; Calc 46mg; Fib 7.2g; Sod 5535mg

p317 | **Pickled cauliflower chillies** (total) Eng 225kcal/935kJ; Prot 893g; Carb 18g, of which sug 17g; Fat 11g, of which sats 4g; Chol 0mg; Calc 111mg; Fib 7.5g; Sod 23629mg

p320 | **Spiced ground rice pudding** Eng 525kcal/2219kJ; Prot 5.1g; Carb 119.4g, of which sug 78.8g; Fat 5g, of which sats 2.9g; Chol 0mg; Calc 56mg; Fib 0.8g; Sod 20mg

p323 | **Pumpkin in syrup** Eng 318kcal/1355kJ; Prot 1g; Carb 83g, of which sug 82g; Fat 0g; Chol 0mg; Calc 57mg; Fib 1.7g; Sod 4mg

p324 | **Baked stuffed apples** Eng 507kcal/2150kJ; Prot 5g; Carb 113g, of which sug 112g; Fat 4g, of which sats 1g; Chol 0mg; Calc 91mg; Fib 4.8g; Sod 52mg

p327 | **Sesame and pistachio biscuits** Eng 406kcal/1701kJ; Prot 7g; Carb 49g, of which sug 20g; Fat 22g, of which sats 9g; Chol 31mg; Calc 165mg; Fib 2.4g; Sod 111mg

p328 | **Sweet pancakes with scented syrup** Eng 474kcal/2011kJ; Prot 4g; Carb 109g, of which sug 80g; Fat 5g, of which sats 1g; Chol 0mg; Calc 61mg; Fib 1.2g; Sod 5mg

p330 | **Dried fruit compôte with almonds** Eng 260kcal/1092kJ; Prot 5g; Carb 36g, of which sug 36g; Fat 11g, of which sats 1g; Chol 0mg; Calc 73mg; Fib 3.8g; Sod 31mg

p330 | **Milk pudding with mastic** Eng 613kcal/2561kJ; Prot 10.1g; Carb 70.5g, of which sug 58.2g; Fat 33.7g, of which sats 17.1g; Chol 63mg; Calc 279mg; Fib 1g; Sod 248mg

p333 | **Cream cheese pudding with syrup** Eng 431kcal/1799kJ; Prot 7.5g; Carb 43.5g, of which sug 27.8g; Fat 28.4g, of which sats 14g; Chol 62mg; Calc 158mg; Fib 1.2g; Sod 124mg

p334 | **Creamed semolina with cinnamon** Eng 420kcal/1771kJ; Prot4g; Carb 73g, of which sug 44g; Fat 14g, of which sats 9g; Chol 36mg; Calc 27mg; Fib 0.8g; Sod 108mg

p334 | **Puréed apricot dessert** Eng 412kcal/1731kJ; Prot 4g; Carb 59g, of which sug 59g; Fat 19g, of which sats 11g; Chol 46mg; Calc 91mg; Fib 5.9g; Sod 51mg

# Index

## About the author

Writer, broadcaster, and food anthropologist, Ghillie Başan has worked in different parts of the world as an English teacher, ski instructor, cookery writer, restaurant critic and journalist. With a degree in Social Anthropology and a Cordon Bleu Diploma, her interest in and research into different culinary cultures has culminated in many books, some of which have been nominated for the Glenfiddich, Guild of Food Writers, and the Cordon Bleu World Food Media Awards. They have also appeared regularly in the 'Best of the Best' and 'Top 50' lists; and she has been described as one of the 'finest writers on Middle Eastern food'. Her food and travel articles have appeared in the Sunday Times, Sunday Herald, Daily Telegraph, Sunday Tribune, Press & Journal, BBC Good Food Magazine, Diet & Nutrition USA, and various Middle Eastern and internet magazines, and she is one of the presenters on BBC Radio Scotland's Kitchen Café.

This edition is published by Lorenz Books
an imprint of Anness Publishing Ltd
www.lorenzbooks.com; www.annesspublishing.com;
info@anness.com

© Anness Publishing Ltd 2020

A CIP catalogue record for this book is available from the British Library.

Publisher: Joanna Lorenz
Design: Simon Daley
Photography: Jon Whitaker
Food styling: Fergal Connelly
Map artwork: Simon Daley
Nutritional consultant: Clare Emery
Index: Marie Lorimer

Previously published as *The Food and Cooking of Lebanon, Jordan and Syria*, updated and revised.

Although the advice and information in this book are believed to be accurate, neither the authors nor the publisher can accept any legal responsibility or liability for any errors or omissions that may have been made nor for any inaccuracies nor for any loss, harm or injury that comes about from following instructions or advice in this book.

## Cook's notes

Bracketed terms are intended for American readers.

For all recipes, quantities are given in both metric and imperial measures and, where appropriate, in standard cups and spoons. Follow one set of measures, but not a mixture, because they are not interchangeable.

Standard spoon and cup measures are level.
1 tsp = 5ml, 1 tbsp = 15ml, 1 cup = 250ml/8fl oz.

Australian standard tablespoons are 20ml. Australian readers should use 3 tsp in place of 1 tbsp for measuring small quantities.

American pints are 16fl oz/2 cups. American readers should use 20fl oz/2½ cups in place of 1 pint when measuring liquids.

Since ovens vary, you should check with your manufacturer's instruction book for guidance.